CLAIMING SUNDAY

CLAIMING SUNDAY

The Story of a Texas Slave Community

Second Edition

JOLEENE MADDOX SNIDER

FORT WORTH, TEXAS

Copyright © 2022 by Joleene Maddox Snider

Library of Congress Control Number: 2022947333

TCU Box 298300
Fort Worth, Texas 76129

Design by: Julie Rushing
Cover art: *Martin at the Gin*. Artist Robert Jones.

To Paul, for over fifty great years,

and our children,

Jessica, Jeffrey, Fazia, and Joe

Contents

Acknowledgments	ix
INTRODUCTION *to the Second Edition*	1

PART I

CHAPTER ONE: Slavery	9
CHAPTER TWO: The Alabama Years	17
CHAPTER THREE: Alabama to Texas	26
CHAPTER FOUR: Early Years in Texas	37
CHAPTER FIVE: Descendants All, 2014	49

PART II

CHAPTER SIX: John Devereux's Legacy	61
CHAPTER SEVEN: Final Decision	69
CHAPTER EIGHT: Ancestors All	83
CHAPTER NINE: Descendants All, 2018	98

PART III

CHAPTER TEN: Cotton, Cotton, and More Cotton	111
CHAPTER ELEVEN: Work, Work, and More Work	120
CHAPTER TWELVE: Brogans, Lowells, and Log Cabins	132
CHAPTER THIRTEEN: Pork Chops and Potions	142

PART IV

CHAPTER FOURTEEN: Descendants All, 2021	157
CHAPTER FIFTEEN: The Dance	179
CONCLUSION	193

APPENDIX I: *Slave Register*	201
APPENDIX II: *Devereux Slave Community Family Trees*	221
Notes	225
Bibliography	247
Index	251
About the Author	259

Acknowledgments

Writing a book takes many people. Writing the same book twice, which is what a second edition of *Claiming Sunday* is, takes even more people. My family has given the most and suffered the most. My mother passed New Year's Day 2020, but she would have loved this. Paul supported me just as he always has. I can't count the times he has walked back and forth across the driveway from our main house to my office in the Casita to check on me, listen to me, bring me tea, or just come see if I was still alive. When we realized we had TCU Press on board for this edition, I fired my son Jeffrey from his lofty position of unpaid design editor and guru of all things technological. I rehired and fired him about four times, but he is back as the badass that makes all this computer-dependent process work, and we will see it through together. My daughter, Jessica, has been my sounding board, and she and Joe are responsible for "Da Beast," a vintage microfilm reader that got me to the end of locating all the footnotes. Fazia listened to me talk through issues of reorganization and made me look amazing in the author's photograph.

Standing on the shoulders of Marianne Reese and Jessica Schneider, the proofreading team from the first round, we reached new heights of editing prowess this time by drawing on the expertise of Dr. Sandra Smith Davidson. Dr. Davidson is way too talented and educated to be doing my lowly work, but she was between opportunities and agreed to give me a hand. She did all the transcripts of the new interviews, sitting in on a few of them, and then turned the talents learned from completing her dissertation at the University of Houston to editing, correcting, and proofreading this edition. Sandra was one of my first-year survey course students, back in the 1990s, who hated history. I corrupted her. She became a history major and did her master's work with us at Texas State University, where she was my teaching assistant. She has been one of those people who pop into your life, and you realize you couldn't have done what you did without them. Thank you, Sandra.

Valerie Arnett, thank you and your former employer, LexisNexis, from the bottom of my little historian heart for the gift of the microfilm in 2004.

ACKNOWLEDGMENTS

Without it I would never have learned the things I have about the Devereux Slave Community the last time—or this time.

I owe a debt of gratitude to my professional family, who provided inspiration for years and years of my life, especially the late Bill Liddle and Everett Swinney. I still owe the late Professor S. Davis Bowman a research paper for a class at UT in 1994. This version would qualify.

Jeri Mills, without you this would be a very different book. If it had not been for you pushing me forward, it might not have been finished the first time. It is because of you that the strong, amazing voices of the descendants are here. I would never have had the opportunity to meet the families of the descendants and share their joy, interest, and passion for those who came before them. Thank you for nearly twenty years of inspiration and treasured friendship.

Pat Scott, thank you for your friendship, support, enthusiasm, information, and everything else. Even though we are separated by over 1,500 miles, you and I form a very special club—we are about the only two who have spent weeks and months hunched over microfilm readers searching for the documents that would tell us about the members of the Devereux Slave Community. You were hunting ancestors, while I was researching the book.

To Robert "Bob" Jones, your artistic talent overwhelms me. So proud to have your work grace my words.

Of greatest importance are the descendants of the Devereux Slave Community. To all of you scattered over the country, I owe you a debt of gratitude for opening your families and your stories to me. I thank you for your time, knowledge, and willingness to share your past. Your passion and pride for your ancestors has been an inspiration. In spite of the difficult questions I was asking, all of you responded with honesty, openness, and friendship. The members of the Devereux Slave Community represented a remarkable group of people, and their descendants are just as remarkable. I treasure all of you and what you have taught me—a hearty and sincere thank you.

Thanks to Cindy Brandimarte, who continued to bug me about this book's appeal to an academic press. And thanks to Dan Williams of TCU Press, who answered his own phone the day I called.

The people at TCU Press have been wonderful to work with. I am astonished at the level of detail and precision with which they have gone over my book. They have made it a much better product than what I sent to them last fall. A special thanks to Molly Spain and Kathy Walton for their guidance and patience.

To Tabby and Scott, thank you for guiding and sustaining your family through many trials and travails. You gave me a wonderful, enlightening, encouraging, and inspiring book populated with amazing people.

No one is more surprised than I that I finished this book, twice even.

Introduction
to Second Edition

This second edition of *Claiming Sunday: The Story of a Texas Slave Community* has enough differences from the first edition to require some introduction and explanation. After all, a good introduction is something all books need. Prospective readers always look at the back cover of a book first. If that appeals, they skim over the introductory materials before making a decision on purchase. For those assigned a book or who need the information contained therein, a good introduction is crucial; how else will they be able to talk glibly about a book they have never read? Therefore, this introduction needs to be substantial and do its duty. I hope it will encourage some to read more deeply into one of the most painful and difficult subjects in American history—slavery.

There are two main purposes of this book. The first one is to tell the story of the Devereux Slave Community in as much detail as the records allowed, thus providing an in-depth look at slavery as it existed on one plantation in Texas. In general, slave history is obscured by the slaves' inability to leave documents and traceable information. However, like many planters, the Devereux family kept copious records—daybooks, work records, medical bills, slave bills of sale, wills, letters, daily diaries, receipts for slave cloth, shoe orders, and an abundance of additional information. I was basically going through white records to get at black lives; it was the equivalent of doing history upside down. After becoming immersed in the records from this plantation over a series of many years; extracting all the information about slaves; organizing and arranging it; and then, as much as possible, interpreting those records from the perspective of the individual slaves and the Slave Community, I gained an enhanced understanding of the daily lives of the enslaved. These were the pieces of information that slowly built the lives and images of individuals and families. These enslaved souls were real people with families, friends, ambitions, tragedies, abilities, dreams, and I hope they come to life through my words. While this is a meaningful outcome in itself, the results should have relevance beyond the immediate work.

The fact that the white Devereux family is a perfect example of Southern planters and slave owners makes this study valuable and applicable in broader terms. Had the Devereux family been on the fringes of planter society, *Claiming Sunday* might not be pertinent to other slaves' lives. Slave owners John and Julien Devereux (father and son) started in Georgia, moved to Alabama in 1817, and then to Texas in 1841. By the time Julien Devereux died in 1856, he was one of the largest planters in the state, with over seventy slaves and more than 10,500 acres in East Texas. After his death, his widow Sarah Landrum Devereux, became one of the few major women planters in Texas and ran the Monte Verdi Plantation until emancipation.

All three plantation owners were very involved in running the plantation on a day-to-day basis. They practiced the most modern agricultural techniques found in journals and manuals written for and consumed by growers of cotton and owners of human flesh. For example, they ordered and tried the most recent hybrid cottonseeds, consulted with their overseers about every aspect of plantation management, and attended to the health of everyone.

Both John and Julien Devereux were recognized as leaders by their peers. Among other public duties, John Devereux served as senator to the Alabama legislature for eleven sessions. Julien followed in his father's footsteps in Alabama and Texas, working to further education, commerce, and transportation. In Alabama, Julien was a trustee of the University of Alabama. Later in Rusk County, Texas, he served for three years as a justice of the peace, and during the last six months of his life, when he was clearly failing, he served in the Texas legislature as a representative from the Rusk County area. Somewhere along the way, he had even acquired the title of Colonel Devereux, following the pattern of Southern gentlemen of the Old South. There was no shortage of paramilitary groups ready to confer military titles on just about any true Southern gentleman who carried the scent of jasmine and magnolia about him and rode their way. I knew this material intimately and was on solid ground in telling the story of the Devereux Slave Community, and I had done it once already.

The second purpose of this book is to establish how profound the history of slavery is to issues of race relations in our modern world. Yet, as profound as that connection is, I meet many people, of all colors, who won't talk about slavery, or who are just woefully ignorant, or both. I am incredulous that there are still Americans who didn't know enough about slavery to fill a decent paragraph if they are asked to write down the extent of their knowledge. But if asked to commit to paper what they know, or think they know, about race relations in this country, they can go on for pages. It is a safe bet that most of what they know, or think they know, about race has its origins in a subject about which they have little to no knowledge—slavery. How to deal with the second goal of connecting the history of slavery and the story of the Devereux Slaves to current race affairs eluded me, but I knew the connection was there. There was just too much evidence bombarding me daily.

The preponderance of evidence increased exponentially in 2016 when Donald Trump managed to identify and harness a massive force of malcontents who were opposed to change, growth, and progressivism in America and turned it into a political movement, complete with his own weaponized, rag-tag army. The Black Lives Matter movement, conflict over the glorification of Civil War leaders, and reactions to demonstrations over police killings of black Americans brought negative reactions from the Trump-inspired right. Violence was built into the prescription, and lives were needlessly lost in various clashes, including at the Capitol on January 6, 2021, when Trump's rhetoric resulted in an attempted coup to take over control of the election results of this country. It is true the mob's aim was to overturn the election of Joe Biden; but it is also true there were few minority faces in the crowds storming the Capitol. So, what did all this turmoil have to do with a book about slavery in the mid-nineteenth century? Turns out, it had a lot to do with it. The past failures of America to confront and understand the history of slavery set issues of race up to be a prime target of ultra-right aggression.

Those same issues of racial harmony—*disharmony* is more appropriate—are playing themselves out politically here in Texas, where state officials politicize the history of slavery by approving textbooks that have referred to slaves as "indentured servants," "African immigrants," and most recently, "involuntary immigrants." The textbook wars are heating up as new adoptions are looming, and Texas school children will likely know even less about slavery in the future. On a more personal level, I am "Auntie Jo" to two young African American women, and I see firsthand some of what they deal with daily. It isn't pretty, but it is more proof of the connection between my work and the world in which we live. How we got to where we are and how do we move on are important questions to ask and to answer. Where race is concerned the history of slavery is ground zero.

Connecting the history of slavery and the story of the Devereux Slaves to current race relations turned out to be solved by happy accident. At the invitation of Devereux slave community descendant Jeri Mills, in 2014, I took my white face along with my camera and laptop and crashed an African American reunion in deep, rural East Texas. The Caddell Family is descended directly from Tabby and Scott. By then, I had known the host and her family for twelve years, but few of the other Caddells knew me or had any warning I was coming. I was very comfortable in their presence. After all, I had lived with their ancestors in my head and heart, if not my DNA, since 1990, when I discovered the Julien Sidney Devereux Family Papers in the Briscoe Center for American History at the University of Texas at Austin. Nobody was impolite, rude, or unfriendly. They were just wary. I realized the ice was showing some cracks when one of the younger descendants got me out on the driveway-turned-dance floor. "Listen to the rhythm, Auntie Jo, listen to the rhythm. I think you got a bit of the 'sista' in you," she told me.

Please understand I didn't just drop in for an hour or so. I stayed all day for nearly four days. On the second day, there was still some uncertainty about my presence, but one of the cousins broke right through the issue of race with honesty, humor, and a healthy dose of pure bravado. Dale Johnson came down the hall from the back door and skidded to a sudden stop when he spotted me washing the dishes. I was working in the kitchen and chatting and visiting with family members when out of Dale's mouth comes, "Jeri, you got yourself a white woman. I want one, too. White people been buying us for years." Suddenly, stone-cold silence replaced all the conversations that had been going around, and every last person was staring at me. When I burst into laughter, the tension dissolved, and we were all laughing. Dale passed recently, and I never got a chance to give him the hug he deserved. I left the 2014 reunion an honorary Caddell.

Over the course of the three-day reunion, I interviewed five descendants (four of which are in the first set of interviews, while the fifth one was recently redone and appears in the third set of interviews). The interviews grew rather organically out of the opportunity and were not as carefully planned out as they should have been. Instinct told me to do them, but later scholarly reflection brought me to understand how vital they were. After my husband and I attended the Caddell reunion in Oklahoma in 2018, I planned a second set of interviews for later that year. I added a third set in 2021 for this new edition of the book. It was the interviews that linked the present to the past like nothing else I could have done. These were real, living people with whom readers could identify. It became possible to see into and through them to their ancestors. The best way to understand the enslaved people and their importance to today's world was to connect them to the living people who were their descendants. And from those living today, I had my connection to current race relations in America. I could tell the story of the ancestors, but no one could tell the stories of the descendants and modern racial connections better than themselves. There was my continuity from the past to the present, the then to the now, nineteenth-century slavery to contemporary racial tensions and issues. The pieces of the puzzle fit.

Thus, with the structural importance of the interviews having been established, it became necessary to use them differently and place them into the text at new and strategic places. Therefore, I removed my questions and comments and changed the format to a one-way conversation organized around specific topics. Essentially, I wanted the descendants to facilitate me in telling both their stories and the story of their ancestors, and the best way to do that was to simply get out of the way. I have arranged the interviewees' words to give their thoughts a topical presentation and to enhance flow and readability. Otherwise, they spoke for themselves.

In addition, this second edition has been revised for a more academic audience, while keeping the tone and approachability of the previous edition. It now includes citations and a bibliography of works that appear in the text, rather than listing every book I've read over a lifetime of studying American slavery. The index has been generously enlarged to make it easier to find specific items the reader might want to locate. The slave register in appendix 1 remains substantially the same because we (my husband is the compiler) found little new material to add.

Throughout the revisions, an attempt has been made to incorporate the words and ideas of other scholars in the field of American slavery. There was a conscious effort to use both older and newer works so that the scope of academic work on slavery over the years is represented. I hope I have selected quotations worthy of transporting into the text that won't impede the flow of the main story of the Devereux Slave Community.

The text is broken into four parts. Part I, which consists of chapters one through five, discusses the early years of the Devereux Slave Community. Readers come to know many of the members of the Community and understand their importance, especially Tabby and Scott, the two slaves whose presence holds the Community together during times of trial and trauma. Part I closes with the first set of interviews, done in 2014.

Part II covers chapters six through nine and details the breakup of Tabby and Scott's extended family as a result of the death of John Devereux. With Tabby and Scott at its center, the Slave Community held together in spite of the breakup, Part II culminates with the second set of interviews, from 2018.

Part III, which covers chapters ten through thirteen, is a detailed look at life on a Texas slave plantation. The specifics about slave life, which emerged with careful study, were mind boggling. Not every fact and detail are used, but enough are present to take the reader into and on the plantation. Specificity does matter.

Part IV ends *Claiming Sunday* with chapters fourteen through sixteen. Chapter fourteen is entitled "Descendants All, 2021" and presents the final set of interviews. Chapter fifteen discusses the dance that slaves constantly performed to gain and exert some control over their lives in order to survive the dehumanizing impact of slavery. I conclude the book with some of my reflections on future work on the subject of slavery.

In closing this introduction, I thought about the slave Henry. In 1846, he told his owner he wasn't going to leave for Rusk County because it was Sunday, and that was his day to look after his own business. That statement gave me the title for this book. When I first ran across that quote, I just sat and stared at it. Who knew slaves had their own affairs? And who ever thought they had the nerve or self-confidence to claim time to attend to those affairs? That was the moment I knew the papers of a white enslaver were revealing things about the lives of the enslaved that I did not know, and that I could draw enough material out of the Devereux records to tell the story of the Slave Community and find a way to bring the story of those people into the world of today. This is the result of that years-long endeavor.

PART I

Chapter One
Slavery

There was never a moment . . . when the slavery issue was not a sleeping serpent. [It] lay coiled up under the table during the deliberations of the Constitutional Convention in 1787. It was . . . more than half awake at the time of the Louisiana Purchase in 1803. Thereafter slavery was always in everyone's mind, though not always on his tongue.[1]

JOHN JAY CHAPMAN, 1921

"The past is never dead. It's not even past."[2] If William Faulkner was not thinking about slavery when he wrote these words, he should have been. Few subjects in American history are more fraught with feelings of guilt and shame, more entangled in modern race relations, and carry more historical baggage than slavery in America.

Slavery is the American stain—the dirtiest, ugliest, and most repellent of the permanent blotches on the fabric of American history. It has been a part of the American story since 1619, when Africans were brought to the Virginia colony, just twelve years after the founding of the first permanent settlement in North America at Jamestown, Virginia, in 1607. Historian Hugh Thomas in *The Slave Trade* estimated that 13,000,000 Africans were taken out of the continent of Africa, and 11,328,000 were delivered to ports in Europe and the New World. The overwhelming majority of those individuals, approximately 10,828,000, were taken to ports in the Caribbean and South America. Only 500,000 or so of those Africans were transported into what would become present-day America.[3] When the northern and southern colonies reached an impasse over the issue of the slave trade at the Constitutional Convention in 1787, a compromise was reached. The trade would be left untouched for the time being, but a clause was inserted that ended the trade twenty years after ratification. Thus, legal protection for the forced migration of Africans

SLAVE MIGRATION OUT OF AFRICA 1500–1900

The preponderance of slaves brought to the New World were taken to South America and the Caribbean. While the American colonies/states received the fewest number of enslaved, its slave population increased its numbers by self-propagation to more than four million by 1860. *Courtesy of Jeffrey Snider.*

for slavery ended in 1808. Smugglers continued to bring in small numbers of enslaved persons for years, however.

At first, slaves were common in both northern and southern colonies. In northern colonies and states most slaves were household workers, artisans, or general laborers, and they were not held in large numbers. In 1810, the northern colonies/states had 418 slaves, and middle colonies/states had 30,840 slaves. In comparison, the southern colonies/states had 1,090,852 slaves. Add in a few odd bits and scraps of inhabited land, and the total number of slaves in America in the first census taken after the external slave trade ended in 1808 was 1,191,302.[4]

By the census of 1830, the number of slaves in America was slightly over two million, and they were nearly all in the South.[5] These enslaved people were the human labor upon which some Southern farmers and planters depended to work their fields and make their profits. By 1860, on the eve of the Civil War, no Northern state had slaves; however, the total number of slaves had grown to nearly four million human beings, and nearly all of them were in the cotton-growing states of the lower South.[6]

Some northern colonies and states, while still racist in culture and society, had begun various methods to end slavery as early as the colonial era. These methods included gradual emancipation and freedom for service in the Revolutionary War. The abolition movement began in earnest around 1830 in the North and East, with immediate and total emancipation as the goal of the American Anti-Slavery Society, the dominant group. The few northern states, such as New Jersey and New York, that still had slaves undertook emancipation in reaction to the abolition movement. In the South, however, abolitionism met with such resistance that it gave rise to the development of the theory of paternalism that defended slavery's benefits to all, black and white.

That defense of slavery centered around the enslavers as paternalistic owners who cared for their slaves and treated them as part of the family. The system was also patriarchal, since the head of the family was nearly always male. In the view of the paternalistic owner, punishment was administered only when absolutely necessary and in the best interest of the slave and the entire community. The theory argued that slave owners protected familial relationships, when possible, spread the Protestant word of God to their slaves, and provided for their slaves from birth until death. In return, the enslaved gave grateful obedience, loyalty, and hard work. In Southern magazines and books published before the Civil War, the South's paternalistic defense of slavery was described in benign and benevolent terms. In reality, it cannot be denied that the system ultimately rested on the threat, if not the actuality, of violence. There was no power to control the baser impulses of the owners, who had unlimited authority to abuse or work their slaves to death.

It is difficult to know how much anyone, black or white, bought into the paternalistic theory. Slaves almost certainly saw through the ruse. If we accept what white enslavers said and wrote, then they believed in paternalism; but if we look at their actions, they only practiced the theory when it was expedient and did not damage their monetary interests. It was a convenient, not to mention romantic, contrivance to combat the increasing strength of the abolitionists and the rising negative attention in the North to the Southern system of slavery. Julien and his father, John William Devereux, and Julien's wife, Sarah Ann Landrum Devereux, were not among the owners who subjected their human property to the horrendous cruelty and depravity described in some Southern documents. The three owners provided decent provisions for their slaves. They tried to protect family integrity when they could, and when it was convenient. They recorded few instances of harsh punishment and counseled their overseers never to punish a slave in anger. In truth, it should be noted there was probably more violence or the threat of violence than the records revealed. The Devereux family recognized the worth of their slaves in terms of both market value and contributions to their livelihood. However, when owning or not owning a slave affected their bottom line, potential profit or loss of profit won the argument. Rarely did the betterment of the slaves or their families determine an enslaver's actions. For example, when Julien Devereux was planning his escape to the Republic of Texas to flee his troubles, he would no more have asked his slaves' opinions about the plan than he would have consulted the cattle and horses he intended to take. He treated his slaves with some kindness because he was, essentially, a kind person. Probably, though, it had more to do with the fact that his enslaved people were the most valuable things he owned.

The system of slavery upon which most Southern farmers and planters depended was a labor system, first, and a racial system, second. Slaves were slaves because they were black, and because they were black, they were slaves. A system which determines status by skin color is the essence of a racist system, and slavery was the ultimate systemic racist system. Historian Edward Baptist in *The Half Has Never Been Told* explained just how integrated into American society, economics, and politics slavery was: "Virtually all white Americans were now [1820] interested, almost all profiting in some way—financially, psychologically, or both—from slavery's growing empire."[7] This growing slave and cotton empire was making the Civil War inevitable. The contradictions between the beliefs of liberty and freedom upon which the nation was founded in the eighteenth century and the reality of a slave empire were becoming unsustainable by the mid-nineteenth century.

While people continue to argue about the causes of the Civil War, of which there is no doubt, Texas was very clear about the reasons for secession. From "A Declaration of the Causes Which Impel The State of Texas To Secede From The Federal Union" in the *Journal of the Secession Convention of 1861* comes the following statement: "That in this free government all white men are and of right ought to be entitled to equal civil and political rights; that the servitude of the African race, as existing in these States, is mutually beneficial to both bond and free and is abundantly authorized and justified by the experience of mankind, and the revealed will of the Almighty Creator."[8] Still, others will argue that the cause of the war was "states' rights." If that is the case (it isn't), then exactly what right of a state or its citizens was so important and in question that it justified secession and war? There is no other answer. Nothing on the political landscape of America was of sufficient consequence to justify civil war other than the right of a white citizen to own black human beings of African heritage. There is no other conclusion to draw: slavery was the cause of the Civil War. Returning to Faulkner's words—the issue of slavery and its role in our history is still very much with us. The past is the present in American racial relations.

The importance of slavery to the Civil War is even more profound when coupled with the value of slaves. When Julien Sidney Devereux died in 1856, he left behind ten thousand plus acres of East Texas sandy loam that was valuable cotton-growing soil. According to his will, he also left seventy-two slaves to his widow and heirs. Those seventy-two human beings were worth nearly twice what his 10,500 acres of land were worth.[9] And Devereux was hardly alone in that equation. Of all the wealth in the American South in 1860, the four million black souls held as slaves were by far the most valuable property whites owned. For many Southerners, their slaves were more valuable than their land, houses, livestock, outbuildings, tools, carriages, investments, and bank accounts combined.

One of the greatest ironies of the Civil War is that the South's best chance to preserve slavery was from within the Union, where it was protected by the Constitution of the United States. Once the South seceded from the Union, committing state treason, that protection was withdrawn, and slavery, especially, was vulnerable if the war did not go the South's way. Had the South remained in the Union, laws could have been passed to limit the spread of slavery, but the abolition of slavery was only made possible by the act of Southern secession and a Union victory in the Civil War. Basically, Southern action doomed what it was meant to protect.

The study of the institution which the south was so determined to keep that it seceded from the Union and went to war to protect has been and still is a field of rich and copious historical research that is constantly growing and redefining historical viewpoints and perspectives. However, it is not an easy field in which to work; historians wrestle with a number of problems not faced by scholars in other areas and for which there are simply no happy resolutions. The thorniest of these are the contradictions inherent in writing about a country founded on principles of self-governance, personal liberty, freedom, and democratic principles that was also a nation of slaveholders. The subject is challenged more than some other subject areas by issues of control, power, white patriarchy, and finally, the unavoidable moral issue of one human being owning another. Finally, historians of slavery face other major obstacles in their work. First, slave history is not an uplifting story. In fact, it is grim with no redeeming virtues. Second, even in current times it is obvious historians of slavery tell a story Americans may not like. Just eight years ago historian Edward Baptist wrote the following: "The idea that the commodification and suffering and forced labor of African Americans is what made the United States powerful and rich is not an idea that people necessarily are happy to hear."[10] Third, the enslaved did not leave the sorts of documents that other groups of Americans did because they were denied the right to learn to read and write, so telling their story is decidedly more difficult. It requires huge amounts of time and tedious work to unearth their lives from white records and other sources. Yet, their stories matter, for they tell the story of slavery which is crucial to understanding who we are as a people and a country.

Black scholars and writers such as Frederick Douglass, W. E. B. DuBois, and Carter G. Woodson were doing modern studies of slavery right after the Civil War. However, it was the white institutions of higher learning that did the early studies of slavery that prevailed from the end of the Civil War era until around 1950, and these depicted a system in keeping with the paternalistic views of the Old South. According to the traditional school of slavery, sometimes referred to as the Dunning School, the enslaved were well-treated, treasured members of the white family, more happy minions than enslaved. It was World War II and the ensuing Cold War that brought about the first of the modern civil rights movements, opening up the historical frontier on slavery for the revisionist group of slavery historians, who depicted a much less benign system of slavery than the traditionalists. Kenneth Stampp's book, *The Peculiar Institution*, was not the first revisionist view on slave history, but it had the greatest impact and opened the gates for a flood of works on slavery. Throughout the 1960s and '70s, the revisionist historians produced so much new material on slavery it could bring a grown historian to tears of both joy and frustration. Still, those academic endeavors didn't establish African American studies programs, nor did they usher in a meaningful number of black scholars. Those programs came with the neo-revisionists in the 1980s and '90s in most topflight universities in the country. But, even now, there is a paucity of black scholars studying slavery. In 2019, there were 2,512 African Americans who earned doctorates in America,[11] but many of those were in subjects other than slavery.

Some scholars have presented the most debased treatment imaginable in books on slavery. One of those was Stanley Elkin, whose work, *Slavery: A Problem in American Institutional and Intellectual Life,* compared slaves to concentration camp inmates, so dehumanized that they had no self-will left. Several current scholars, especially those historians whose work concentrates on the Mississippi Valley, portray slaves as so overworked and abused that they had no lives other than work, punishment, and starvation rations. No doubt some owners did treat their slaves with unbelievable inhumanity. However, any people so beaten down and deprived as some studies depict would not have managed to build families and increase their numbers over the centuries in the South. This tendency—to present only the worst of slave treatment—has seemingly arisen from a philosophical belief that for the system of slavery to be bad, the treatment of slaves had to be egregious. Slavery did not have to be bad to be bad. Regardless of treatment, slavery was inherently a degradation. The fact that it allowed for the unrestricted power of ownership by one human being over another was sufficient to leave open the door to the worst of the system. It was not what an owner *did* to his slave property that became the operative problem; it was what that owner *could* do to his slaves that was the pertinent question. The answer was that an owner *could have done* just about anything he wanted to his slaves.

The emphasis on the worst of the worst in slavery, as if being a slave is not victimization enough, is that it further victimizes African Americans who were held in bondage against their wills. Slaves were victims, there is no doubt of that. However, many thousands of slaves battled daily against that victimization by leaving the products and results of their labors and talents still visible across the New South, by building families they hoped and prayed could be kept together, and by constantly pushing and shoving at the boundaries of the system that enslaved them.

When Washington, DC, was preparing for the first inauguration of Barack Obama in 2008, a reporter discovered that slaves had built the older parts of the White House. The story took off with such intensity one would think it had been announced that beings from outer space had built some of the official presidential residence. Much of white America, and some of black America, were shocked to know that slaves built any part of official Washington. In reality, slave labor built not only much of our nation's capital before the Civil War; that same system of slavery supplied the labor to build most of the American South in the antebellum period. Frederick Douglass called the South the land which the slaves "had watered with their tears, enriched with their blood, tilled with their hard hands."[12] Slave labor cut the trees; broke the ground; made the bricks; built the structures; drove the wagons; fenced the fields; managed the livestock; and planted, raised, and gathered the crops. Additionally, slaves were carpenters, blacksmiths, cooks, brickmasons, crop specialists, seamstresses, ginning and baling managers, midwives, designers, engineers, and builders.

To not recognize and give full credit to what black Americans accomplished during slavery is to further victimize them. *Claiming Sunday* is the story of a remarkable group of people who rose above their enslavement to build families, homes, farms, and plantations. They did not surrender their self-respect to the system of slavery. On the contrary, they worked their entire lives to maintain their humanity, even though they were in a system designed to rob them of their humanity, self-worth, and self-respect.

It is impossible to fully understand what it meant to be a slave. On the other hand, to not make the effort to understand and depict the lives of the four million African Americans held in perpetual bondage is to admit those lives are lost to us as a society. That is unacceptable. Therefore, *Claiming Sunday* portrays the Devereux Slave Community with facts and honesty, while maintaining an understanding that the existence of slavery is unacceptable, especially in a democracy based on liberty, freedom, equality, and self-determination.

The story of the Devereux Plantation is too important and too good not to tell. It is the story of people who lived all or part of their lives in the ownership of the Devereux family. It is not the story of every enslaved person or enslaved community, but it is the story of many of them. It is the story of America, both past and present.

Chapter Two
The Alabama Years

'Reconsidered the matter, declined making a crawfish

of myself and finally came to Texas.[1]

JULIEN SIDNEY DEVEREUX, 1840

John William Devereux was already forty-eight years of age in 1817 when he took twelve-year-old Julien and sixteen-year-old Albert and moved from Georgia to Alabama.[2] John's oldest child, daughter Louisiana, remained in Georgia with other family members. Also with John were Slave Community matriarch Tabby and patriarch Scott and their children, all of whom had been born in Georgia. John established himself as a cotton planter at several locations in the new state, but finally settled permanently in Covington County. Given his age, it was clear he planned to slowly turn operation of his enterprise over to Albert, but at age twenty Albert contracted yellow fever on a business trip to Florida and died with his father at his side a few days after returning home.[3]

Thus, at age sixteen, Julien was the only son left to help manage and, ultimately, take over what John was building. Likely, he began to assume some management duties for his father's plantation and slaves at a much younger age than either father or son had planned. By the age of twenty, Julien was already involved in financial aspects of the cotton business, cosigning a note with his father to borrow $200 from John Ramar.[4] At twenty-four, he hired the overseer for the year.[5] By 1830, Julien was in charge of the entire plantation operation. By 1832, when he was twenty-seven, he was buying slaves for himself.[6] Taking on such a high level of responsibility at such a young age may have contributed, in part, to his later irresponsibility.

When Julien married Adaline Bradley on December 28, 1826,[7] the union combined two of the largest plantation operations and most prominent planter families in the southern half of Alabama. At the ripe old age of twenty-one,

Julien had a major plantation to run, a marriage to build and sustain, and a large group of people whose very survival depended on how well he managed his affairs. Four years later, when Julien was twenty-five, the United States Census of 1830 showed him with thirty-seven enslaved African Americans;[8] however, by 1840 he was listed as owning seventy-two enslaved people.[9] Some of those legally belonged to his father; some belonged to his wife, and some may have belonged to his sister, Louisiana Devereux Holcombe. That did not lessen his responsibility for all seventy-two people.

In the early part of the 1830s, Julien rode the tide of good times and easy credit, investing in cotton lands and slaves. But the hard times were just around the economic corner, if anyone had cared to look. Julien's money issues were tied to the Panic of 1837 and the depression that lasted through much of the 1840s. Economic collapses are complicated. In the South, the Panic of 1837 was closely related to the rampant, uncontrolled speculation and buying of slaves and lands seized from Native tribes by the government. Money for both land and slaves was readily available, but interest rates of 8 to 10 percent and higher steadily climbed after 1830, making payback more and more difficult. Interest rates at New York banks were "rising from 7 percent annually to 2 to 3 percent per month" during the resulting banking crisis in 1837.[10]

All that available land came as a result of the Indian Removal Act in 1830, which forced what was left of the Five Civilized Tribes (Choctaw, Seminole, Creek, Chickasaw, and Cherokee) living east of the Mississippi River to the west of the Mississippi, leaving behind some of the best cotton lands in the lower South available for sale to white Americans. When all of this land hit the market at once, it created a massive bubble in real estate and a quagmire of issues relating to legal property rights for years to come.[11]

It also left behind opportunities for chicanery. Howard Zinn, in his book *A People's History of the United States,* quotes a Georgia banker who wrote, "Stealing is the order of the day."[12] It is unclear how deeply Julien was involved in the deception to purchase lands belonging to the descendants of the late Cherokee Indian Pin Hadjo.[13] There is no doubt Pin Hadjo's descendants were tricked into selling their lands for a pittance. Julien may or may not have been a major player in the plan to bilk Hadjo's descendants, but he was certainly associated with the men who were the principal players in the deception. And Julien did end up claiming the land.

The affair was reported to the Bureau of Indian Affairs, along with thousands of other similar cases, and the bureau opened an investigation that placed ownership of the property in limbo for years. Several times it appeared that the federal government was prepared to file suit against Julien for what he did or did not do in the crooked real estate deal.[14] It went on for years until the Commission of Indian Affairs settled the matter in Julien's favor in April 1840.[15]

Before the economic bubble burst, states also got in on the good times. The Erie Canal had opened in 1825, and proved a great success story. It was funded in part by the federal government but also with money acquired through the sale of bonds issued by the state of New York. According to historian Gene Dattel, "All"—did he really mean *all*?—"the Erie Canal bonds were sold to Europeans."[16] The canal operated with enough profit to pay the bonds off at their maturity, bond owners made money, the state got its internal improvement, and everybody was happy.

Impressed by the Erie Canal's success, other states issued bonds or borrowed money directly from foreign governments, mostly Great Britain, for internal improvements. While some bonds were bought within the United States, most were purchased across the pond. According to one contemporary estimate, by 1838, state governments were indebted to European banks for one hundred million dollars.[17] That is a huge debt load for states; it translates into about three billion in today's money. By July 1841, the states began to default on their bond payments. Starting with Michigan, a total of eight states and the territory of Florida defaulted and declared bankruptcy by December 1842.[18] That was a third of the states in the Union!

And here was the triangle that defined much of the American economy in the first half of the nineteenth century—slaves, cotton, and England's money and mills. Slave labor and cheap, fertile lands were essential to raising cotton in the Old South. Cotton was valuable and made whites rich—the more land and the more slaves they owned, the richer planters became. Even though American mills around Lowell, Massachusetts, began to absorb more and more southern grown cotton in the 1840s, the primary market for all that cotton was the mills of Liverpool, England. According to Sven Beckert, "By 1850 one British observer estimated that 3.5 million people in the United Kingdom were employed by the country's cotton industry."[19] Textiles were the basis of the English industrial empire in the nineteenth century.

By 1838, "the mountain of debt that had been accumulated to purchase land and slaves brought an avalanche of financial failures."[20] Lenders were tightening credit, states were defaulting on bond payments, banks were finding it harder and harder to collect payment on notes made in better times, and sources of foreign capital were drying up. Julien Devereux, like many others, was going broke. In 1840, the Bank of Charleston agreed to grant him "the indulgence requested . . . to furnish a new note for the balance of the debt" of $4000 he owed.[21] There is no indication he ever repaid that money or money owed to any other creditor. Some creditors were more demanding, including the president of the Bank of Milledgeville, Georgia. He wrote Julien on September 4, 1840, "I take the liberty of reminding you of the promise made to me in Montgomery and also in the letter of the 22nd of July last, that when you did sell your land the debt due by you to this Bank should be the first paid out of the proceeds of the sale." He then added, "Inform me by return mail when I may calculate, with certainty on your payment."[22] If Julien responded truthfully to the banker, he would have said, "probably never." To compound his situation, the people who owed Julien could no more pay him than he could pay his creditors.

The money woes were only a portion of his problems. Julien Sidney Devereux was in personal trouble, and his slaves had probably known it for several years. Segregation and the separation of the races after 1865 has masked the knowledge of just how much black and white lives intertwined under slavery. Enslaved black people worked and often lived in their white owners' houses. They raised white children and nursed sick white family members. White enslavers checked on sick and infirm slaves in the quarters, called physicians to treat them, and noted their marriages, births, and deaths in their journals and daybooks. Owners and their families traveled with their slaves. Black and white children played together. On small farms, masters and slaves worked side by side in the fields. The human property knew intimate details of white lives, and one of the details the Devereux Slave Community knew about Julien was that he was stepping out on his wife.

The quarters also knew about some of his financial troubles. White owners were often very casual and unguarded in their conversations around their slaves. To quote Edward Baptist, "Enslaved people trained themselves all their lives in the art of discovering information from white people,"[23] and they were very astute in making sense of the information they gleaned. So, in 1838 when Julien and his cousin Alfred Devereux left for a trip to Texas, the Slave Community probably had all the pieces they needed to put together the puzzle of what was happening. In an affidavit filed in April of that year in Houston, the Republic of Texas declared Julien's "intention to become a citizen of this Republic."²⁴ It is doubtful any of the enslaved knew about his declaration in Houston, but they knew enough. And what they knew was not good for them.

Adaline Devereux, Julien's wife, certainly knew by 1838 that her husband had a mistress. That was the year that Julien and Barbara Scott Way had their first child and named her Antoinette, after a sister of Julien's who had died as a toddler. No doubt, Adaline knew Barbara Way. She was the sister of Andrew Gilbert Scott, who worked for the Devereux Plantation, which probably accounts for Barbara's nearby presence. Shrouded in mystery is the story of Mr. Way's absence, but it may account for why Barbara was apparently living with her brother.

By the summer of 1840, when everything caught up to Julien, he put what was really John Devereux's plantation up for sale for $21,500. Robert and William Doughtery of La Grange, Georgia, agreed to his price, arranged to take possession of the property on January 1, 1841, and remitted half of the amount due.²⁵ Julien's family, both black and white, were leaving, but needless to say his black family members had no choice in the matter, nor would they have any control over who went and who stayed behind in Alabama with Julien's wife and her relatives. In late 1840, Devereux moved his black and white families into temporary quarters in Montezuma, Alabama, where he had connections and housing available until he left for Texas in mid-1841.²⁶ On January 1, 1841, Julien wrote a receipt to Robert Doughtery for $14,014.14.²⁷ This was the first payment for the property, and it included the corn and fodder Doughtery asked Julien to leave behind for his use. In later years, Doughtery and Julien squabbled over the remaining money due.

Throughout 1841, the demands for payment on debts continued to roll in for Julien. For example, on February 12, 1841, another demand arrived from a lawyer named Thorington calling in a loan for $1,384.65, which Julien had cosigned with several other business associates.²⁸ Three days later, on February 15, another demand for payment arrived. At least it was polite: "I am also under the necessity of asking of you the amount of your note as I fear I shall not be able to pay the 20 per ct required [of me] without it."²⁹ This request was from E. Hamon, who held a note from Julien and his brother-in-law, Henry Holcombe.

As late as July 1841, Julien's obnoxious brother-in-law, Henry Holcombe, was offering advice to Julien on his situation. Holcombe was about the last person in the world Julien wanted to hear from, but Holcombe knew more than most people about going bust. He had done it repeatedly. On July 7, 1841, Holcombe advised Julien, "Your course is plain. . . . Go ahead & see into the very bottom, deep as it may be . . . take papers; notes, negroes, lands, or anything. I really am afraid it is a scrape."[30] Holcombe urged Julien to sell his enslaved property and stay in Alabama. He wrote, "It will not do for you and your father to leave Alabama. Louann [Louisiana Devereux Holcombe] solemnly protests against it and says it must not be so."[31] Holcombe was whistling in the wind. Julien's land was already gone, and he had made up his mind to go to Texas.

This is where Julien's story turns a bit strange. Of course, there is no way to know what was going on in his mind from fall 1840 until his departure for Texas one year later. On September 3, 1840, Robert Doughtery, one of the two men buying the Devereux Plantation, wrote Julien about the move. He wanted to purchase some corn and fodder that Julien would leave for him and he had a message for Julien's wife, Adaline. Considering that Julien had a two-year-old child by his mistress, Barbara Scott Way, the message Doughtery wanted conveyed to Adaline Devereux seemed odd, though. Doughtery wrote, "Please to Mrs. Devereux, that I will take all the poultry she may have to dispose of." And then Doughtery closed with "Give my respects to your Lady."[32] Julien might have wondered, "Which one?" However, Doughtery clearly meant Adaline, and his message implied he thought she was leaving for Texas with Julien. Julien, however, was leaving his wife behind.

And what of the other lady not in residence in the big house? This part of the story gets even more disturbing. Julien had hired Andrew Gilbert Scott, Barbara Scott Way's brother, to take a team of mules, two wagons, and at least one horse and head for Texas about three months before Julien's departure. Scott left the Alabama plantation around June 12, 1841. It made good sense to have a reconnaissance front man, but nothing about Scott's trip indicated that was the purpose; in fact, his journey defied logic. In addition to a few slaves, Scott carried in the wagon Julien and Barbara's firstborn child, three-year-old Antoinette, under the care of a slave girl named Rhody.[33] It is difficult to believe Barbara Way would have thought it just dandy to be left behind in Alabama while sending hers and Julien's three-year-old daughter to Texas, solely in the care of a ten-year-old slave girl and the toddler's uncle. You don't normally take a toddler and her child caregiver on a scouting mission to a new country, so what might have so affected Julien's plans?

Part of the answer to this mystery surfaced from a hint in Andrew Scott's letter to Julien on June 22, 1841, while Scott was on the trail to Texas. He wrote, "It is a fine thing that muther did not come" due to the condition of the roads and other hardships. There were no other mothers who could have been included in this particular trip, except Barbara Way, so it seems reasonable to assume that Way had originally planned to go to Texas at this time. Such a plan made more sense than tossing Antoinette and the ten-year-old child Rhody into the wagon and saying goodbye. So why wasn't Barbara Way in the wagon?

The answer turned up in simple human biology and a good look at the calendar. Clearly, Julien was making conjugal visits to Barbara Way because she was pregnant with their second child, to be named Julien Sidney for his father, but he carried his mother's maiden name as his last name until Julien had it changed to Devereux. Records on Sidney's birth are confusing and contradictory. Removing the outliers, it appears he was born around the end of 1841 and the beginning of 1842. Nothing gave a month or day for his birth, not even his gravestone in Texas. His Confederate enlistment in 1861 has him as twenty, and 1841 as his birth date. The 1860 census shows Sidney living with his sister, and he is listed as nineteen, which also indicates an 1841 birth date. Nothing indicates who decided that Barbara Way would not go to Texas with her daughter. However, given the timing, it seems Julien made the decision himself, possibly when he found out he was to be a father for the second time. Backtracking from Sidney's probable birth date, Way would have conceived around early to mid-April and realized she was pregnant sometime in May. It is conceivable that Julien had planned for Barbara Way and their child to go ahead to Texas until he found out about the second pregnancy. It is only supposition by this author, but it appears as if Julien scooped Antoinette up and left Barbara Way pregnant with their second child.

There are no records that Barbara Scott Way ever saw her daughter again, and she and Julien fought for years over Sidney.[34] It is clear that Sidney was in Rusk County by around 1848, when he was about seven, because he started at the school Julien had established. Later, Julien paid for the building of the Forest Hill Academy for both male and female students, probably to school his own children.[35] Julien had the Texas legislature pass a resolution to legitimize both Sidney and Antoinette, and he left them property in slaves in his will. Sidney's grave marker in Texas reads, "Julien Sidney Devereux, Jr., Son of Barbara Scott Way, 1842–1890, A Veteran of the Civil War." At one point, Barbara Turner (she remarried) hid both herself and Sidney's whereabouts from Julien. When she failed to return Sidney to Texas after he visited her, Julien sent notices out to sheriffs in areas of Louisiana where he thought she was located.[36] When one inquiry bore fruit, Julien sent Jesse and Howerton to bring Sidney back to Rusk County.[37] Sidney lived most of his adult life in Texas, married a Texas woman,[38] and was buried in McKnight Cemetery in East Texas.[39] Children, just like property, slaves, and women, legally belonged to the white men in the family.

What an injustice Julien did Rhody, who was taken from her family and thrust into the wagon with even less preparation and concern than were given Antoinette. She was going to have to leave her parents soon anyway, but if Julien had waited until the others were sent to Texas in September 1841, she would have been transported with four of her brothers, a fact that would certainly have made the trip easier for her. She endured the trip to Texas alone, torn from family, responsible for a three-year-old, whipped for falling asleep, and having to endure a three-month wait for the rest of the community. Scott could have found a job; so could the enslaved adults on the trip, but Rhody had to take care of Antoinette all that time and hope that others provided for her while they were providing for Antoinette.

It was a tall order for Julien to find a place where he would be safe from the people he had wronged. A wagonload of creditors and lawyers; a betrayed wife; and an abandoned, pregnant mistress made formidable enemies. The new Republic of Texas had been founded in 1836, when it won its independence from Mexico, and it offered Julien advantages that a state in the Union would be unable to provide. Texas was legally a foreign country, so the Republic put him out of the reach of his creditors, his irate wife and her relatives, and Barbara Way: at least for a while, Texas fit his needs beautifully.

The rather Solomon-like decision Julien Devereux had to make about his land and slaves must have been difficult. If he remained in Alabama, he would have been forced to sell most of his slaves to help repay his debts. If he did that, he would not have been able to work his land. On the other hand, if he sold his land and kept his slaves, he would have had no place for them to live and no way for him and his families—both black and white—to make a living. He owed many individuals and at least four banks in three states. He had to make some serious decisions, and what he decided would profoundly affect his human chattel.

It appeared he made those decisions in a businesslike manner and selected slaves to bring to Texas who would be of the most benefit to him. It is unclear how many enslaved Julien owned in his own right. We do know from the extant documents that he purchased a total of two women and eight children in 1832 and 1833, and he purchased Jack before he left Alabama from his brother-in-law. The core of the community—the family slaves—were owned by Julien's father, John, and they were all relocated. A complete list of who stayed in Alabama and who came to Texas and who owned them is not in the records, but we can piece together some things.

Compounding the confusion are the enslaved who came as part of Adaline Bradley's marriage to Julien. Whether they were loaned, given as wedding gifts, or just there for a one-time chore or event, if they were in Julien's presence when he left Alabama and he wanted someone who belonged to the Bradleys, he likely would have taken them. The old adage that possession is nine-tenths of the law is applicable here. Laws did not protect women's property in a marriage, so slaves on the Devereux plantation that had belonged to Adaline Bradley Devereux were the property of Julien Sidney Devereux.

Basically, the family slaves who belonged to John Devereux all went to Texas. Julien Devereux then selected the most productive members of the enslaved community on the Alabama plantation, sent the less useful back to his wife and her family, and spirited away a few others who may or may not have been his property. Louisiana Devereux Holcombe and her husband Henry B. Holcombe never accused Julien of taking any of their slaves; however, he clearly took Gincy's children. How he managed that is unclear. His choices broke up families and decades-old friendships among the enslaved workers owned by the extended Devereux family. He had no good options, and by virtue of his actions, his slave property had even fewer.

Chapter Three
Alabama to Texas

Up one hill and down another all day till it is a nuff

to kill the mules and horses.[1]

ANDREW GILBERT SCOTT, JULY 1841

The most notable thing about the new country, to which Julien was forcibly removing many of the slaves he controlled, was its size. Today, even by modern standards, it is just too big. Crossing the state in any direction by automobile requires twelve hours. Travelers from our past were fond of repeating the old Texas adage, "The sun has ris' and the sun has set, and we is in Texas yet." It encompasses more distinct geographic areas than any other state. Out of the ten largest cities in the United States, four are in Texas. Expand that list to the twenty largest cities, and Texas heads the list with six. The size of the state has caused an identity crisis for its modern inhabitants. We cannot figure out whether we are Southerners, Coastal folk, Westerners, Plains people or something in between. Even for residents it is sometimes hard to know what to make of a state where the temperature in the northern part of the state is below freezing with blowing snow, while dwellers on the coast are wearing shorts, T-shirts, and flip-flops. Many coastal and valley Texans have never seen snow, much less shoveled it, and some Texans in the Panhandle have never tasted the salty waters of the Gulf of Mexico.

The question of state identity that plagues modern Texans was easier to answer before the Civil War. Until after the 1870s and the near annihilation of southern Native American tribes—mostly Comanche, Kiowa, and some Apache—the western half of Texas, which gives modern Texas so much of its identity, was considered dangerous by settlers who feared attacks by tribes who resented white encroachment onto their lands. The ninety-eighth meridian, which runs approximately from Wichita Falls south through the Hill Country just west of Austin and on down to the Gulf Coast near the Nueces River and modern-day Corpus Christi, was the line that divided eastern Texas, identified with the Old South, and the western half that was Comancheria—Comanche country. It was not until 1875, when Quanah Parker surrendered himself and his rapidly diminishing, half-starved band of Quahadi Comanches, that Texans started to settle western Texas.

Make no mistake about it, before the Civil War Texas was in and of the South. It was the land of cotton and slavery, of rich, sandy soil and abundant rainfall, largely settled by people who migrated from the southern sister states of Louisiana, Alabama, and Mississippi. These adventurous souls came to grow cotton, get rich, gain prestige and power, and they brought their slave labor force with them to do so. To anyone who thinks Texas was something other than Southern during the period of 1840 to 1860, it is wise to consider

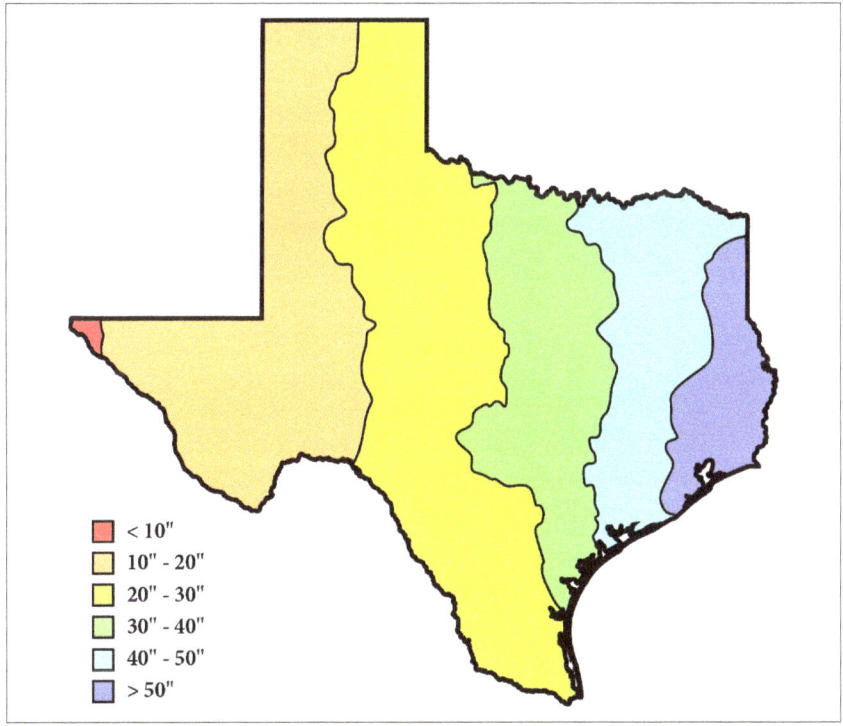

AVERAGE ANNUAL RAINFALL 1980–PRESENT

Texas's many rainfall zones correlate to the different geographical regions of the state. Since thirty inches of rain annually is the minimum amount for agricultural success, it is obvious why East Texas was the western zone of Southern cotton culture. Heading west, the land becomes increasingly arid and finally merges into the Chihuahuan Desert in far West Texas. *Courtesy of Jeffrey Snider.*

this fact: In 1860 the percentage of the population in Texas composed of slaves was 30.22 percent.[2] The percentage of the slave population in Virginia—The Old Dominion, the heart of the South, the colonial settlement to which slaves were first imported—was 30.74 percent,[3] almost the same as that of Texas. Slavery's roots were deep into Texas soil.

Until 1821, the Spanish government allowed slavery in its most northerly state of Tejas, or Texas. In that year, Mexico won its independence from Spain, and the new nation prohibited slavery in its new constitution. However, until 1830, Mexico was very lax about allowing Americans to bring their slaves into the Mexican state. That year Mexico passed a law with the unassuming name of the Law of April 6, 1830,[4] which prohibited Americans from bringing slaves into Texas. The Mexican legislation did grandfather owners who already had slaves in Texas, allowing them to keep their slaves. The Texians, as they were called, were Southerners to the core and committed to the South's "peculiar institution" of slavery. After 1830, hostilities over slavery and import taxes worsened steadily between the national government in Mexico City and the northern state of Texas until they boiled over into the Texas Revolution in 1836.[5]

The Texians were successful in achieving their independence in April 1836, and quickly established the new Republic of Texas. There was little doubt at the time that Texas was meant to become a Southern slave state. However, the abolition movement had reached sufficient prominence in the North and East to block Texas's entrance into the Union for nine years. When pro-expansionist James K. Polk won the presidency in 1844, Texas was waiting for an invitation to join the Union like a southern belle in her ball gown waiting for young men to ask her to dance.

When Texas entered the Union in 1845, the state was on the move toward its greatest decade of growth in the antebellum period. From 1850 to 1860, thousands of settlers across the South would carve the initials "GTT" for "Gone to Texas" on the doors and walls of their cabins and farmhouses and head west to Texas for some of the best and cheapest cotton lands available in the Old South. In that ten-year span, the population of the new state of Texas grew from 212,000 total habitants, 58,000 of whom were slaves, to 604,000 total population, of whom 183,000 were enslaved.[6] Julien Devereux was ahead of the curve in his removal to Texas. However, he had more push than pull factors than most emigrants.

Once he hoisted his toddler Antoinette into the wagon with the slave girl Rhody and waved Andrew Scott down the long road toward Texas, the die

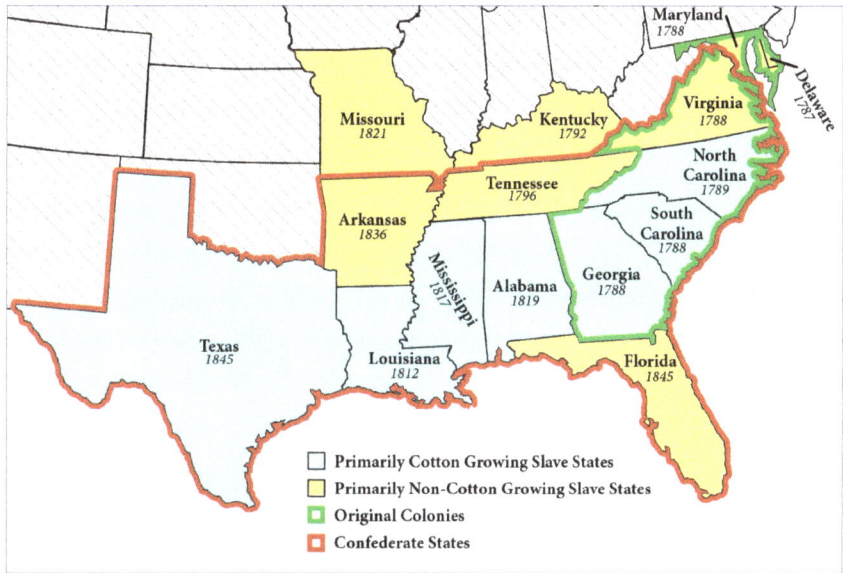

In the lower South where most slaves lived, cotton dominated agriculture. In border states where there were fewer slaves, more diverse agriculture was practiced. When the Civil War began, the border states remained in the Union. *Courtesy of Jeffrey Snider.*

was cast. Julien Devereux, the core of the Devereux Slave Community, and assorted others were about to be among those emigrants going to Texas. There were still issues to be settled. First, the move would separate families and create heartache and pain for many members of the Slave Community. As Julien sorted out those he wanted to transport to Texas, he separated families and lifelong friends. Some had connections to the slaves owned by the Holcombe and the Bradley families, and some individuals had relatives on neighboring farms and plantations. These relationships suffered the pain of the separation and the likelihood of its permanency.

Another question involved John Devereux, who was nearly seventy-two years old in 1841. If he did not kick, scream, and stomp the floor, he probably wanted to and had every right to do so. Julien had chased women, money, land, and slaves until he drove John's life's work straight into ruination. John Devereux contemplated not going to Texas with Julien. The purchaser of the plantation in 1840 wrote Julien, "Say to old Mr. Devereux that he may keep possession of his house & his flowers and his fruits . . . as long as he pleases—that it would be acceptable to me if he would become a member of my family. I would freely board such a man for his company."⁷ However, John's choices were as limited as Julien's. Pitching in his lot with people he hardly knew was not inviting. Staying in Alabama with his daughter Louisiana and her brood meant staying with son-in-law Henry Holcombe, and that was never going to happen. John Devereux would go to Texas, but not until the spring of 1842.⁸

The trip that carried Julien and Barbara Way's daughter, Antoinette, to Texas was the first of five trips to the new country. The second and third trips occurred nearly simultaneously in the early fall of 1841. The first trip included nineteen enslaved people under the direction of William Baker Bond (see Table 1), with the second trip under the control of Alfred Devereux, one of John's nephews. In April 1842, Bond sued Julien for the expenses he incurred

TABLE 1. SLAVES UNDER COMMAND OF WILLIAM BAKER BOND

SLAVE NAME	AGE	SPOUSE	PARENTS
Jack	Older	unknown	Purchased from H.B.Holcombe
Lucius	30		Gincy
Martin	28	Louisa	Gincy
Maria	26	Levin	Gincy
Martha	24		Gincy
Jack	5		Maria
Green	1		Maria
Levin Jr.	11		Maria
Juba	8		Maria
Richmond	1		Martha
Joanna	4		Martha
July	16		Mindah and Jerry
Jim	14		Mindah and Jerry
Stephen	15		Mindah and Jerry
Joe	11		Mindah and Jerry
Judy	16		Kizzy
William	13		Kizzy
Alleck	10		Kizzy
Allen	10		Kizzy

returning to Alabama.⁹ Bond claimed he left Alabama on the thirtieth of September.¹⁰ Table 1: "Slaves Under Command of William Baker Bond" details the names, ages, and parents of the slaves who went west with Bond.¹¹

There is more information in the records about the people on this list. Jack, the machinist, was probably the oldest of the three men. "Machinist" was a nineteenth-century term for a blacksmith with mechanical and engineering skills. The previous year Julien's brother-in-law, Henry B. Holcombe, had written Julien to "try and sell Jack" so he could pay a note. Julien bought Jack from Holcombe for $1280.¹² Jack probably left a family somewhere in the exchange. Martha, Maria, Martin, and Leven were children of Gincy. The ten-year-old Rhody, sent ahead to care for Antoinette, was a sister to Stephen, July, Joe, and Jim.¹³ These five were the children of Jerry and Mindah, who along with their daughter Elmina, remained in Alabama with the Bradley family.¹⁴

On the same day, September 30, 1841, John Devereux noted in his memorandum book that "Alfred Devereux started from Hobson's Choice in Macon County Alabama with 20 slaves of mine and 4 of his and 11 of Juliens—35 total."¹⁵ The group was bound for Jasper County in Texas. According to John Devereux, Alfred had a large "waggon drawn by 6 fin mules to carry forage & possessions" and a "light waggon with two mules."¹⁶ Alfred Devereux had the Devereux family's one-horse carriage. Wonder who got to ride to Texas?

Five years later, in the spring of 1846, Julien and John Devereux and Alfred Devereux sued each other over expenses related to Alfred's role in the trip. The individuals who were with Alfred are listed in the lawsuit, which can be found in the *Record of the District Court Book of the County of Montgomery, Texas* (see Table 2).¹⁷

The majority of the enslaved under Alfred's charge appeared to be John's and a few of Julien's. However, there is no doubt that Julien sent individuals to Texas that he did not rightfully own; in fact, the Bradley family later claimed he stole some of their slaves.¹⁸ In the summer of 1848, Julien's former wife, Adaline, learned of the lawsuit over John's will and inheritance and tried to recover some of her losses. A man named Robinson, working on Adaline's behalf, wrote Henry Holcombe seeking information about Julien. Robinson claimed Julien's creditors had taken all he "left her," and Adaline intended "to pursue" him "with her claims" for compensation. Louisiana wrote Julien,

TABLE 2. SLAVES TAKEN TO TEXAS BY ALFRED DEVEREUX[19]

SLAVE NAME	AGE	SPOUSE	MOTHER
Tabby	54	Scott	
Henry	33	Maria	Tabby
Maria		Henry	
Mary	30		"
Ham	4		Mary
Anthony	2		"
Amey	22	Jesse	
Charles	5		Amey
Mahala	3		"
Daniel	16		Tabby
Randal	10		"
Polly	21		"
Cyrus			Polly
Lucy			"
Flora	19		Tabby
Colin			Flora
Cynthia	18		Tabby
Louisa	14		"
Diana	13		"
Matilda	12		"
Anderson	27		"
Katy	24		
Little Tabby	7 months		Katy
Tom	4		
Jane	1		
Jesse		Amey	
Eliza	16		Maria
Peninah	9		"
Simms			
Amos	5		Maria
Walton	3		"

"Mr. H would have nothing to do with it."[20] Louisiana reported to Julien that Adaline had contacted her directly and "made her case lamentable but did not say in her letter what she intended to do."[21] Nothing further was mentioned about it.

It is, however, interesting. John Devereux's diary recorded "14 Negroes to Brooklyn [Alabama] which with 9 there will make 23 for his wifes share of the spoils."[22] The average price of a slave in 1840 was $500, so Julien left her with property worth approximately $11,500; that is hardly penury, provided she could keep it. Putting the pieces together, I suspect Julien took some of the Bradley slaves he wanted and left Adaline some of his whom he considered less valuable and useful. Then his creditors took from Adaline those slaves legally belonging to Julien.

Julien practiced law in Alabama, so he had to have known the state's laws on women and property. He was still married to Adaline until 1843, so *all* the slaves could have been sold at auction to cover his debts. It just defies credibility that Julien did not understand that, in addition to leaving Adaline destitute and utterly dependent on her family for support, he was sacrificing the lives, families, and futures of those twenty-three people he handed over to her. Once again Julien's actions wreaked havoc upon the enslaved population he left behind, breaking up their families even further. So much for Southern paternalism.

Others in question included the children of Gincy. It appears that Gincy belonged to Louisiana Devereux Holcombe; legally, her children and grandchildren should have been Louisiana's property, although there is no record of when or under what circumstances John Devereux gave ownership of Gincy to his daughter. Amey, Jesse, and their children were also on the list of those with Alfred Devereux. Jesse was a vital and integral part of the Devereux Plantation in Texas, and presumably in Alabama, but his origins were unclear. Who did he belong to?

The fourth trip began on October 8, 1841, when "Julien started with a waggon & 6 mules."[23] John Devereux had a wily sense of humor, which shows in his account of learning that news of Julien's departure was going around the neighborhood. John wrote that one neighbor, Will Waddell, reported that Thompson, another neighbor and former business partner of Julien's, went to "Montgomery probably to spread the emigrating news and to offer his services as a debtor catcher to the Bank."[24]

An overland trip in the 1840s from southeastern Alabama to Texas was an arduous undertaking. Andrew Scott wrote several letters to Julien Devereux from the trail in the summer of 1841, and from those letters, a great many details about the journey emerge. Most of the slaves walked to Texas, at least for most of the way. In fact, most emigrants—black and white—walked across the South to their destinations. The records indicate Andrew Scott left the Devereux Plantation around June 12, 1841. The group was eight miles shy of the Mississippi border on June 22, 1841. They crossed the Mississippi River on July 8, but only after they "cut a road about a qarter of a mile through the swamp" because the mighty Mississippi had "caved and taken in the road."[25] Andrew Scott had a "Big waggon" and "the Jersy," both of which broke on the trip and required on-the-road repairs. A Jersey Wagon was basically a box on wheels that was pulled by one or two horses. It was mostly for forage and supplies. In addition, Scott's group endured "a vary Bad storm in the pine woods" with "the nearest house . . . three miles" away.[26] The roads were rough and the land hilly. After they landed in Louisiana, they found "it almost imposable to pass our money."[27] That would have made acquiring food and fodder very difficult. They would have gotten to Jasper, Texas, by about July 20, 1841. Julien did not arrive until November of that year, so Andrew Scott was on his own for five months with a three-year-old child, her ten-year-old caregiver, and a group of slaves he had to care for.

If the group headed by Andrew Scott left the Alabama plantation, Val Verdi, around June 12 and, estimating optimistically, were in Jasper, Texas, by July 20, the trip took slightly more than a month. This estimate of just over one month to make the trip to Texas is supported by the trip records of William Baker Bond, who later sued for expenses he believed to be Julien's responsibility. Bond left Alabama on September 30, and on October 30, he crossed the Sabine River into Texas. He was still three days away from Jasper. Four to five weeks appeared to be an average time for such a trip.

About half of the internal slave trade was like the Devereux slave migration—with white owners and their families traveling with some, if not all, of the enslaved families they owned. Slave transfers of this nature were still disruptive and destructive to slave communities, but hardly as much as the slave trade conducted by professional traders for profit, with enslaved peoples bought at auctions or rounded up in local countrysides. Historian Steven Deyle wrote, "The domestic slave trade, in all of its components, was very much the lifeblood of the southern slave system, and without it, the institution would have ceased to exist."[28] Southern gentlemen like Julien Devereux would have taken offense if anyone had called them slave traders, because professional slave traders were considered lower class and distasteful. However, the Julien Devereuxes of the South were as much slave traders as the professionals they bought and sold to all the time.

Professional traders and enslavers commonly moved slaves in coffles, groups of enslaved African Americans chained, roped, or yoked together to prevent escape. On any trail or road, coffles of miserable, brokenhearted men, women, and children could be seen trudging their way across the American South. They were being driven to slave markets in the interior of the South, where farmers and planters were hungry for more slaves. The land in the older eastern states was playing out, and in those areas slave owners' most valuable commodities were their slaves. By 1850 or so, eastern seaboard states like Virginia, particularly, were hemorrhaging slaves to the western areas of the South. The trade was so common it gave rise to the old adage of "being sold down river" or "gone down the river." It also provided Harriet Beecher Stowe with some of her most disturbing and memorable images for *Uncle Tom's Cabin*.

The rate of travel for slaves in coffles being moved for sale and profit was much more brutal than the Devereux slaves' experience. Edward Baptist stated, "There are 1,760 yards in a mile—more than 2,000 steps. Forty thousand is a long day's journey. Two hundred thousand is a hard week."[29] He was estimating a twenty-mile day, which would have been a grueling pace. It is approximately five hundred miles from southern Alabama, near present-day Andalusia, approximately where the Devereux Val Verdi Plantation was located, to Jasper, Texas. Based on the time and space, it is more likely that the Devereux Slave Community covered between twelve to fifteen miles in a day. That pace would have gotten them there in about four to six weeks.

Baker Bond's lawsuit provides a fascinating and enlightening look at the trip. For one, it was not cheap to make a month-long trip across the American South with nineteen dependents in the 1840s. Bond's account does not relate what Julien had already paid him, but it does relate that Bond believed Devereux still owed him $1,014.04. It included $20 for eleven pairs of shoes for slaves; no doubt walking across all or part of four states would wear out a pair of shoes.[30]

The ferry crossing of the Mississippi River was $28.50, while crossing the Sabine River was another $8.75. Food purchases included two gallons of whiskey, a bushel of potatoes, 600 pounds of beef, four pounds of sugar, and an astonishing 242 pounds of bacon. The standard package of bacon in a grocery store today is twelve ounces, so the twenty people ate the equivalent of nearly 323 packages of bacon! With the beef added, a minimum of 842 pounds of meat were consumed on Bond's journey—42.1 pounds per person. If the trip took thirty days, that gave each person 1.4 pounds per day on the trip. The supplies with which the group started and what they may have acquired on the road are unknown, but certainly it was some amount. Many of those travelers were children and women, who would not have consumed the average. The amount may seem excessive, yet the protein and calories needed for the journey were enormous.[31] Walking for ten hours on level ground, the average person will burn 2,100 calories. Factor in the activities of this business of crossing the country in the nineteenth century: they would have included, but were not limited to, climbing and descending the hills, navigating the bad roads, crossing rivers, repairing vehicles, getting stuck and unstuck, loading and unloading each day, setting up and taking down camp, feeding and caring for the stock, and then doing all this day after day for four weeks, maybe longer for some groups, and you get the picture. It increased the caloric need to between 3,000 and 4,000 calories each day—not just calories, but protein calories.

Of greatest interest is the two gallons of whiskey.[32] That is 256 ounces of brew. The average shot glass is 1.5 or 1.0 fluid ounces, depending on the barkeep. Either Baker Bond consumed 4.5 to 6.4 shots a day, or the slaves were imbibing some of the whiskey. Of the nineteen people with Bond, six were under ten years of age. Only three were grown men. It appears somebody went to Texas half lit. The total of the lawsuit also included one doctor's visit and Bond's return trip to Alabama. There is no record of whether the booze and the doctor's visit were related.

Julien Devereux and his various groups of slaves under the direction of Baker Bond and Alfred Devereux entered Texas at Jasper, where Julien became a citizen of the "Republic in the Year 1841 and the County of Jasper sometime in November 1841" and the "oath of alegiance . . . was duly & formally administered."[33] Julien Devereux was officially a Texan and, by virtue of his oath, so were his and his father's enslaved property.

Chapter Four
Early Years in Texas

Henry & Tabby arrived safely on Saturday night.
The negroes were glad to see their mother.[1]

DR. WILLIAM TAYLOR, MAY 2, 1851

This was the element of slavery the enslaved dreaded most: the permanent separation of family and friends by sale, inheritance, financial distress, or death of an owner. Using the Works Progress Administration's Slave Narrative Collection, Robert William Fogel estimated that a third of all enslaved single-parent households were the result of the sale or transfer of one partner or the other.[2] Approximately one-third to one-half of all slaves could expect to be separated from family and friends at least once in their lifetimes. According to Edward Baptist, the "cumulative risk of being sold at some point in the course of the three decades of one's 'salable' years was close to 50 percent for each individual."[3] The Devereux Slave Community was no different in those facts of separation, but because of Tabby and Scott they had a much-enhanced chance of overcoming the trauma of the move to Texas.

Because of their profound effect on the Devereux Slave Community, it is important that readers know about Tabby, the matriarch, and Scott, the patriarch. It was Tabby and Scott who gave the Devereux Slave Community the strength to overcome all the heartache and pain of the move to Texas. Their guiding presence mitigated the effect of the transfer to Texas in the earlier years, and it would become even more vital eight years later when a worse disaster hit the community. We know for certain Tabby and Scott were not born in Africa, but there is no way to know how far back their African roots went or who their ancestors in their home country were. Based on the dates and locations of their births, it is certain their American roots date back to the Revolutionary War. Tabby was born in Wilkes County, Georgia, in 1787.[4] That was the same year that the leaders of the country to which her

Mahala was the daughter of Amy who was the daughter of Tabby and Scott. She was called Helen, a variation of her name, in slavery. After emancipation she used the name Helen exclusively. She married Anthony Caddell and raised a family.
Courtesy of Lynnda Caddell Stephens.

ancestors were forced to come wrote the Constitution. That document legalized and entrenched into statute the system that held her, her mate, and all her descendants in bondage for life. Scott was younger than Tabby. He was born in Columbia County, Georgia, in 1792.[5]

The couple probably "jumped the broom" in 1807, when Tabby was about twenty and Scott was only sixteen or seventeen. "Jumping the broom" was a ritual constituting a couple's marriage that originated in African tradition and came across the Atlantic with the human cargo packed into slave ships.[6] The rite probably had something to do with the broom as a symbol of housekeeping and indicated the formation of a household. At any rate, the ceremony came to America with African slaves and has endured in African American culture to this time. Jumping the broom was as official as slave marriages ever were. They could be torn apart as an owner determined. It was not until after emancipation in 1865 that slave marriages were registered and legalized under a provision of the Freedmen's Bureau's duties and responsibilities.[7]

Together, Tabby and Scott raised eleven children to adulthood. Tabby was twenty-one years old when she and Scott had their first child, Henry, in 1808. Mary was born in 1811, Anderson in 1814, Amy in 1819, Polly in 1820, Flora in 1822, Cynthia in 1823, Daniel in 1825, Louisa in 1827, Matilda in 1829, and Randle in 1831.[8] They welcomed numerous grandchildren and great-grandchildren into the family as the years continued to accumulate.

After Henry's birth in 1808, the children continued coming every two to three years, with the exception of a five-year break between Anderson in 1814 and Amy in 1819. Their last child, Randle, was born the day after Christmas in 1831. Tabby would have been twenty-one when her first child was born and forty-four when her last was born. Chances are high that she lost a child at birth or miscarried at least one time, maybe more. Such maternal losses may account for the five-year gap between Anderson and Amy. The extant documents show that Tabby spent almost twenty-five years of her life gestating or lactating (eighteen months was used for lactation).[9] These numbers help illuminate the lives of enslaved women.

The 1860 Census Slave Schedule listed a sixty-eight-year-old black male slave on the Devereux plantation. That slave was Scott. A seventy-three-year-old black female slave was listed; this was Tabby.[10] Tabby lived into her seventh decade, and Scott may have also lived that long. If Scott lived to be seventy-three years old, he would have seen the end of slavery. For several reasons, Scott and Tabby were major keys to the success and cohesion of the Devereux Slave Community throughout the years, and not just in difficult times. First, they lived long lives, and thus were able to exert considerable influence over the community for a long period of time. Second, they also had many children who lived to adulthood, integrating them into every family grouping on the plantation. Thus, over a span of many years, they were a symbol of marital and family success. Scott and Tabby carried wisdom resulting from decades of survival under the South's oppressive system of slavery. Probably more than any other slaves on the plantation, they communicated their knowledge of how to endure slavery to younger and more impulsive slaves.

We have no idea what Tabby or Scott looked like, exactly when they died, or precisely where they are buried. No doubt they are buried near the plantation, but the graves remain undiscovered at the time of this writing. When all the mentions of Tabby and Scott in the Devereux Family Papers were assembled, they began to reveal a life that had texture and substance—a life lived by real people. How they reacted to the events, joys, and heartbreaks of their lives is unknown, but considerable detail about their lives and their kinships is available in the records.

Tabby came to Texas in the fall of 1841, but Scott came in the spring of 1842, with John William Devereux. They traveled first to Mobile, Alabama, where John "laid out" twenty dollars "for cloathing . . . for myself & Scott."[11] Then, the two went by steamboat down the Mississippi River to New Orleans. While in New Orleans, John bought a set of handguns, a hat, and a knife for himself and "for Scott small things" for which he paid "62 cents."[12] The two men boarded a schooner for Galveston, Texas, where John paid ten dollars at the Old Capitol Wharfage for their trip.[13] The two men ran up a bill of $7.50 at the Houston House where they stayed in Houston while they gathered provisions for the trip to Lake Creek in Montgomery County.[14]

John Devereux made an additional purchase in New Orleans. He recorded he carried "2 dollars" given to him "by Dougherty for nice fabric for Tabby."[15] John Devereux recorded the money as "sum pd. for callico . . . for Tabby,"[16] and he selected it for her. We do not know exactly why Robert Dougherty was giving Tabby calico fabric; however, it may have been her sewing or culinary prowess that he found endearing. She was the cook for the Devereux family for most of her adult life, and Robert Dougherty had stayed on the property several times while the purchase and transfer of the plantation were being finalized, so Dougherty probably sampled her cooking. When Julien Devereux was in Montgomery County and Tabby in Rusk County, he blamed his loss of appetite on his "having been so accustomed to Tabby's kind of cooking."[17] Certainly, the civilizing influence of a woman who could cook was nothing new in human existence.

However, Tabby's most important and all-consuming duty was to help care for the Devereux children born to Julien and his second wife, Sarah Ann Landrum Devereux. She wrote to Julien on November 22, 1855, that "granna [Tabby] fell down in her house and sprained her wrist very badly so that she could not use it to sew or do any but walk about after the children."[18] No doubt Tabby had a hand in the upbringing of all the Devereux children and was attached to them. In 1851, Tabby went to Marshall, Texas, for a visit to her children who belonged to Louisiana Devereux Holcombe by that time. Louisiana's son-in-law, William Taylor, was a physician, and he wrote Julien on May 2, 1851, that all had arrived safely.[19] Apparently, Tabby was concerned about a

On the Porch. **Artist Robert Jones.**

rash the Devereux baby had. Taylor added to his letter, "Tabby has describe the eruption on your babe's skin to me," but he had no long-distance diagnosis or remedy to offer.[20]

However, it was the last Devereux child, Charles, born in 1855, who was clearly her favorite. When Charlie was born, Tabby thought she might be allowed to name him. She maintained that hope for a while. On December 15, 1855, Antoinette Devereux tacked a note onto Sarah's letter to Julien while he was in Austin on legislative duty: "Granma says she thinks that she will get to name yet and that she is looking for a name every day."[21] In addition to the four Devereux sons, Tabby raised her own children and probably helped with the rearing of her grandchildren and great-grandchildren. It is not inconceivable that Tabby had a major hand in the upbringing of as many as one hundred children or more, white and black, over the years of her adult life.

That, in addition to her sewing, cooking, and housekeeping, would have been a remarkable and substantial contribution to the Devereux family's well-being. Her contributions to the enslaved were so widespread and of such long duration that they are simply incalculable.

Scott, for his part, had an equally integral role on the plantation. Though the early years in Montgomery County are not as well documented as later years, we know Scott was there by 1842. Sometime in 1845, Scott was relocated to Rusk County—probably when John Devereux went there. Scott began the new year of 1846 in charge of the enslaved workforce. John wrote on January 1, 1846, that "Negroes under management of Negro Scott no overseer young Reed's time out."[22] (Reed was the previous overseer.) Scott assisted John Devereux with various duties for the rest of the year. John recorded he "had to get Scott to help" when he and three other slaves burned an area in preparation for planting.[23] When he wasn't doing something for John Devereux, Scott performed many services. He often went to send and retrieve mail from the tiny hamlets of Anadarco (modern spelling is Anadarko) and New Salem. He also drove the wagon and carriage, picked the garden, and assisted Tabby in the care of the children when needed.

When Julien Devereux commented on the role of the two older slaves on his plantation and in his life, he always mentioned them together. On June 23, 1854, while he was on a trip east for his health, he wrote Sarah from Kentucky that he hoped "Tabby & Scott will continue to assist you in taking care of our boys."[24] A year later, while he was in Austin, he wrote Sarah that he hoped "Scott & Tabby will take good care of them all and especially Albert,"[25] who had been ill. All the Devereux children were boys, and Scott probably had a more essential role in their upbringing as they matured into older boys.

Tabby and Scott straddled the line that divided black enslaved from white enslaver and served both groups in different capacities. As the oldest of the family slaves and household servants, the two were the eyes and ears of the white enslavers in the Big House. Their positions carried some responsibility to keep the master informed about the affairs of the slave quarters. However, their home was in the quarters, and the inhabitants of the quarters were family, both by blood relations and by kinship of situation.

Walking the fine line between the Slave Community and the Devereux family must have required the acumen of modern-day diplomats. Almost certainly, Tabby and Scott carried more information back to the quarters from the main house than they carried the other way. However, making decisions about what information went in which direction was crucial to their positions. If they misjudged and failed to tell Julien or John Devereux something that resulted in a problem, the owners might hold them responsible. If they were indiscreet in the information they relayed from the slave quarters, the quarters might bear repercussions for their misjudgment.

Early slave studies from the 1970s recognized the importance of the slave quarters. *The Slave Community*, a classic written in 1972 by John Blassingame, recognized the quarters as the slaves' primary environment that imported "ethical rules and fostered cooperation, mutual assistance, and black solidarity" among the community members.[26] It is clear that Tabby and Scott—along with Martin, Jesse and Henry—had closer associations with their white enslavers than did the majority of the slave community. In the opinion of the author, those individuals would have taken on some responsibility for protecting the quarters and preserving as much of the privacy and integrity of the Slave Community as they could.

Working more as a sociologist than a historian, Herbert G. Gutman calls people like Tabby and Scott cultural "links between generations of different families."[27] In reality, they were probably more important as keys to continuity and endurance. It is possible they frequently made judgment calls on whether to share information they learned or not. For instance, Scott and Tabby were in a position to be the first slaves to learn that Julien was pulling up stakes and moving to Texas. While we have no way of knowing exactly how they handled that information, it is possible they decided to keep quiet until they knew more.

In clause 8 of his will, Julien Devereux rewarded Tabby and Scott for their lifetime service, not with their freedom, but with care and consideration for their final years. They were bequeathed to his sons Albert and Julien, and "in consideration of the long and faithful services of the old negro Slaves," they were to "be exempt from compulsory personal labor—further than to give such attention as they may be able in nursing and taking care of my children after my death."[28] Considering that his sons had not reached their majority when Julien died, the fate of Scott and Tabby was left to Julien's wife, Sarah, and his other executors. According to Devereux records, Tabby had died at Monte Verdi by the end of 1860.[29] Scott's last years are unclear; he may have lived to see emancipation.

The connections of families on the plantation were complex; however, the community all centered around Tabby and Scott. The community survived a number of difficult periods throughout its life and managed to repair itself in times of trial and stress. Its strength and cohesion came from within, and doubtless emerged under the guiding hands of Tabby and Scott. There was simply no other entity with the ability to wield such influence and power as it must have taken to survive and recover the separations. Think of the Devereux Slave Community as a woven cloth, with the crisscrossing of all the various people as threads that compose the fabric. The more numerous the threads are and the tighter the weave, the stronger the piece of fabric becomes. The strength of the Slave Community, woven in large part by the hands and hearts of Tabby and Scott, was tested in the move to Texas, but the test the Slave Community was to endure eight years after coming to Texas was even greater.

No doubt Tabby and Scott made the transition to Montgomery County easier than it might have been without their guiding presence. By late 1841, Julien Devereux had settled the Slave Community led by Tabby and Scott at Lake Creek in Montgomery County, Texas, just north of present-day Houston. He purchased the established plantation of Cyrus Dikeman on December 3, 1841.[30] The trip had been long and taxing. Settling into a new place that was in newer country and did not have all the comforts of the Alabama plantation was another challenge. Additionally, the enslaver's finances were still in disarray. Most of the money Julien received from the sale of his Alabama plantation had disappeared rapidly, used for the costs of their move and the purchase of the Lake Creek property.

As early as January 1842, Julien was begging for credit. He hired Flora out for a month's credit at the store in Montgomery County.[31] Texas merchants were not shy about reminding Julien he owed them real money, and they expected to be paid promptly. One Houston merchant, whose signature is unreadable, wrote Julien on March 3, 1842, "you will remember that we Texians have no credit in the States to purchase our goods & that we have to pay the cash for them."[32] Julien's troubles all flowed downstream from Julien to his enslaved property.

On February 10, 1843, Julien petitioned a Texas court for a divorce from Adaline Bradley Devereux. Julien swore in the petition that the failure of his marriage was Adaline's fault. He stated Adaline was "irritable and violent" of

TEXAS LOCATIONS OF DEVEREUX ACTIVITIES

Various members of the Community made numerous trips to and from Lake Creek and Rusk County and from Rusk County to Shreveport, Louisiana. *Courtesy of Jeffrey Snider.*

temper with "excesses of passion . . . and such outrageous conduct as . . . to render the life of your petitioner one of Extreme Misery." Julien swore he had been "a true faithful Kind and affectionate husband."[33] John Devereux backed up his son in the Texas court, and no one brought up that unpleasant little matter of Barbara Scott Way and Julien's two illegitimate children. The petition was filed on February 10, 1843,[34] and granted on March 20, 1843.[35] In June 1843, thirty-nine-year-old Julien Devereux married Sarah Ann Landrum,

PART I

 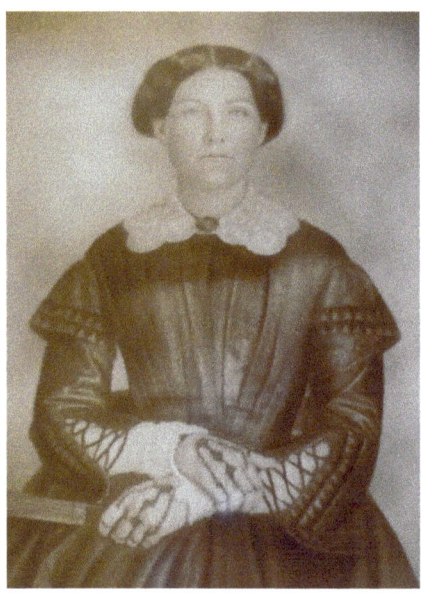

These pictures of Julien Sidney Devereux and Sarah Landrum Devereux were probably made around the time of their marriage in 1843. Sarah appears very young, and while his hair was thinning, Julien was still a handsome man and probably what Sarah's family considered a good catch. Both photographs hang in the central hall of the Monte Verdi Plantation House. *Courtesy of Paul Snider with permission of Joe Koch.*

the sixteen-year-old daughter of Texas Revolution veteran John Landrum. Landrum's farm bordered the Devereux Plantation. Sarah was twenty-three years younger than her husband; however, she was a level-headed, practical young woman and devoted to her husband. The marriage once again gave the Devereux Slave Community a mistress.

None of the Devereux family cared much for the Lake Creek area. The malaria-carrying mosquitoes, scorpions, swampy conditions, and deluges of rain (rightly termed "frog-stranglers") were all too common. The persistent fogs and mists contributed to additional weather-related illnesses. Everybody complained about the miasmas that made the place such a trial. Miasma literally translates to "bad air." The term was widely used in the nineteenth century, and miasmas were blamed for all sorts of illnesses. John Devereux was especially critical of the Montgomery area and ready to go; his comments were vociferous and funny. If only he had known what air-conditioning was going to do to that area of Texas, now home to the third largest city in the nation.

Deo Volente (God Willing) I will take myself away from middle Texas... June next—I'll be seen no more between San Jacinto and Lake Creek—I have been three years in this poison'd atmosphere—drank bad water and breath'd foul aire—have borne northers and scorchers—inundations drouths—pestilence endemic and epidemic—chilld with cold & moisture and again panting and exhausted with hot sirocco air surcharged with malaria from stagnant lakes—the sun is obsur'd every morning until nine oclock and constant rains from October until June and drouth from June until October—we frequently experience a feverish heat like a day in July and the next hour a norther as cold as we might expect in January—however a man may distrust his own judgement in other matters he can at least guard against the tyranny of climate and not do violence to his common sense by continuing... in the most variable of all variations the weather in Middle Texas.[36]

Since yellow fever, cholera, and malaria were all swampy types of diseases and leading causes of illness and death, John's claims were not too far-fetched. Julien, John, and Sarah were all ready to permanently depart from the area and resettle in deep East Texas in Rusk County.

John Devereux was there with part of the Community as early as December 1845. Julien Devereux was at Lake Creek, negotiating the sale of his land and planning the complete move. On February 4, 1846, Julien wrote his father in Rusk County from Lake Creek, "I have no fear of being troubled with any of them [the Slave Community] when I move."[37] Even Anderson, a slave who did not want to go to Rusk County, told the overseer "that he thought more of his master than his wife and was ready to go whenever the rest was carried."[38] However, Julien's confidence had limits, because he wrote he had said "nothing about selling as it might discourage Howerton [new overseer] and the negroes."[39] It seems inconceivable they had not figured it out. After all, half of them were already in East Texas clearing fields to plant crops and building outbuildings and slave quarters.

Apparently, the final move did cause more consternation in the Community than Julien had anticipated. On March 7, 1846, Julien wrote John that "Dock remains here for the present and is very much averse to going at all."[40] Julien realized it might be necessary to sell the slave, so he asked his father, "What is the best you will take for him if it becomes absolutely necessary to sell him?" Julien did not relate all the problems with the slaves, but he did tell John, "Mr. Howerton (the overseer) can explain our difficulties with the negroes."[41] Unfortunately, John did not record "the difficulties" in his memorandum book.[42] It was interesting to note that Scott and Tabby were not at Lake Creek the entire time the move to Rusk County was developing. Their presence might have helped to calm some of the difficulties of the move. Scott, particularly, might have had some influence on Dock's decision not to go. According to several family members, Dock was sold in Montgomery County.

The difficulties with the Slave Community that Julien Devereux referenced encountering in the move from Montgomery County to Rusk County were less disruptive than the earlier breakup in Alabama. No doubt the presence of Tabby and Scott and their descendants helped to calm the uncertainty that accompanied each of the moves, but one can wonder if it dawned on the Devereux enslavers that not having Tabby and Scott at Lake Creek during the preparation for the move to Rusk County had been a mistake. The worst crisis to come struck straight at the heart of the Slave Community from 1847 to 1849. It decimated Tabby and Scott's immediate family and left the core of the Community sorely jeopardized and at risk.

Chapter Five
Descendants All, 2014

My momma told me, "You know, your grandmother only cleaned those steps. She never had a chance to sit there. And you are sitting there." So I just lay down on them.

CORETTA WILLIAMS, 2014 CADDELL REUNION

This collection of interviews was done in 2014. Most of the descendants knew some of their history and were interested in learning more. Even though modern descendants of the Devereux Slave Community have moved all across the country, a remarkable number of them still live in and around the Texas counties of Rusk and Nacogdoches, quite near where their ancestors were enslaved on the Monte Verdi Plantation. The families are close, and their family reunions are well attended. Many descendants are kin to multiple branches of the original families. For example, a Caddell can be a Bowens; a Bowens a Henry; a Henry an Anderson: an Anderson a Freeney, and on it goes through the list of families descended from the community. When all the cousins are factored into the equation, the kinship connections grow exponentially. The close proximity and familial connections made it an ideal setting for interviewing descendants. Even after more than a century and a half, the presence of Tabby and Scott could be sensed in the interviews with their descendants.

Individuals were chosen at random. The words are all theirs; I combined material to get the topical arrangements and make their thoughts read smoothly. Otherwise, I just made sure the recorder was running; no way could I compete with what these individual descendants were saying.

CORETTA WILLIAMS INTERVIEW
Coretta Williams is the producer for the morning show on CBS19 in Tyler, Texas. I interviewed her on June 7, 2014. She traces her roots to Tabby and Scott through Mahala (Helen), daughter of Amy and Jesse.

HER HERITAGE

Our big family reunion was back in 2001, and I learned a lot then. [We all] visited the plantation, and I crossed the steps onto the porch, and my momma told me, "You know, your grandmother only cleaned those steps. She never had a chance to sit there. And you are sitting there." So I just lay down on them.

I had the opportunity to go to the cemetery where Helen and Anthony were buried this last October. The headstones—it's incredible. His headstone is right next to hers and you can still see the inscription on it. It's very visible. I posted it on Facebook and one of my former bosses said, "They would be so surprised about you now. You are such a hard worker. They would be really, really proud of you right now." The station [I used to work for] did a piece on Monte Verdi Plantation. So I was able to air it on the show that I produce, our morning show. I emailed my bosses on it. And they emailed me back and said, "Don't lose track of your heritage. That's amazing."

My sister has a friend and she has a little girl [who] is five. She has a picture on Facebook of her and her little girl, and her mother and her grandmother. The relationship between this little girl and her great-grandmother was like how me and Helen [Mahala] would have been. I began comparing myself. I could have been five, and me and Helen would be in the picture. That's how I visualize it. I'm proud of them, just to know some of the things they had to go through, and then where I am today. They might not have felt proud of their heritage, but I am. I kind of see them like superstars, like celebrities. The fact that I'm a young black woman in the position I am.

RACE

Two years ago I was in the store buying some outfits, and the lady asked me what was I getting ready for, and I told her. We talked about the family reunion, and I showed her some of the pictures. She started crying, "I'm sorry what they went through." White people will want to hug me. And I'll tell them it's okay. They will apologize. In a way, they are sorry what my great-grandparents went through being slaves. So, I guess, just sort of apologizing, I guess in a way, make things right.

[So] we've come a long way but I'm not sure if both sides can talk about it [race] yet.

I love my president [Barack Obama], and sometimes it is so hurtful to hear the comments made toward him from other races. One of my friends commented, "I've seen all this stuff on Facebook, and I wonder what they would really think if we had lunch together in the cafeteria." And I wrote her, "Good point." But having a black president, I've never seen so much controversy over it. I've never seen so many negative comments about him. About any president ever. It hurts. I can walk through the stores in the entertainment section, and they may have the TVs on CNN and people walking by will say, "There's that old president." And I'm like, "Don't you see me standing here?" I'd think they'd see me standing there and have a little bit of respect, but they just go by and having all these comments. And some of it on Facebook. I'm like shocked. It's coming from the opposite race, and I'm thinking, "What's with these people?"

Coretta Williams.
Courtesy of Coretta Williams.

I look at my job. They respect me because I am the producer. The people I work with, we've been together like ten years. They are all I've ever known. And they respect me. The general managers are always saying, "You're doing such a good job." And at work do I ever feel threatened? No, sometimes, but no.

CYNTHIA TATUM INTERVIEW

Cynthia Tatum, a Caddell descendant, did not realize until the interview that she had the same first name as one of Tabby and Scott's children. Cynthia, the ancestor, was transferred to Louisiana Devereux Holcombe in the 1848 lawsuit that split the Community. Cynthia Tatum's granddaughter is named after the original Tabby.

HER ANCESTORS

We were not here under our own will, and we didn't have permission over our surroundings. We didn't have a lot of choices to make.

Everybody made choices for us. I do think about it a lot. I'm going to talk about Helen. She was a slave there. I don't know who her father was, but she didn't come out looking like her mom and dad. I think that's why we keep coming out looking like we do.

Some of us look awfully light to be African American. I used to work for the city of Fort Worth in the voter's registration office, and I loved my job. My best friend was African American. I mean she looked African American, but they treated us totally different. And I didn't like the way they treated her. On the other side where I looked a little different. So I eventually changed jobs.

Cynthia Tatum.
Courtesy of Cynthia Tatum.

HER LIFE

I wanted to be a cosmetologist. I practiced for fifteen years. But I've always loved children so that's my occupation now. I'm a childcare director. A licensed daycare center in Fort Worth, Texas, and I've been doing it now for fourteen years. I love children. I'm only licensed for fifty children. I have ten employees and about thirty-five parents.

I think they [our ancestors] would be glad that we keep in touch with each other. You know I think the Caddells love children and we love family. My daughter had a little girl, and she named her Tabby. We had just learned of Tabby. I'm proud that they [our ancestors] lived the way they did because a lot of us have really did well. So I'm proud of them.

MARTHA HAMMONS INTERVIEW

Martha Hammons's mother died when Martha was five. She was raised by her maternal grandparents so that her father could leave to find work. Her mother's death left her living a much different life from what she had been accustomed to living. She had stories to share about her life as a black woman that were missing from the interviews of the younger people.

HER MOTHER

It was extremely hard for me. My mother and daddy had lived in the city. In the country it was much, much harder for me. Before my mother passed, I didn't work in the fields. After my mother passed my grandmother had me work in the fields, and we would get up early in the morning and work all day in the hot sun. I would be so glad when it rained or when it would come a freeze, and we didn't have to work at all that day. I was so elated I didn't know what to do. I stayed with them until I was eighteen when I finished high school. The most enjoyable thing I had was when it snowed. We would go out and get fresh snow and if grandma had some vanilla flavoring we'd make snow ice cream.

As a child I cried a lot because everybody I knew had a mother, and I didn't have a mother. A lot of time when I did go to school I'd go out into the woods and sit on a log and just cry because I didn't have a mother. And I just hated the country. It was just so much work and I didn't like picking cotton. I didn't feel like I should be out there picking cotton 'cause I knew if my mother had lived I wouldn't be out in the fields. My mother was a schoolteacher. Her name was Ada Ross. And Jeri [Mills] was telling me that she found in the records where my mother was chosen for some new school that they had built. I remember Dad told me that they would have to go around to the back to get her check. She could never go into the front of the school.

HER SCHOOLING

Yes, I was going to school some days if someone was coming to pick us up to go to school, but not all days. A truck, great big truck, and a white guy would be driving and we'd sit on the truck and go to the school. I didn't get to go to school as often as some of the children. But whenever the white guy would come through on the truck that day I'd get to go to school. [Other days] I'd either pick cotton or pile those peanuts up into a big pile. And then they would come and get the peanuts in the pile and put it on the truck. I don't know what they would do with it. My prayer was always, "I hope it rains." Anyway, that was always my prayer that it would rain or turn cold, if it was in the winter time.

I went to Texas College [in Tyler, Texas]. And I was in college for two and a half years, and I got married, and I never did go back to get my degree. I had a son and we moved to Fort Worth. Then I had another baby. And she was a year and three months younger than my son, and after that I gave it up 'cause I knew I wasn't going to be able to go back to school.

HER FAMILY'S EXPERIENCES WITH RACE IN AMERICA

And I remember after I got married, we moved to Fort Worth, and the store still had black and white water fountains and restrooms. After my husband and I got married, we liked to travel, and we'd go to Houston or San Antonio. So we would take our vacations at the same time. We would

Martha Hammons.
Courtesy of Martha Hammons.

always have to set up a plan how far we would be at a certain time so we could spend the night with some of our relatives because we were never allowed to go into the hotels. And I remember one year my husband was not going with us. He found out at the last minute that he couldn't get off. So my son and my daughter and my baby decided we were going to go to San Antonio. We saw a sign that said Johnson Ranch, and [Lyndon B.] Johnson was president at the time. It was right after [President John F.] Kennedy was killed. The kids were telling me they had studied about Johnson's Ranch being in Texas, so we decided we were going to go see it. We couldn't get in so we stood at the gate [and] made pictures of Johnson's Ranch. On the way back we stopped at a store. It was an old run-down building, but still a store. [For years there was an old building that was a mercantile business and a post office at Hye, Texas, very near the Johnson Ranch. The Secret Service agents at the Johnson Ranch picked up the presidential mail there.] And me and my three kids went in and we wanted to buy newspapers, books, and stuff with Johnson on them, and the old white man called his wife. And he just stood and looked at us like we were crazy. Junior, my son, said, "Do you think we can buy these books in here?" And the old man said, "Yes, you got the money you can pay for 'em."

We couldn't eat on the way, so we took food. We didn't prepare enough food so we stopped at a store, and there were four white guys sitting out there. My son was sixteen, he was driving, so when we drove up the guys stopped playing dominoes and they just sat around and looked at us. So we went into the store, and we bought some bologna, crackers, and candy and they sort of followed us to the door like, "What are these black people doing out here?" My aunt and I had been communicating by letter about where we were supposed to stop. We sat in that park until my aunt got off from work and stayed until she could come and get us and carry us to her house. It was kind of rough in those days.

We were going to Atlanta, Georgia. We were on the road all day and all night because we couldn't stop in the hotel. We stopped at the park somewhere and ate, but we ran out of food. We stopped and wanted to use the restroom. The children and all wanted to use the restroom and the man hollered—"blacks go to the back." Anyway, we got back in the car and drove on down the street where we could stop on the road.

I remember when one summer we were going to California and the kids were small, and my husband had told us that in California you could go to the front door, and you could do this, and you could do that. And finally we crossed the state line and my husband said, "Okay, the first time we go to a cafe or restaurant we go in the front." For those kids, I think Junior was nine and Brenda was eight, and the baby is six years younger than Brenda. Anyway, those kids got out and ran right in the door of the restroom and the café, and they were so elated. The lady came to the door and said, "May I help you?" And then she started asking what they wanted to eat. And then she started playing with the baby, and the kids were surprised. They didn't remember white people being nice to them. All she had was some soup, I remember. And they had green beans and my husband said, "I've eaten so many green beans in my life I don't even want my kids to eat 'em."

This part [of the south] is a little bit better than Louisiana or Shreveport I'm told. Now in Atlanta, we didn't have any problems there. My son and his wife moved there. You know, my son worked

Martha Hammons on the dance floor with her daughter Brenda Sadler and author Joleene Maddox Snider. *Courtesy of Paul Snider.*

for Gulf Oil for years in several positions. There was no prejudice toward him. As a matter of fact, they liked him. He was sent down there to hire blacks, and they had this big, beautiful house. But they were threatened in a storm, and Henry was at work and these white ladies befriended his wife and children. They [the white neighbors] went up and told them they needed to move. They befriended them, because he was living in a white neighborhood. Some places are not as bad, even though the state may be bad. But they were really nice to them.

There were some blacks that did real well back in the day. I know my mother's people did. They did real well. There were others who suffered. It just seems like there are some who have, and there are some who have not. Those who have usually strive extremely hard to have whatever they have accomplished. But there are those who just don't, and, of course, I find that to be in any race. There are those who strive to be successful and some just lazy.

BRENDA WILLIAMS INTERVIEW

Brenda Williams is Coretta Williams's mother. Brenda is the supervisor and chief cook for a school cafeteria. She worked her way up to the position over the years. Her other daughter was graduating with her RN degree that June 2014.

ON HER PAST

Oh, [I know] just what my dad has told me. My mother and my dad, they wouldn't go into too much history of things like that. Some of the things I can remember came through my Uncle Tom, who lived with us. He was like an in-law in the family. Aunt Nannie had just passed away, and Uncle Tom was mourning over her death so much that my daddy said, "I'm going to stay a few weeks with him until he kinda gets settled." And then he stayed until Tom was ninety-five. He stayed there with him, and they worked the farm together. They were farmers.

One day daddy told him, "I'm going to get married." He says, "Okay." Daddy says, "I don't have anywhere to bring my wife." He said, "You can bring her here." That was my mother Corine. They all stayed together, worked together, shared the bills together. I was the baby. He was more like a grandfather to me. And he loved us as grandchildren. That's what he called us. He'd say, "These are my grandchildren."

He ended up staying there after I was grown. He always said he didn't want to go to a nursing home and he turned everything back to Daddy. So my mother told me he would never go to a nursing home. And we all worked. My mother worked in the cafeteria. She worked there [Henderson] until her retirement, and at that time Daddy retired and his health was getting real bad, so my mother went home and said, "I'm going to take care of him."

Johnny, my husband, and I got married about two years later. Three months after that he [Uncle Tom] passed away. He was ninety-five years old. I always said that hurt me worse than almost my daddy, because I would stay there with him when my mother would go out to visit with a neighbor or go somewhere. I preferred to stay at home, because he

Brenda Williams.
Courtesy of Brenda Williams.

was always there. I learned some things—he'd always tell me about his wife. And he'd call her Mother HeLa [Mahala/Helen], too. That was just some of the things I could remember.

And then there was Lucindy. She lived in a big house not far from us. It was one of those kinda houses that every room went into the hall. She passed away when I must have been like a senior in high school. And we used to stop by every once in a while, when she was on the porch. All I knew was "Aunt Cindy"—that was what they called her. And I knew her children, 'cause one of her daughters taught me down at Concord School. But I didn't know that this was history. If I'd a known that I'd a sat down and talked to her.

Then there was the baby girl named Marinthe. She lived down in Jacksonville, and she just passed away cause Coretta remembered her real good. We used to go and visit with her. She was the youngest one, and I always enjoyed her so much. I just loved Aunt Marinthe. She was the last one to pass away. She was born in 1892.

ON HER HERITAGE

I heard of Tabby, but I never heard of Amy. And I knew that she was over there on the Devereux farm, and that was where she was raised. And where she is buried. We went in there. There were graves all over the place, and the prettiest flowers growing. Nobody had been there to plant them; they were just growing in the wild. Then they named it "Cemetery Campground Springs," and that is what it is named today. Then Anthony Caddell helped to start the church where we all was raised. And it was not a bury ground so we started burying in the Miles Cemetery.

All I know about Tabby was that she came from Georgia and that two slave owners brought her here to the plantation. I thought at one time that Tabby was Helen's mother, but she wasn't. She had Amy and then Amy had Helen. But I guess they were all born there on the plantation. She was known as Grandma Caddell. So you could put that. That's what they called her.

PART II

Chapter Six
John Devereux's Legacy

Heard the hands carrolling their melodies

and at 12 heard their large horn.[1]

JOHN WILLIAM DEVEREUX, MEMORANDUM BOOK, 1847

John Devereux spent the entire year of 1846 in Rusk County, often alone with the slaves and the overseer. After his death, whether he was lucid and sound of mind during his twilight years became a crucial issue. In Louisiana Devereux Holcombe's legal challenge to her father's 1845 will, she claimed her father was not in his right mind because of his advanced age and because her brother, Julien, had undue influence over him. It is very doubtful that the Texas court that heard the case considered the last few years of John William Devereux's life. If they had, it might have changed the outcome for Tabby and Scott's children and grandchildren.

John Devereux was a learned, intelligent man, and many things occupied his mind. He read voraciously and wrote often in his diaries and journals. He was a seeker of knowledge about the natural world, Earth's creation and solar system, and historical events. He did have a dark side and penned many a poem, essay, and sermon that dwelled on death, loss, and mourning. Considering he had buried two wives, three infants, and one grown son, the tone of his writings makes sense. In many ways, loss defined much of his life, but he was a busy and productive man all his life, including his last two years.

The elder Devereux was involved to an astonishing degree in the establishment of the new plantation in Rusk County. He laid out the ground for new slave cabins, hosted new neighbors who came to call, paid for various services and goods, commented on work routines, recorded the daily weather, noted the health of the plantation's inhabitants and others in the surrounding area, planned his garden, and planted the starts and seeds others acquired for him.

There were days when he was unwell and did little. Then he would be up and about, absorbed in some project or another. He did much of his own planting, sometimes with the help of one of the slave men, sometimes not. In one such digging, he unearthed the skeleton of an infant, which he assumed was a Native American child who was born and died on the land.[2] He rode the countryside a good bit. Occasionally, he rode alone to Mount Enterprise for business or pleasure. An amazing amount of company came and went from the Devereux Plantation, and they often stayed for dinner and a night's lodging. One evening, he recorded seven at table. All the visitors placed an extra burden on the enslaved, who had to cook, clean, wash, and tend to the visitors' animals, but John seemed to enjoy the company. On Monday, June 1, 1846, he complained, "I remain solus—no white person on the plantation but myself."[3] Later, on June 16, 1846, he lamented he "dined alone"[4] (that is, lacking white companionship). However, he was never without some company from the slave population. Henry, Scott, July, and others were often mentioned in his daily writings.

His memorandum book for 1846 is detailed and shows no signs of dementia. To the contrary, it documents his lucidity. He was funny at times; commenting about the continued rain, he said, "it was, it did, now go."[5] Other times, he was thoughtful and compassionate. For example, on January 2, 1846, he wrote, "Henry continues to suffer."[6] On January 6, he noted Henry was better and commented, "Henry able to ride about."[7] He kept a close watch on things, especially the health and well-being of the slaves. He recorded births and deaths for the year and found their midwife, Mrs. Wornell, something of an entertainment. On Monday, May 25, 1846, he wrote she was as "busy as the old one in a gale of wind."[8] During the sick season in August, he tried to sound optimistic, writing on the eleventh, "we sail with hope on our bow."[9] However, by the fifteenth, the weather was hot and damp and very "unfavorable to sick and the convalescent—we have some bad cases yet of relapses."[10] On the eighteenth, he wrote, "we have about ten cases of Fever at this time and as many more unable to go about or do any thing."[11] This level of attention to detail and involvement in plantation affairs contradicts Louisiana's claims that John was an individual of feeble mind.

John Devereux's yearlong quest to stay abreast of the ups and downs of the functionality of the Lylly' Mill, a local business, was enough to be a full-time job. Cornmeal was the core of the southern diet, and it was the same for the group at Rusk County, so a working mill was a necessity. On Tuesday, February 10, 1846, he wrote, "day rainy and dark hands can't do any thing but beat meal in a mortar—all mills broke."[12] On February 12, he recorded "mill at Lyllyville mended and we have got meal."[13] On Monday, February 16, things once again looked bleak: "Mill broke again worse than before they say she will not grind again in less than two or three weeks—we have the mortar a going to get our dinners."[14] On February 19, "Heard and Dan return'd from Graysons mill with two bags of meal."[15] The subject then dropped out of his entries for a month or so. On April 9, however, he wrote, "mill stop'd grinding by high water—near neighbours grinding on our steel mills."[16] The problem slowly improved over the year.

After Julien arrived in the spring of 1846 with the last of the slaves from Montgomery County, John was never without company. In November 1846, he wrote that he went up to the house Julien and Sarah occupied as the "family wanted me to join them for Thanksgiving Dinner."[17] He enjoyed seeing his grandchild William, called Billy, who was named for him (John's middle name was William), even going so far as to assist in the care of a pet fawn for the entertainment of the child.[18] There were times, however, that he tired of the family and craved his own company.

His level of mobility and activity is demonstrated by a trip he made with Julien, Jesse, and Martin to Shreveport for business. On Friday, July 17, 1846, seven months after he wrote the 1845 will and was supposedly impaired in body and mind, John accompanied the others and a man named Gage on the way to Shreveport. He was seventy-nine at the time. He rode horseback or in one of the wagons the entire trip. His memorandum book recorded the journey. On Friday, they "started with 2 waggons . . . and camped near his [Gage's] house 15 miles."[19] Presumably, Gage remained at his home while John and the others moved on. On Saturday the eighteenth, they "went 25 miles and encamped for the night."[20] On Sunday, they "went 15 miles,"[21] crossed the Sabine River by ferry, and then went ten more miles before stopping for the night. On the twentieth, they traveled "26 miles and stayed at the 4-mile Spring."[22] The next morning, a Tuesday, he and Julien rode the four miles into Shreveport "to breakfast," and the "waggons arrived soon after."[23]

They spent two nights in town and departed early on July 23, 1846, for the return trip. The evening before, they sent the wagons and drivers "out to 4 mile springs,"[24] so they had to get an early start the next morning to meet the wagons and travel "20 miles."[25] On Friday, they traveled another twenty miles. On Saturday, the twenty-fifth of July, the "waggon broke down in the morning."[26] John Devereux "left Julien to go home and send"[27] the overseer. Presumably, John had the other wagon and at least one of the slave men. That day they traveled twenty-two miles and another twenty miles on Sunday. On Monday, July 27, 1846, John arrived "home about 3 o'clock and started Howerton to meet the waggon,"[28] so he would have traveled another ten to fifteen miles that day.

In eleven days, he had traveled nearly two hundred miles, all by horseback or freight wagon. This trip occurred six months after he wrote the will his daughter and son-in-law contested because of his disabilities, and a year before his death. It was July in a hot Texas summer, and there was little time to rest in between the going and returning trips. He traveled with Martin or Jesse for two and a half days and camped on the road nine of the eleven nights. On Tuesday, July 28, 1846, John Devereux recorded in his memorandum book that he was "very feeble & sore with jolts but thankful that I am no worse."[29] He may have been sore and tired, but mentally deranged and physically wasted he was most assuredly not.

Even before he went to Texas, he had begun to think about the disposition of his property following his demise. In January 1841, he wrote to his daughter Louisiana Devereux Holcombe, "I would like very much if Mr. H [Henry B. Holcombe] would have some property in land and slaves so situated that they would not be liable to be taken from you in case he should fail or die to which I would add half of my negroes at my demise which cannot be long."[30] Six months later, in June of the same year, he informed Louisiana that he would "keep a will in the hands of a confidential friend that, provided that half of my family of negroes will be for your individual benefit during your lifetime after my demise."[31] It is important to note that John, in this second letter to his daughter, did not specifically say he was giving half his slaves to her; rather, he said she would have the "benefit" of them.

If John Devereux wrote a will in 1841 or 1842, it did not survive. The first extant will was written, signed, and witnessed on December 30, 1843, in Montgomery County, Texas. The will reads as follows: "Its my Will that my twenty two Negroes and their increase shall remain and continue in the possession of my said son Julien S. Devereux for his uses during his life time under the care of the Court."[32] John provided for his slaves after Julien's demise by designating certain ones that would go to the four youngest children of his daughter Louisiana. They were "Anderson, Polly and her three children Cyrus, Lucy and Ossian. Flora and her child Collin, Cynthia, Louisa, Diana and Matilda to decend to the four Youngest Children of my daughter Louisiana A Holcombe."[33]

In this will, John clarified what he had meant by "benefit" of his slave property for Louisiana. Julien was "required to make an allowance of what may be reasonable and paid annually to my daughter for her own uses."[34] In essence, John left *all* of his slaves to his son Julien for their use in Julien's lifetime, and then gave Louisiana's half to her children after Julien's death. In other words, he skipped over his daughter Louisiana in bequeathing his wealth. Why, one wonders?

The answer is in the will. John Devereux did not like or trust Henry B. Holcombe, his son-in-law, and did not want him to have any control over Tabby, Scott, or their descendants. In 1843, neither the property laws of Texas nor Alabama allowed women to own property exclusive of their spouses. It is the legal principle of "coverture" or covered. Women's legal rights and existence were legally covered under the laws that recognized and applied to the men to whom the women were attached. In simple terms, anything and everything a woman had or owned was the property of her husband; upon marriage women simply ceased to exist as independent human entities. John Devereux knew the law in Alabama: he was involved in public affairs and served multiple times in the Alabama legislature. To will half of the family slaves to his daughter would have meant leaving twelve individuals at the mercy of Henry Holcombe. Property laws governing women in Texas, where the will was probated, granted separate property rights to married women in 1846, but this was not the case in Alabama. There, wives could legally own property; however, husbands still had control of it. John Devereux knew that any family slaves he left to his daughter would essentially be Henry B. Holcombe's property, and to do with as he pleased.

Today some might call Henry B. Holcombe a visionary, but to John Devereux he was his thoughtless, ne'er-do-well son-in-law. Holcombe tied up every penny he had in city real estate. To his credit, he saw the way the urban areas were developing, and he gambled on it. He was a man who was too far ahead of his time for his ventures to be successful, and besides, he lacked the personal traits to be an accomplished businessman. Holcombe was always involved in a new business, a new get-rich-quick scheme or a new position, and he was always lamenting about previous adventures that had not worked for him. His failures were always the fault of someone or something other than his own actions.

John Devereux was adamant that his son-in-law have nothing to do with the family slaves. In the section addressing guardianship of the slaves intended for his Holcombe grandchildren, John unloaded on Holcombe. He wrote, "It is probable my son in law Henry B. Holcombe . . . may claim a preference to the Guardianship of the property of his children."[35] John strenuously objected to that. "It is my Will and desire that the court having the appointing of Guardians may not appoint him."[36] John Devereux then lost his manners completely, and family civility took a hike. Devereux wrote that Holcombe "has no feeling or regard for the comfort or the morals of slaves but would take them to Houston or Galveston and let them to the highest bidder."[37] John followed with an indictment of Holcombe's management style: "he did so with his own and has consequently gotten scarce of slaves several of them died in Augusta and very little increase of those intended for my daughters children."[38] John then laid out his other wishes. He did not want the slaves hired out to cruel masters or to masters in cities. They were to live in the country where their morals could be protected. City life provided too much opportunity for moral laxity for the enslaved, in John Devereux's opinion.[39] He skirted the issue of the extra freedom and opportunities that city life offered for slaves.

Two years later, on September 4, 1845, he wrote his final will, making the previous one null and void. In it, he came up with a totally new wrinkle. The slaves were still to be in the "possession and for the use and benefit of my son Julien Sidney Devereux for and during his lifetime."[40] However, upon Julien's death, the slaves and their issue were to be divided as closely as possible according to families and inherited by only two of Louisiana's children, "the two sons of my Daughter Louisiana."[41] John named both grandsons in the will, and then required each of them to change their last name to Devereux before they could inherit the slave property. Further, he stipulated that if they refused to do so or if they changed their names back to Holcombe at any point, they would lose ownership of the slaves and Julien's heirs could sue for their return. If only one grandson agreed to change his name, then that grandson would receive both his and his sibling's slaves. If neither grandson agreed to change his name, then all slaves remained with Julien Devereux's heirs or in guardianship for them.[42]

If John Devereux was not in his right mind, then he was crazy like a fox. He had found a novel way of disposing of Henry Holcombe to the extent that the name Holcombe would not go forward in future generations. Just in case Holcombe tried to intervene, John left instructions that excluded Holcombe from any possible control by guardianship. The slaves were not to be placed in Holcombe's "possession as guardian or next friend of his sons or under any pretext whatever, not that he is severe or hard to Slaves but that he would put them in the hands of such"[43] that would jeopardize their well-being.

Clearly John Devereux's twists and turns in his 1843 and 1845 wills were driven by his dislike and distrust of his son-in-law, Henry B. Holcombe. Gincy and her children were part of the "family slaves," and it may have been Holcombe's use of them that set John's teeth on edge. It was the lives of Gincy and her children that financed many of Holcombe's business escapades, and John knew it. On one list of slaves are the names of three other individuals that were no longer part of the Devereux Slave Community. The context indicates that they belonged to Holcombe. Out to the side is a note that read, "Dead, all dead."[44] The handwriting is John William Devereux's.

By late 1847, it was clear his health was failing. Chronic heart problems and persistent dysentery had troubled him for months. On April 6, he "rode to the Old Garden" but paid for it with severe leg pain that afternoon.[45] On April 9, 1847, he wrote in his journal, "I am not long for this world."[46] Only opiates allowed him some relief from the pain and discomfort, but his mind seemed sound. He complained about the doctors, his persistent dysentery, and swollen feet and legs.

Most of his journal for the last months of his life dealt with doctors and his illnesses, but he addressed other things as well and was clear and mentally alert. He may have realized the clarity of his mind would be an issue after his death. On April 21, 1847, he wrote, "dark, damp cool dreary—Lucid—."[47] On Sunday, April 25, 1847, he wrote, "I have been annoyed with wives, Children & friends and kept besieg'd by spoiled children. But it has to be so."[48] Apparently, relatives and friends were coming for final goodbyes. In mid-May, his writings started to dwindle off, but he made it until the "tenth day of June," when he wrote, "adieu."[49] He left behind one son, Julien; one daughter, Louisiana; and numerous grandchildren—legitimate and illegitimate. What hung in the balance were the lives of twenty-seven African Americans held in slavery who still belonged to him. When he passed away on June 22, 1847,[50] he went to his Maker doubtless secure in the knowledge that he had provided for and protected those individuals he owned. He was wrong.

Chapter Seven
Final Decision

No, I say that his [John William Devereux] mind was not right if he made it so unlike anything he made before which makes me say it could not be his will.[1]

LOUISIANA DEVEREUX HOLCOMBE, 1847

John Devereux did not plan on his daughter, Louisiana Devereux Holcombe, contesting his will, thus placing the fate of his property in the hands of a Texas Court. As the white litigants jockeyed for position, hired counsel, and argued about money, the families and lives of the black humans involved were nothing more than property in the eyes of the law. There was absolutely no control or willpower they could exercise over the situation.

The relationship between Julien and his sister, Louisiana, is relevant because of how it affected Tabby, Scott, and their descendants. John Devereux's will was very specific about the property in question:

> a family of slaves belonging to me being at this time twenty-four in number and known as a negro man named Scott his wife Tabby and their children Henry Mary Anderson Amey Polly Flora Cynthia Daniel Louisa Matilda and Randal their Grand children Diana Ham Anthony Phebe children of Mary and Charles Mahala and Sam Children of Amy and Cyrus, Lucy and Ossian, Children of Polly and Collin son of Flora.[2]

By the time the division was made, John W. Devereux had twenty-nine slaves, and they were all subject to the court's jurisdiction.

It is important to focus on the individual people in the Devereux Slave Community whose futures were at stake. The following paragraph identifies the individuals, all of whom were subject to separation from family and the larger community. They had spouses, families, and friendships that had developed over a lifetime. They had names, relationships, lives, homes, jobs, and a presence both as individuals and as part of the whole.

Since status in terms of slavery was determined by the mother, Scott and Tabby's male children were in jeopardy of being separated from their families, but their spouses and children could not be included in the transfer. Both Scott and Tabby fell under the control of the will. Mary and her children Diana, Ham, Anthony, and Phebe were subject to transfer, along with Diana's children Jesse and Harrison, who were Mary's grandchildren and Scott and Tabby's great-grandchildren. Amey and her children Charles, Mahala, and Sam; Polly and her children Cyrus, Lucy, Ossian, and Little Scott; Flora and her son Collin; Cynthia and her daughter Betty; and Matilda and her son Anderson were all subject to the will. The children of the five daughters—Amey, Polly, Flora, Cynthia, and Matilda—were Scott and Tabby's grandchildren. Also included were Scott and Tabby's children Daniel, Louisa, and Randle.

It is possible that some of the enslaved preferred the transfer for personal reasons. We do not know if they did or if they did not. What we do know is that none of the enslaved people had a choice in the matter. The division was imposed upon them by the misstep of a collection of individuals and entities. First, John William Devereux failed to find a more equitable and protective solution to the dispensation of his human property. Second, Louisiana Devereux Holcombe and her husband Henry B. Holcombe contested the will without regard to the fate of the human property involved. Third, Julien Sidney Devereux did not arrange a better pretrial solution or provide leadership to the estate's legal team for an effective defense. Lastly, a Texas court erroneously ignored John Devereux's will and accepted his daughter's argument that her father was deranged and under Julien's thumb.

Louisiana Devereux Holcombe came to Texas after her father's death, so she was probably at Monte Verdi in July and August of 1847. Julien had their father's will, but he waited until Louisiana was literally walking out his door to go home before he gave her a copy. She wrote Julien in August 1847 after her return to Mobile, "I did not until the last minute before I left your house know that you had the will in possession."[3] Louisiana wrote Julien a number of letters in the months following John Devereux's death and before the court ruled in her favor in November 1848. It is the letter of August 1847, however, that is the longest and most informative. It contains all her future arguments with her brother.

Louisiana concentrated on several recurring themes. She reminded Julien over and over that he was "rich as the world would call it" and she "very poor as regards property"[4] and with a large family. Nearly all her letters reminded Julien he had it in his "power to do" her "justice."[5] Additionally, Louisiana repeatedly reminded Julien there were but two of them "and no third party or person to interfere with it."[6] This statement related to her repeated desire that "Mr. H" not "have anything to say in the matter."

It did not matter what Louisiana thought, wrote, or wanted. As a married woman, whatever she did in either Texas or Alabama had to be conjoined with her husband Henry B. Holcombe. It was over halfway through the twentieth century before married women could singularly and in their own right undertake legal redress in a court of law in Texas. Louisiana was a century too early to contest her father's will or own her inheritance in her own name. It was in the "January Term 1848" that Louisiana and Henry B. Holcombe filed a petition for a redress of their grievances with the "Judge of the 6th judicial District." The petition stated:

> John W. Devereux at the time he made his said last will and testament was of very advanced age to wit of the age of eighty years and much impaired in his mind and was not of sound and disposing memory. That he had been for the last ten years of his life entirely under the control of his said son Julian S. Devereux with whom he lived at the time of his death.[7]

Of course it was not Julien who had influenced John Devereux; it was the behavior of Louisiana's husband, Henry B. Holcombe.

Julien appeared to be somewhat unconcerned with the case. If he answered his sister's letters, she did not receive them, for she repeatedly mentioned she had not heard from him. It was likely he elected not to write back. (Even from this distance, Louisiana is a bit tiresome and whiny.) On April 16, 1848, Julien wrote a friend, H. F. Stern, that "an attempt is being made to break the will—the Executors have the best counsel in the country engaged in the defense and are fully assured that the will—will be sustained." Julien added: "Let the case go as it may it will not effect me seriously in any way."[8] It certainly affected the slaves, and he elected to ignore that fact.

This seems strange considering the value of slaves in 1848. Julien knew exactly what the people were worth because the twenty-seven slaves had been appraised on April 23, 1848, at the request of Julien or someone else (see Table 3).[9] Three men's names appeared on the appraisal: William Reagan, Enoch Spivy, and Selanus Everett.[10] All three were associated with the Devereux men in other matters. Everett was a near neighbor who did blacksmithing work for the Devereuxes. Reagan was one of the witnesses to John Devereux's 1845 will, and Spivy's name appeared in several letters, as well. The three men evaluated the slaves in the following list:

TABLE 3. **INITIAL APPRAISAL OF JOHN DEVEREUX'S LEGACY**[11]

NAME	VALUE (IN $)
Scott (an old man)	300
Tabby (an old woman)	200
Henry (negro man diseased)	300
Mary & 3 children Ham, Anthony & Phoebe	1200
Amy & 3 children Charles, Mahala & Sam	1200
Polly & 4 children Cyrus, Lucy, Ossian and Little Scott	1350
Flora & child Collin	800
Cynthia & child Betty	700
Daniel	650
Louisa	500
Matilda	500
Randall	500
Diana & 2 children Jesse and Harrison	750

The total assessment was $8,950, so there is no doubt Julien knew what the people were worth. It is also certain he knew the dispute mattered a great deal to the slaves, as their lives would be profoundly affected by the outcome. Taking into account the inaccuracy of money extrapolation from then to now—and assuming it was even possible to place a dollar evaluation on a human being—the enslaved owned by John Devereux were worth nearly one-third of $1 million.[12]

In his April 1848 letter to Stern, Julien wrote he "had been advised to attack the will" himself "upon the grounds that" he had "paid taxes for the property for twenty three years and otherwise executed entire control over it."[13] He had

LANDS OWNED BY JULIEN S. DEVEREUX IN 1855

By the time of his death Julien Devereux owned over 10,500 acres, far in excess of the amount his slave workforce could have cultivated. *Courtesy of Jeffrey Snider.*

also fed, clothed, provisioned, and cared for the persons he called "property." At the very least, a counterclaim might have recovered enough funds to have kept a person or two in the Community. An even stronger argument was that John Devereux was not mentally impaired. His copious writings and notes from 1846 and 1847 proved that. Additionally, there were many people available to testify to his sanity in those last years.

Julien was ordered to "appear before the Honorable District Court . . . for the County of Rusk in the Town of Henderson . . . On the first monday of July next (A.A [D]. 1848)" to "answer the demands"[14] of his sister and her husband. When the final judgment was issued in November 1848, the court ruled in favor of the Holcombes. The court first nullified the will: "Where as the said parties are well advised and are of opinion that the said will so far as it divided the Negroes therein specified is contrary to the law of this state and therefore void."[15] Next, the court ordered the slaves be evaluated: "It is further agreed that the Court appoint three disinterested commissioners to examine the specifics in said will and report the value of each slave to the Court."[16]

In two rather legalistic sentences, a Texas court had undone all of John W. Devereux's carefully laid plans to protect his enslaved souls from the whims and get-rich-quick schemes of Henry B. Holcombe. Essentially, the court equally divided the value of the property, with no regard to family units, kinship, or the deceased owner's wishes. The division was purely monetary. The ruling went on to state, "Julien S. D(evereux) shall have the privelege of selecting for said slaves any individuals & number the value of which shall not exceed the one half of the value of the whole number by more than twelve hundred dollars and it is agreed that the slaves so selected by said Julien shall be decreed to him as heir."[17] The remainder of the slaves "shall be decreed to the said Louisa [Louisiana] as heir of said J [John]. W [William]."[18] The ruling addressed a few more outstanding details and then, presumably, the court moved on to the next case on its docket. Under Southern laws, enslaved human beings were property and, as such, Southern courts ruled with cold efficiency.

On November 29, 1848, the appraisal team, composed of Mark Stroud, Elijah Dodson, and Slade Barnett, issued their figures and indicated which of the individuals (they now numbered twenty-nine) Julien Devereux had selected. By default, those who remained were Louisiana and Henry Holcombe's property (see Table 4).

The total value of the twenty-nine slaves listed in this appraisal was $500 lower than the April estimation for twenty-seven slaves. The average price of all twenty-nine individuals was $291.37. The slaves selected by Julien averaged $275, and the slaves selected by Louisiana averaged $318.00.

The value of the slaves brings up an obvious question: why did Julien not buy the slaves from his sister? The total value of the slaves Louisiana won in court was $3,500. If Julien was as financially sound as his sister believed, he could have purchased the people in question. Or could he? Maybe yes, maybe no. Julien Devereux was like most Southern planters—cash poor, land and slave rich. Planters and farmers who raised cotton tended to roll profits from their crops back into land and more slaves. Certainly, that was what Julien did. He was not buying many slaves, but he was purchasing land at a feverish pace in those years. If his records are a good indicator of readily available funds, he

TABLE 4. FINAL APPRAISAL AND SELECTION OF SLAVES[19]

NAME	L. HOLCOMBE	J. DEVEREUX	VALUE (IN $)
Scott		Yes	300
Randal		Yes	650
Daniel		Yes	650
Tabby		Yes	100
Henry		Yes	50
Mary		Yes	400
Ham		Yes	300
Anthony		Yes	250
Phebe		Yes	150
Amy		Yes	200
Charles		Yes	250
Mahala		Yes	250
Sam		Yes	200
Polly	Yes		500
Cyrus	Yes		300
Lucy	Yes		250
Ossian	Yes		200
Little Scott	Yes		150
John	Yes		50
Flora	Yes		500
Colin	Yes		300
Cynthia	Yes		500
Betty	Yes		200
Louisa	Yes		550
Matilda		Yes	550
Anderson		Yes	50
Diana		Yes	350
Jesse		Yes	150
Harrison		Yes	100
Total Value			$8,450

might not have had the money. Besides, he did not think he had to buy slaves whom, as far as he was concerned, he already owned.

Basically, the burden of trying to keep mothers and their children together rested with Julien. It was an impossible feat, since all the people were direct descendants of Tabby and Scott. It appears Julien selected some slaves of little or lesser value to keep as many together as possible. Yet there was still heartache and tragedy in the selections. Louisa was married to Martin, Julien's slave manager and driver and probably his most valuable human property, yet she went with Louisiana. Polly and her four children were destined for transfer to Louisiana, but Polly died before the transfer, leaving her four children orphaned with new owners. The Community had barely a month to prepare themselves for the inevitability of separation. It could not have been a merry Christmas that year.

William Taylor, Louisiana's son-in-law, handled the transfer on her behalf. He wrote Julien on January 25, 1849, that he could not come himself as "he could not possibly leave home"[20] at that time. His letter was carried to Julien by Taylor's nephew, Thomas Poe. Julien may not have taken kindly to Taylor phrasing his letter in terms that read more like an order than a request. "I have sent over for Mrs. Holcombe's negroes. You will please to deliver them to him [Poe]."[21] Taylor also wrote that he "was sorry to hear that the negro woman Polly was dead. I will see that her children are well taken care of."[22]

It was the last sentence of Taylor's letter that reveals his understanding of the pain he caused the enslaved blacks he was transferring. He wrote, "I will be obliged to you if you will get Mr. Howerton to go a part of the way with the negroes he knows them well and will understand best how to get them across the bad creeks between your house & Henderson."[23] Supposedly, Taylor wanted Howerton to help guide the group across the creeks. Since Poe had just gotten to Monte Verdi across those same creeks, it seemed unlikely that he needed Howerton to get back across. And what did Howerton's having significant knowledge of those being ripped away from their homes and families have to do with getting across a few swollen creeks?

As much as white Southerners liked to pretend that slaves were just property to be bought and sold and to work the fields, there were times when the humanity of the enslaved could not be ignored. Neither Devereux nor Taylor wanted to be a part of the transfer. Being part of the transfer meant witnessing the slaves' goodbyes to family and friends and listening to pleas to keep a family together. Most poignant and heartbreaking was the situation of Polly's children. They had just lost their mother, and now they were separated from their father and grandparents, Tabby and Scott. It must have hurt to observe such pain and sadness. The employee Howerton drew the black bean of presiding over the separation—something neither of the more affluent white men wanted to do. In truth, Howerton was asked to go along to keep order, calm the people leaving, and make the transfer as peaceful as possible.

In the long run, the slaves who remained on the Devereux Plantation fared far better than those taken away. Early on, it was Louisiana's plan to "let William [Louisiana's son-in-law] buy" her "a piece of land and put them [her slaves] on it"[24] in Texas. She wrote Julien, "As you say Papa's object was to keep the negroes together his wish could be gratified" if she moved to Texas.[25] Louisiana and William Taylor did buy a place near Marshall, Texas, fulfilling Louisiana's wish that "the property [the enslaved] should never be brought out of the state and I would move out there."[26] For a time, her plan worked. Then the realities and risks of an agricultural venture set in, and Taylor "found he could make nothing by farming."[27] Taylor moved back to Mobile to practice medicine.

By fall of 1852, Louisiana had also moved back to Alabama. On September 12 of that year, she wrote Julien, "We bought a farm in Texas with a view of moving out and settling permanently there."[28] Louisiana was disappointed when the plan didn't work. As she explained later to Julien, in a letter dated March 12, 1853, she had her mind made up to move to Marshall, Texas, and if they had been successful, "while the negroes were there, it would probably have been eventually our home."[29] But by 1853 the slaves she won in the contested will were on a plantation or farm in Alabama owned by Henry B. Holcombe.

Louisiana assured Julien she had given the slaves nice cabins and arranged for good living conditions.[30] However, we only have her opinion on that issue. She "brought Louisa down" as her "Body maid and seamstress," while Ossian was her houseboy. "I never saw better servants,"[31] she wrote to Julien. Probably hoping to quell Julien's fears of the fate of the enslaved black laborers in Henry Holcombe's control, Louisiana stated, "I would like to hear how you all get along very much and [about] the relations [relatives] of the negroes [I own]. As regards the servants I own I have no idea of parting with them while I live or of bringing them to the city."[32] Louisiana then closed her letter to Julien with one of those passages traditional historians of slavery quoted to exhibit the benefits and harmony of the system: "They [the slaves] enjoy their music and seem very happy. I tell you all these little things for Scott and Tabby's [?]

benefit."[33] Antebellum Southerners had a talent for making a system of human bondage sound quaint and pastoral.

By March 12, 1853, Henry Holcombe had sold the plantation and his slaves to his son Homer, who was hiring his mother's slaves as well. The sale of the plantation did not sit well with Louisiana. She was "for sometime distressed about Mr. H selling."[34] Louisiana and Homer agreed "that if the negroes are disposed to live together as husband & wives, should keep them hired or I am to buy back the husbands or Gincy's children. I am better reconciled to the sale as Homer is as much attached to them as I and would not seperate them."[35] She asked Julien to assure Tabby and Scott that "their children and grandchildren are well and appear happy."[36]

A year later, on February 7, 1854, Louisiana wrote Julien that "Homer wrote me that they [the slaves Louisiana inherited from her father] were all well clothed, and fed and seemed contented & happy."[37] Louisa was still Louisiana's cook and Ossian a house servant in Mobile. In this letter, Louisiana brought up Julien purchasing her slaves. "If I should ever take a notion to dispose of the negroes, I would like for you to have them."[38] This letter, which exuded sentiment and concern for the slaves she owned, ended on a jarring note, raising questions about just how genuine her concern for her slaves was. Those words—"take a notion to dispose"—of the slaves seem callous and cold. A notion is a whim, an impulse, a fleeting thought that one may or not act upon. And then "to dispose" of these human beings who have been a part of her world for an entire lifetime? We dispose of the trash. Louisiana was prepared, on a whim, to throw out the trash, it appears.

However, there are other possibilities that explain her actions. She may have seen the inevitable coming and was embarrassed to admit to her brother that her husband's business activities were once more mired in debt and failure. To tell Julien the entire truth was to confirm her father's beliefs about the man she had chosen to spend her life with and who had fathered her large family. So her language was an attempt at being coy and sound out Julien on the possibility of his buying the slaves back.

We cannot read Louisiana Devereux Holcombe's mind, but there is a third possibility that is well supported in her surviving letters. It was clear from the beginning of the disagreement over their father's will that Louisiana wanted Julien to pay her for her share of the slaves. She mentioned that possibility to Julien in nearly every letter she wrote him, repeatedly reminding him of his wealth and position and her, the poor sister, with a big family and a husband who was a continually unreliable provider. Not once in any of her letters did she express affection or support for her husband. Quite the opposite, she expressed frustration and anger at him on several occasions. If she had the money for the slaves, she might have believed that it could give her independence from Henry B. Holcombe. Indeed, she would have to have left Henry if she expected to hold on to the money or have any say in how it was used. Like everything else, Henry owned all of what was Louisiana's; in reality, he owned Louisiana and their children. Her letters always contained her trials and travails with her husband and her children, their spouses and the many grandchildren often staying with her for months on end. Someone was always ill, pregnant, unable to manage their children, in financial difficulty or some crisis, and everyone depended on her to care for them. Financial independence was about her only way out of the situation. She could buy herself a little peace and help her children if she had the money. Getting to know this woman through her writings makes me think she never wanted the slaves at all; she wanted the money from the beginning. In truth, gaining control of the slaves only increased her burden as a caregiver. She could not bring herself to sell them and violate her father's wishes, and she did care for them in her own way. But all the lawsuit accomplished for Louisiana Devereux Holcolmbe was to add more people to the list of those for whom she felt a responsibility. The enslaved people who had the misfortune to end up in her care probably understood all of this, too.

It was in 1855 that the bottom fell out for Louisiana and the slaves she owned, and as John Devereux had feared, Henry Holcombe was the instrument of the downfall. Louisiana admitted to being "much provoked with Mr. H for selling them [Gincy and her children]"[39] to their son Homer. Holcombe had "invested every thing in real estate which has fallen much in value with interest on it & taxes I fear will place it out of his power to buy them back."[40] In addition, he had sold the note he had taken from their son Homer, and Homer was unable to make the payments to the new loan holder. Louisiana very much wanted Julien to buy the slaves from her, writing "if you conclude to buy them write me and make me the best offer as I am now entirely dependant on them for a support."[41]

It is interesting that Louisiana made it plain to Julien that he was dealing with her and not Henry. She wrote, "If I think propper I alone will read your letters.... Mr. H had no business to sell and lock up every thing in real estate."[42]

When a scourge of yellow fever decimated Mobile's real estate markets, it laid waste to Henry Holcombe's investments. The epidemic devastated the lives of Tabby and Scott's children and grandchildren just as surely as the disease itself would have. This was only six years after the Texas court had given the slaves to Louisiana Holcombe.

Louisiana wrote Julien several more times in 1855, but the news did not improve. Two letters written to Sarah after Julien's death give clues about the slaves living with Louisiana. The first letter indicated that things were fairly stable. Louisiana told Sarah, "Let us hear from Tabby & Scott and the relatives of my negroes."[43] Following that was an accounting of the Alabama Devereux slaves. Cynthia had two more children and a stillborn child in the winter of 1855–56. Louisa and Ossian were still house servants. "The others are hired on the plantation that Homer bought from his Father. Gincy and her 3 children are all there as well."[44]

The last surviving letter Louisiana Devereux Holcombe wrote to Sarah on the subject is a badly damaged one dated January 29, 1857. Her missive was primarily to ask Sarah for a favor from John Landrum, Sarah's father. Louisiana wanted him to locate and send the proof of her ownership of the slaves. Even with the damage, Louisiana's words speak for themselves:

> At the time we are all unsettled Homer . . . [illegible] sold his land and has been to look at Texas . . . [illegible] thinking of stay here. . . . Mr. H has never had any thing to do with the negroes I hired them to Homer and now I want to bring them down until I can get a farm in the country and I want to have the property well secured in case of . . . [illegible] as I have no other means to look to for support but . . . [illegible]. Mr. H has been unfortunate in his business and now have to depend on these negroes decreed . . . [illegible]. I have a certificate and it is recorded here but the proof . . . is not attached . . . what is necessary to secure the property against debt. . . . It is unpleasant to be placed in such a situation but is no less true. I think all will be right after a while. . . . I hope I shall be able to keep what I have a right to.[45]

In a number of letters, such as the one above, Louisiana repeatedly claimed her husband had nothing to do with the slaves. Apparently, she was attempting to establish her sole legal ownership. In the face of Alabama's patriarchal property law, she might have felt she was talking to a brick wall.

In 1846, Alabama granted women the right to own property but not to control it. Three years later, the state allowed women to own and manage property in their names if the husband was incapacitated. It was not until 1867 that the state allowed single women full property ownership rights. Between 1865 and 1876, most Southern states legalized women's individual property rights due to the upheavals of the war and the economy in the South. The Civil War freed the enslaved and, to some extent, Southern women.[46]

What exactly happened to the individuals involved—Cyrus, Lucy, Ossian, little Scott, Flora, Collin, Cynthia, and Louisa—is unclear, but census records do provide some information. The 1850 US Census Slave Schedule shows L. Holcombe in Texas with two female slaves, aged fifty-five and fifteen. L. Holcombe was listed in Alabama with two slaves of the exact same ages—presumably the same two people. The first one may have been Gincy, but who was the second female? And where were Louisa and Ossian? Louisiana told Julien in 1854 that Louisa and Ossian were her house servants. In the same census, H. B. Holcombe was listed with fourteen slaves, ranging in age from sixty to six. Gincy may have been represented in H. B. Holcombe's group as well.[47] But some of these people appear to be the slaves won in the lawsuit in 1848.

By 1860, the Slave Schedule recorded only five slaves belonging to H. B. Holcombe— three females aged thirty-six, forty, and forty-five, and two males aged sixty-five and sixteen.[48] None are listed as being owned by Louisiana D. Holcombe.[49] However, H. [Homer] Q. Holcombe of Washington County, Alabama, possessed forty-nine slaves.[50] Homer did own slaves in his own right, so there is no way to know if the Devereux slaves are among his enslaved. One can hope that the slaves taken from family and friends by the contesting of John Devereux's will ended up in Alabama with Louisiana's son, Homer Q. Holcombe, until emancipation. However, if they were not with Homer, then Henry Holcolmbe had done exactly what John Devereux thought he would do—"let them to the highest bidder."[51]

The people put in jeopardy by the dispute over John Devereux's will represented the most essential part of the Devereux Slave Community. The damage and danger that threatened those ripped out of the center of the community—Tabby and Scott's children and grandchildren—were obvious, but all of those left behind were jeopardized as well. Scott, Tabby, and their family were the very center, the core of the Community: they were what held together the entire circle of individuals who made up the whole of the Devereux Slave Community.

Human affairs do sometimes mirror natural law. A slave community was a living, breathing organism, and like any living thing, it had a center without which it could not continue undamaged. The Devereux Community could and did survive many changes; in fact, probably its most constant event was change itself. People came and went, were born and died. Geography changed, living arrangements changed, marriages were made and ended. But these were the normal ebbs and flows of life and did not usually jeopardize the Community. However, a serious disruption to the core of the Community, such as the rupture caused by the lawsuit, had the potential to inflict lasting damage, and this crisis may have done just that. Nevertheless, the Community survived as far as we can tell from the evidence available to us. It is a fair and reasonable judgment to assume one of the main reasons it did survive intact was the steadying influence and continued presence of Tabby and Scott.

This episode in the life of the Devereux Slave Community cannot be closed without some attention to the nagging question left dangling—how did the people affected think about their owner after this? It is a question to which we have no answer, but it must be considered. The family slaves were placed in a special category on the plantation. For one thing, they were owned by John Devereux, not Julien, and John did not want them separated or sold. Records abound showing that slaves knew more about white affairs and how they factored in those white lives than whites ever realized. That knowledge and sense of security that the family slaves had was shattered with the lawsuit and separation. They must have asked themselves questions. Why didn't Julien fight harder for them? Why didn't he make arrangements to buy his sister's share of the family slaves? Julien Devereux had status in the community; he could have borrowed enough money to pay his sister or he could have worked out a payment plan with her. Why didn't Julien argue the issue of his father's lucidity? The enslaved around John Devereux knew he was not demented. They may have even told Julien as much. And, finally, the question for us is how much did their enslaver really believe in the theory of paternalism that governed his relationship with his enslaved people?

Chapter Eight
Ancestors All

In order to know our future we need to understand our past.

We need to take pride in the legacy in which our history was cast.

One of the things that gives us pride is remembering that the strength,

that incredible strength and perseverance came from within.

They were living in a broken system, but it didn't break them.

SHEILA SPENCER, DESCENDANT

ASALH (ASSOCIATION FOR THE STUDY OF AFRICAN AMERICAN LIFE AND HISTORY, INC.) ANNUAL CONFERENCE, 2015, ATLANTA, GEORGIA[1]

By the 1830s the Southern defense of slavery called "paternalism" was well entrenched in the philosophy and thought of the South. Historians Eugene Genovese and Elizabeth Fox-Genovese in *Fatal Self-Deception* (the title says it all) concluded, "Decades of study have led us to a conclusion that some readers will find unpalatable: In most respects, southern slaveholders said what they meant and meant what they said,"[2] and what they said was they believed in paternalism. Among those believers were the owners of the Devereux Slaves. The concept rested on family, and the white master was the leader of both the white and the black family, and he and/or she ruled with firmness and caring. The Genoveses defined the concept this way: "The master provided protection, sustenance, and religious guidance in return for the slave's obedience and faithful service."[3]

Integral to the belief in paternalism was the concept of family slaves like Tabby and Scott and their direct descendants. The term "family slaves" refers to slaves that had been in the family a long while, slaves with whom the owners may have grown up and who had given faithful service for many years. Many, like Scott and Tabby, were house servants and had more contact with owners and their families than field hands. The concept of "family slaves" was also a philosophical necessity because the idea that slaves were part of the owner's broader family was vital to the Southern defense of slavery.

Family slaves were even more firmly in the fold of paternalistic care than other slaves who came to the community later, either by purchase or by birth. In his 1843 and 1845 wills, John Devereux, ever the proper paternalist, invoked the deity for the ownership of his slaves and took responsibility for their futures, "That I may be better prepared to leave this world by arranging certain property in slaves which has been committed to my charge by divine providence so as to leave them as comfortable as their situation will admit."[4] He made it clear that he believed it was his Christian responsibility—his paternalistic duty—to provide for his human property after he was gone. It appeared that John William Devereux believed what he said. Whether he realized the hypocrisy of it is debatable.

Gincy's owner, Louisiana Devereux Holcombe, provides another excellent example of paternalistic behavior and thought. On July 11, 1848, Julien Devereux received a letter from his sister concerning Gincy's visit to Julien's Plantation. She wrote, "I have given Gincy permission to go down to see her children."[5] However, transportation from Marshall, Texas, to the Monte Verdi Plantation (a distance of more than sixty miles) proved to be a problem. Louisiana wrote, "I am sorry that I could not procure her a conveyance But in the Grand City of Marshall no vehicle but an ox waggon can be procured."[6] Louisiana shoved the return transportation onto Julien. "You will be so good as to send her back after she makes her visit."[7] However, in the next sentence she expressed her sense of responsibility and duty to Gincy: "I have long promised her that she should if ever an opportunity offered to visit her children once more which I felt my duty."[8] Louisiana understood her relationship as one where she had a duty to provide for Gincy, and Gincy in turn had a responsibility to give faithful service. On September 1, 1848, Louisiana wrote Julien, "Gincy arrived safely on friday."[9] Apparently, Gincy stayed with her children on the Devereux Plantation for at least a month and maybe a bit more.

Southerners deluded themselves into believing that slaves bought this ruse of paternalism. The arrangement fell apart when slaves challenged the master's dominance, and then the ugly underbelly of slavery showed itself, and it was slaves who saw and experienced the force and violence, overt and covert, of white over black when paternalism met reality. Paternalists were right about

Aaron Henry, son of Walton, son of Henry, son of Tabby and Scott. Henry's line took their father's first name as their last name. Many of the Henrys moved to California during the Depression. *Courtesy of Aldra Henry Allison.*

one thing, however. Families were very important to all slave communities, not just the Devereux Slave Community, but not for the reasons that paternalistic white owners believed. Families were the first agent of socialization in all societies, but among slave societies that socialization was much more important than among non-slave social units. Families gave slaves the ability to survive the horrors of slavery. Slave families were instrumental in training new members of the slave community in the ways of their masters and mistresses; slaves who had been on the plantation awhile knew the best ways to approach and deal with them. Slaves could inform newcomers about how to slack off work just enough to get some much-needed rest but not get caught and punished for indolence. They communicated tried-and-true methods of earning rewards that could be converted into rights and privileges, just as Henry claimed Sunday for his own affairs.

Among the other duties of the slave community and family was teaching slave children how to endure the injustices visited upon them at very young ages by white enslavers. The wisdom of older men and women who had the respect and esteem of the entire community was instrumental in helping children and parents who found themselves separated. The wisdom, patience, and coping abilities of Scott and Tabby's generation could make the difference in surviving or not surviving. Slave children learned early that they were property to serve the economic needs of their owners.

On April 12, 1825, John and Julien Devereux signed a contract to borrow $200 from John and Daniel Ramer and used two young enslaved girls as collateral for the loan. The first "was a negro girl named Martha between seven and eight years old to secure the payment."[10] Her sister Maria was hired out at the time to someone else; however, sometime between December 26, 1825, and January 1, 1826, she was sent to replace Martha for the last four months of Martha's contract. That extension meant Maria was hired out for sixteen months straight. At the time of Maria's delivery, "the said Girl Martha shall be return'd to said Devereux's."[11] The contract specified that "the said Negroes are to be taken care of . . . and cloath & fed as customary"[12] for people of their status and color. Additionally, the Ramers were to employ the girls "in one of their own families or upon one of their own farms" and not be hired out "without the consent of said Devereux." The Devereuxes were "at liberty to return said two Hundred dollars and receive back the negro Girl."[13] There is no indication that Martha and Maria did not stay the required time of the contract.

Records confirmed their ages. Martha was younger than Maria by two years, being born on Christmas Day in 1817 in Mobile, Alabama; she was eight at the time she was used as collateral for the loan.[14] Maria was born in 1815 in Georgia and was ten years old.[15] Records indicate that Martha and Maria lived out their lives in the ownership of the Devereux Family, and became integral and supportive members of the Community through several generations. Maria married Levin and raised a family.[16] Martha, too, raised a family, but there is no mention of her mate.[17]

Certainly, Maria and Martha were not the only enslaved children who were forced to learn the lessons of slavery at very young ages. Another child was Charity, and her situation was even more poignant and heartbreaking than Maria and Martha's. Charity was not one of the family slaves, so she did not have the support network they did. She was first sold on March 9, 1844, by James R. Vickers, the trustee for the estate of Eliza P. Pitts, to Mrs. E. M. Simonton for $187.50.[18] Then, eight months later, on October 11, 1844, Simonton sold Charity to Julien Devereux for $250.[19] Charity was described as "a negro girl by the name of Charity ten years old wich we warrant sound in body and mind."[20] Just four days later Julien Devereux sold Charity to Dr. E. J. Arnold for $300. A note on the back of an envelope read, "Dr. Arnold failed to pay."[21] There was no mention of any family members being sold with her or that might have been in contact with her. There was not a successfully executed bill of sale for her in any of the later records, nor was she mentioned in any of the lists of slaves owned by John or Julien Devereux. She just vanished from the records without a hint of what the future held for her. One hopes that she received at least some love, affection, and attention from the Slave Community during the short time she was on the Devereux Plantation. Sadly, there were many children like Charity across the South. Essentially, she was bartered and sold as a speculative commodity. Her value rose from $187.50 to $300 in a period of eight months, an increase of $112.50, or about 28 percent. Slaves were so valuable they were often used as payment for debt or to purchase investment property. A female at the age of ten had tremendous potential to reproduce and create more wealth for the owner. Additionally, the owner not only had the labor of the woman for a lifetime, but he or she also had the persons and productivity of her children.

Many slaveholders preferred not to sell or buy young children away from their families simply because it might cause irreparable damage to what could be a valuable and expensive property with strong investment potential. The younger the child, the greater the chance of depression, loss of appetite, disease, difficult behavior, abuse by others, or other problems that could harm a young child's immediate or future value. John and Julien Devereux, like most other slave owners, dealt in the purchase of children at various points, however. One of the last slaves Julien Devereux purchased was a young girl to be the body servant for his wife. John Landrum, Sarah's father, gave money to Julien to purchase the girl as a gift for Sarah. Julien fulfilled his father-in-law's desire on March 31, 1854, when he purchased "a certain negro girl I have named Jenny of black complexion & age about eleven years. To have &

to hold the said Slave Jenny & her future increase unto her the said Sarah A. Devereux."[22] It was clear Devereux recognized the investment potential of the purchase when he referred to Jenny's "increase" and noted Sarah Devereux's heirs would inherit Jenny and her "increase."[23] The child was not even allowed to keep her birth name.

Probably the most essential lesson of slavery that slave communities taught was the ability to hold one's tongue and temper in the face of white arrogance, ignorance, or cruelty. Slaves who lost their tempers or spoke back to owners or overseers usually paid the price. If they did it consistently, slave owners would sell or rent out those slaves, ruining family and future.

While Tabby and Scott's descendants dominated the family lines, they certainly were not the only family units. On February 15, 1832, Julien Devereux bought "Five Negroes Kizzy and four children Judy William Alfred and Albert."[24] He changed Alfred's and Albert's names to Allen and Alleck, presumably because Alfred and Albert were Devereux family names. In adulthood those children formed a family line beginning with Kizzy. Their bill of sale was one of those documents that could only be found in the antebellum South. All in one sentence and one receipt were five human beings, four of them children, and "two mare mules one a blue mule called Kate and the other a cream colored mule."[25] Presumably, the "Eleven hundred and thirty

The original bill of sale for Kizzy, her four children, and two mules as it appears in the original papers. Kizzy and her four children stayed with the Devereuxes for the rest of their lives or until emancipation. Judy named one of her daughters Kizzy for her mother.

Courtesy of Julien Sidney Devereux Papers, di_11544, The Dolph Briscoe Center for American History, University of Texas at Austin.

one Dollars" Devereux paid included the price of the mules as well as the enslaved children and their mother.

Other family lines included Joe, July, Jim, Stephen, and Rhoda, the children of Jerry and Mindah, who were left behind in Alabama in 1841. There were a few male individuals who were bought singly but who probably left family behind on another plantation. The single men later joined the family lines listed above and formed new lines on the plantation. The family lines were constantly in motion and flux, making it very difficult to trace the heritage of slave families. Probably the two greatest deterrents were the failure to give slaves last names and the failure to identify fathers and husbands. Since the slave status of children was determined by the status and color of the mother, identification of fathers was of lesser importance to owners.

The failure to link fathers to mothers and children disguised some of the most distasteful aspects of slavery. Since families were more likely to be separated because husbands and fathers were sold away from wives and mothers, leaving men out of the picture diminished some of the perception of family break-ups. Another reason for the practice was to hide the identity of the father in the event he was a white man. No one was more intuitive and perceptive about the issue of mixed race on Southern plantations than Mary Boykin Chesnut, who wrote, "every lady tells you who is the father of all the Mulatto children in everybody's household, but those in her own, she seems to think drop from the clouds or pretends so to think."[26]

The young Charity discussed earlier comes back into our discussion at this point. At ten, Charity was on the cusp of sexual activity. We have no idea what she looked like, but she may have been developing into a beautiful young woman. If she had, it would have increased her value substantially. To deny or turn away from the reality of the sexual uses made of enslaved girls and women by Southern boys and men is not realistic. Basically, any sexual relationship involving a young girl or boy that was literally the property of the aggressor has to be considered rape. Of course, there were some consensual sexual relationships of white and black in the South, but how consensual can such a relationship be when the power to give or withhold sexual access was nonexistent on one side? By 1850 and 1860 the U.S. Census Slave Schedules were testimony to sexual relations between the races. It doesn't take a handful of quotes and authorities to document the number of mixed-race slaves in the South. Anyone can look up the records and scroll down the

Mary Devereux, the older woman sitting in the middle, was the daughter of Anthony, who was the son of Mary, who was the daughter of Tabby and Scott. She was named for her grandmother. She is surrounded by eighteen of her great-grandchildren who were all cousins. Pat Scott is the tallest on the back row, the second from the right.
Courtesy of Patricia Bowens Scott.

column for color and count the number of times the census taker recorded an M for mulatto.

The 1850 Schedule showed Julien Devereux with sixty-nine slaves and only two mulattoes.[27] Julien Devereux died in 1856. By 1860 the schedule indicated that the Slave Community of Julien's widow, Sarah Landrum Devereux, had grown to seventy-five slaves with seven mulattoes.[28] The overall increase appeared low, but this is because Julien's widow, Sarah, had transferred ownership of the slaves Julien bequeathed to Antoinette and Sidney Devereux, his children by Barbara Scott Way. However, the growth in the mulatto population was a bit surprising. The Devereux mulatto population may have been underreported in 1850, or it simply increased. It was impossible to know if Sarah believed the mulattoes on her plantation fell from the sky, as did the other Southern mistresses to whom Chestnut was referring.

Another major line was that of Gincy and her children. Although it was unclear exactly how Gincy's line fit into the family slaves, there was a definite connection. It was possible Tabby and Gincy were sisters. Gincy's son Martin was married to Scott and Tabby's daughter, Louisa.[29] Martin was significant to the Devereux Plantation, so much so that Artist Robert Jones's artwork entitled *Martin at the Gin* was chosen for the cover of this book. Modern slave studies would call him a "driver," the term for a slave who managed other slaves and attended to a variety of managerial duties on the plantation. Martin's abilities, sense of responsibility, and determination made him a notable subject for study. He supervised the ginning of the cotton and made regular

> My dear Sons & Daughters –
>
> I expected to have seen you all before this time as we came to Texas in Feb. last, we got here to Mars hall the very day that your folks arrived. They said Mas Julien had promised that you should all come up to see me, do come Christmas if Mas Jule will let you. I have lived in hopes that you would come up Christmas if not sooner. I will be mightly disappointed if you all dont come, All are well here now – I suppose you all heard that Bettie Cindy's child died last summer, also little John Polly's baby. Bettie died before Mas William could get to her – She had some thing like the Cholera and died very suddenly – John was sick two or three days with the same disease. We expected Master or mistress out this fall but they have not come and now we dont look for them until next Spring. We have made no crop this year and as we had nothing to do on the farm Mas Jno hired most of the servants out – I am hired to Mr Field the gentleman who will take this letter to Henderson, I like them very much. George has taken Cinthia for a wife, and

Courtesy of Julien Sidney Devereux Papers, di_11545, The Dolph Briscoe Center for American History, University of Texas at Austin.

runs to surrounding towns for supplies. Periodically, Martin made longer trips to Shreveport by wagon to take cotton to a mercantile store owner or a factor, who was basically a cotton broker, to sell cotton and pick up items that included groceries, cloth, trinkets, even pig iron for plows and building supplies. Martin was trusted with the wagon he was driving, with additional wagons, with money for expenses, and with the supervision of other slaves. He was also trusted with himself. The Devereuxes assumed he would return to his enslaver's home and ownership.

Martin's mother, Gincy, gave us one of the most remarkable letters from a slave that ever bubbled up from white records. Like most slaves, Gincy did not read and write, but she did talk. The handwriting in the letter matched other letters from Dr. William Taylor, the husband of Virginia, daughter of Louisiana Devereux Holcombe. No doubt Gincy dictated her letter to Taylor, her mistress's son-in-law, and he wrote it for her. It must be remembered that everything Gincy said was filtered through white eyes, ears, and mind, so she most likely chose her words with care. Gincy's letter, written around 1850 on blue paper, is printed here in its entirety:

> My dear Sons & Daughters I expected to have seen you all before this time as we came to Texas in Feb. last. we got here to Marshall the very day that your folks arrived. They said Mas Julien had promised that you should all come up to see me, do come Christmas if Mas Jule will let you. I have lived in hopes that you would come up Christmas if not sooner. I will be mightly disappointed if you all dont come. All are well here now. I suppose you all heard that Bettie Cinthy's child died last summer, also little John Polly's baby. Bettie died before Mas William could get to her. she had something like the cholera and died very suddenly. John was sick two or three days with the same disease. We expected Master or Mistress out this fall but they have not come and now we dont look for them until next spring. We have made no crop this year. and as he had nothing to do on the farm Mas Wm hired most of the servants out. I am hired to Mr. Field the gentleman who will take this letter to Henderson. I like them very much. George has taken Cinthia for a wife, and Richmond has taken Flora. Louisa has given Mart out sometime, and will get married again I reckon. Mas Wm tried to get Mas Jule to sell him to master and master offered

eight hundred dollars, but since he would not sell him Louisa has given him out. Tell Scott and Tabby their children are very anxious to see them and look for them too on Christmas, beg Mas Jule to let you come up. Mas Wm has bought a nice farm 1½ miles from town and we could enjoy a holiday together very much. I am going out there after the 10th of Dec and will be ready to see you all. God Bless you all my dear children. I hope to see you all next Christmas If you and I live to see it. Some one of you must send me a letter by Mr. Field. I am your affect mother.

Gincy

Courtesy of Julien Sidney Devereux Papers, di_11546, The Dolph Briscoe Center for American History, University of Texas at Austin.

While the letter is of interest because it was so unusual and rare, it also speaks volumes about slave families. Even after the passage of 170 years this letter provided positive proof that mothers are mothers in any era, race, or circumstance. In universal mother fashion, she chided her sons and daughters because they had not come to see her. Or did she? Maybe she was laying a guilt trip on the white masters and mistresses because they had not arranged a trip for her family to visit. After all, she realized her children could not come visit her without the permission and assistance of their owners. Her second sentence made it look even more likely she was scolding Julien for the lack of a visit, for she singled him out for comment and added her disappointment if her family did not come. Reading between the lines, she was clearly disappointed with Julien.

The second part of the letter discussed who had died; both children listed were Tabby and Scott's grandchildren. Other news related marriages. Both Cinthia [sic] and Flora had taken husbands who were Gincy's sons. Louisa, however, had given up on Martin, but not married again. Gincy related how "Mas Wm" (William Taylor) had attempted to buy Martin from Julien and offered the sum of $800.[30] Considering the appraisal on Flora and her son Collin was $800 and on Louisa $550, $800 for Martin was ludicrous. Martin was worth at least $2,000 at any slave market in the South. However, it was all Taylor and his mother-in-law could or would offer.

Strong families meant strong slave communities, and the Devereux Slave Community was strong, resilient, and flexible according to all the available indicators. This study utilized several factors to evaluate family strength over time: success repeated through time, repetitive use of given names, and family stability during extreme stress. One method of judging the strength of slave communities was to study the strength of the family in post-emancipation times.

An example was the Caddell family, direct descendants from Scott and Tabby. Overall, their personal history exhibited an extraordinary level of success. They were economically successful in freedom; prospered early in terms of position and power in the black community; achieved educations and positions of respect and integration into white society; and retained strong family ties as free people. The current descendants are proud of their heritage. Some are very knowledgeable about their ancestors, and many other descendants want to learn more. A family as cohesive as the Caddell family

This photo is the Caddell Family Reunion, 2012, in front of Monte Verdi.
Courtesy of Randy Mills.

had to have forged some cohesion in the pre-emancipation era and carried those values forward into freedom. It takes generations to build such strong family characteristics and group dynamics, and create a real sense of who they are and from where they came. The Caddell family has such unity and cohesion. Probably their most memorable family reunion events were the two trips to Monte Verdi, the Rusk County Plantation their ancestors made. It was a symbolic return of the family to the site of their enslavement and their home.

The Caddell family is the rule, not the exception. The same traits observed in the Caddell family were repeated in the Bowens family (descended from Mary), the Henry family (descended from Henry and Maria), and the Freeney family (descended from Martin and Katy). The Bowens family also comes together every two years and has made the pilgrimage to the Monte Verdi Plantation. The owners, Joe and Cecilia Koch, have been gracious and generous in sharing the grounds of their home with the Devereux Slave Community descendants.

The continuation of family names in both slavery and freedom is another indicator of family strength. Alwyn Barr recognized the significance of

Bowens family reunion at Monte Verdi, 2010. *Courtesy of Patricia Bowens Scott.*

repeating names in a small book probably designed for public school use or tourist purchase at the Institute of Texan Cultures. He wrote: "Parents often gave their children the names of grandparents to affirm family connections."[31] Although Barr understated the use of family names, he certainly had the right idea and mentioned it when many authors did not recognize the significance of the tradition. In the Caddell family the name Tabby lives on in the personage of a vivacious twenty-year-old. Two hundred and fourteen years separate the birth dates of the two Tabbys. The name Tabby has not come anywhere close to running its course in the Caddell family. The repetition of family names is also found in the slave records. Julien Devereux purchased Kizzy and her daughter Judy and three of her siblings in 1832. Judy was taken to Texas in 1841, but Kizzy was not, so when Judy had twin girls on September

The current Tabby in 2021. A span of 214 years separates the birth dates of the two Tabbys. *Courtesy of Cynthia Tatum.*

18, 1848, she named one of the children Kizzy for her absent mother. Other names that repeated in the records were Adaline, Amy (Amey), Ben, Betty, Elisa (Eliza), Frank, George, Henry, Jack, Jesse, Jincy (Gincy), Jinny, Joanna, Joe, Levin, Maria, Martha, Mary, Ossian, Randle, and Scott. Some repetition of names was to be expected, but this many was beyond what might be considered coincidental.

Another indicator of Devereux Slave Family strength was exhibited in the growth and continuity of the family under extreme stress. Each of the major crises had the power to destroy or severely damage the family. However, the records indicate that the family and the Community managed to repair itself and move forward. There were no indications of major disintegration of the Slave Community during the two crises: no uptick in punishments, no breaks in the work routines, no increases in runaways nor any other indicators of decline and distress. Births do not seem to have declined, nor did productivity on the plantation.

The Devereux Slave Community, like many, many other slave communities, has been misunderstood, underestimated, and underappreciated in terms of its resiliency and adaptability. Herbert G. Gutman published his classic study *The Black Family in Slavery and Freedom, 1750-1925* in 1976. However, what he wrote on this subject is as true today as it was then. He noted that "family models" greatly minimized and sometimes entirely ignored "the adaptive capacities of African slaves and several generations of Afro-American slaves."[32] Many scholars of slavery still underestimate the strength of black families, the depth of their commitments to each other, and the ability of the community to endure and eventually prevail.

Chapter Nine
Descendants All, 2018

I look at what my ancestors had to do to survive in terms of slavery. It was a struggle, it wasn't easy, but they did what they had to do in order to make it to the point where I am now.

PATRICIA BOWENS SCOTT

Each time I interviewed descendants, I found myself looking closely at them. Did they resemble their ancestors? A few had pictures of great-grandparents, and I was especially drawn to those images. Were there any hints in those pictures? What about personality traits? Did they act like any of the ancestors I had spent years and years studying? Certainly, they identified with those ancestors. That fact was evident. One descendant so closely identifies with his ancestor Martin that he took the nickname of "Little Martin." His phone calls to me still come in with that name. He saw Martin as smart, resourceful, and magnetic—a doer and an entrepreneurial sort of man. Mostly, Little Martin was tenacious and decisive, and he saw the original Martin as the same.

There was no denying that, as a group, the descendants had achieved amazing things in the last four generations. I ran the list just to see what Tabby and Scott had wrought in this world. There were at least three registered nurses, an ICU specialist, preachers, a wardrobe designer in Hollywood, PhDs, a dean at a major university, a retired head counselor at a community college, a retired lieutenant commander in the navy, a National Merit Scholarship Finalist, a president of the Tournament of Roses in California, a university board member for her alma mater, a retired accountant and self-taught historical researcher, a TV news show producer, a playwright of church productions in her eighties, and the list continues.

So each time I looked into a face or listened to a voice, I was seeing into the eyes and listening to the voices of earlier years. The then was now. The past was the present. The ancestor was the descendant. The descendant was the ancestor. The circle was complete.

HENRY HAMMONS INTERVIEW

Henry Hammons is retired but was previously employed by several major petroleum companies, where he worked to increase minority employment. He is the son of Martha Hammons from the 2014 group of interviewees. He is Junior in her story of the trip to San Antonio. I interviewed Henry by phone in the fall of 2018.

HIS FAMILY

I'm just glad to know where I came from. But I'm proud of it. I grew up in an all-black environment—black family, black neighborhood, black schools, black church. All that. It was a good background. A good family. Both parents. A brother and sister. A Christian background. We saw our family in East Texas a lot, too. I'm proud that someone wants to write a book about my family and I'll know more then. That's why I'm so excited about reading the book.

I was in California when I retired. For us it was economic. It is a beautiful state, just beautiful. But the cost of living was so expensive. We just couldn't do some of the things we wanted to do as retired people. So for us, it [Texas] was economic. That and family. Our family was here. My mom and my sister and others.

For us it was like most retirees— near a big airport, hospitals and medical facilities, shopping, all those things. But we lived all over. Each time I got a promotion we moved. I was with Gulf and then Chevron.

Henry Hammons.
Courtesy of Henry Hammons.

HIS COLLEGE YEARS

I was a National Merit Scholarship winner. When it happened, I didn't think much about it being special. I didn't know exactly what it was. Now I realize it was something really special.

I was accepted at Cornell, but I really wanted to stay in Texas. I was also offered a position at West Point, but I didn't want to do that.

My mother sure did want me to but I didn't. So I told my parents I really wanted to stay in Texas. The year before I came somebody went to the top of the Tower [at UT-Austin] and shot a lot of people. My folks were concerned. Black people didn't do that. Everybody thinks black neighborhoods are crime-ridden, but that just really surprised us. We came up to Austin and went over to Huston-Tillotson [College] first. I spent the night there. My folks checked into a hotel. When they got back the next morning I had already enrolled in HTC.

I was a political science major. I wanted to go into politics and I decided I needed to go to the best school in Texas and then I was going on to UT Law School. I used to live across the street from the law school and I'd walk through there on my way to class. After I got my BA in 1970, I decided I'd work awhile and make some money and then, I just never went back. You know. You start making the money and then you have a family and you just have a life.

It [University of Texas] was hard some of the time. But black people are highly adaptable. We just adapted. Oh, there were some things that happened. I went to class one day, I think it was a sociology class, and the professor came up and asked me to step outside. So I did. I was standing out there in the hall and one of the other students came out and I asked him, "What's going on in there?" And he said, the professor was talking about if I should be in the class or not. So I just went back in and sat down. He didn't ask me to leave again. And then he made an assignment to write an essay, so I wrote my essay on the black elite. And I turned it in and it got a lot of discussion.

It has changed a lot. When I went back one year, I noticed all those racist statues, like they have been taking down everywhere, were all on the north side of the campus. And I noticed now there is a statue of Martin Luther King and some other black, I forget who.

There were so few of us it was hard to socialize. I helped found the first black fraternity at UT. Just for companionship and social reasons. And it was good networking and you can go anywhere and find a chapter now. And we participated in the Panhellenic Council and everything. We just had our fiftieth anniversary. It doesn't seem that long.

I think UT prepared me, though, for the world. I had to learn to be friends with everybody and to work with everybody. UT taught me a lot. I think I remember maybe two African American students graduating a year, though. Well, more were admitted as freshmen, but each year there were fewer and fewer. Then, there were no black football players. Then they got one. Then after Alabama beat them and Alabama had black players, they decided they needed some more black players.

ALDRA HENRY ALLISON INTERVIEW
Aldra Henry Allison is descended from Tabby and Scott's firstborn, Henry. So it is Aldra's great-great-great-grandfather who gave this book its name. For that reason, talking to Aldra was exciting for me. I was starstruck, in fact. Her branch of the family has resided in California for decades and doesn't have much contact with Texas relatives. This interview was conducted by phone on April 2, 2018.

HER DESCENDANTS
I've traced my family, and I've found slaves and then I've found free people of color in 1830. I've done my DNA and I'm 14 percent European, which obviously means somebody got raped, but I'm still trying to find that side of my family. I've gone to family reunions and that's how I met Barbara Spencer Dunn at a family reunion in '87, and since '87 we have been communicating little bits and pieces here and there, putting the whole puzzle together. The interesting thing about what I've found through Barbara Spencer Dunn is the fact that—my last name is Henry. And the reason it's Henry versus Devereux is the fact that his sons decided to honor him and take the last name Henry, and not take the plantation owner's name. So from you telling me about Henry's claiming Sunday, I realize I come from a family of strong, independent thinkers and doers.

One of the things I've found because of that Anadarko Community, that Freetown Community, that Laneville Community—education was important, religion was important. To this day, if I knew a Henry or a Freeney, nine times out of ten they belonged to the Disciples of Christ Church or the Church of Christ, and if they tell me they are from Texas I could guarantee that I'm related to them. And I think because of the church our family was able to hold onto the faith and believe in something that was greater than them. Henry's grandsons, there's about four of them, were very active in the Disciples of Christ Church, including my great-grandfather, Aaron Henry. So it's remarkable that one generation out of slavery produced learned men. It all can be traced back to that Anadarko church and that Anadarko school.

TRACING HER ROOTS

My family's story starts off in Rusk County. My father's father was a minister, and he was born in Henderson. He ended up with a church in Corsicana, Texas, where my father was born. In 1937, during the Depression, they left Texas. They were one of the first generations of blacks in California. So my father actually went to high school here in California. I was born in California. And my grandparents moved to California. So going back to Texas, there really weren't many people back there except some distant cousins; and my grandmother's brothers and sisters stayed in Corsicana. The Henrys it seems like came here.

Aldra Henry Allison.
Courtesy of Aldra Henry Allison.

HER FAMILY

It [her research] is all over the house so they know what I like. For Christmas my daughter got tickets to the African American Museum in Washington, DC, so I flew to DC to go to the museum. It was beyond fabulous. It takes you through the whole experience of the African diaspora. Right from the beginning they put you in the elevator, and they wait until the elevator is packed. Then it takes you down into the basement of the museum as though you are on a slave ship. It is three dimensions—it hits you from what you feel, what you see, what you smell, what you touch. And then they have an exhibit where you get to see the actual coffin that Emmitt Till was in, and then they line you up to go to it, and they have Mahalia Jackson singing "Precious Lord" and you would think you were at the funeral.

HER FUTURE

I'm in affordable housing services. I am very active in the Los Angeles area in social and civic affairs. I'm thinking of retiring to Austin. Do genealogy full time. I've never been in Austin, but it is the blueberry in the red state. I could live in Austin. Go to South by Southwest.

ART BOWENS INTERVIEW

Art Bowens is descended from Anthony, the son of Mary, another of Tabby and Scott's children. His interview was conducted by phone on April 9, 2018. I met Art in person in the summer of 2018, when he came from his home in Denver to San Antonio for the Bowens family reunion.

HIS CAREER AND LIFE

I was career Air Force, and I did police work and, also, I did logistics. I was enlisted. Between Air Force and National Guard—twenty-nine years. I came out here in 1968 with the Air Force, and I stayed here until 1970. Left, went other places, and I came back here in 1977. I decided, okay, go to Texas or stay in Colorado? By that time, I was married, so I ended up here in Colorado.

Art Bowens.
Courtesy of Art Bowens.

I think we all need to learn where we came from. I belong to a group here in Denver called the Black Genealogist Search Group, and all the people who have done the research and the DNA test have found out what part of Africa their ancestors came from, and they've even been back to Africa. They [whites] went to Africa and brought the people over. It is my understanding that in Africa it was the Africans, the black people, who sold their people to the British or whomever in order to bring them to the United States. I think that part was wrong. But, you know,

I'm glad that my ancestors came to the United States and that we can live a decent life right now. There's nothing I can do about what my ancestors went through, but I also know that had it not been for my ancestors coming over here on the slave ships then I wouldn't be here today. So I think it's good history.

HIS HERITAGE

What I've read about the Devereux slaves they were treated pretty good. As I do my research I look and see. For example, 1865 slavery was over and 1870 a lot of the slaves, or free people now, are living right next door to the former slave owner. And yes, slavery was over, but once it was over the former slave master needed people to work the fields, and even though they were free, they just stayed there. They had a place to live and to make provisions for their food, and I think that was good.

HIS FAMILY

The children are not interested; the grandchildren when they have to do a school project, they are interested. I do it for fun, I guess. I've learned a lot of tricks of research, and every time I find something good it makes me feel good.

The fact of the business is I was at a birthday party for a three-year-old, but I was talking to some of his great-grandparents, and I was talking to this one lady and I was telling her about the Devereuxes and she said, "I know about some Devereuxes." So she said she was going to look at her stuff and compare it to what I had. So she was telling everybody, "We're cousins."

PATRICIA BOWENS SCOTT INTERVIEW

My interview with Patricia Bowens Scott was conducted by phone on April 6, 2018. She is a close friend, so this interview was a bit more casual than the others. Pat was related to Tabby and Scott through their grandson, Anthony, son of Mary. Since she works in Washington, DC, Pat has often walked down to the Library of Congress and viewed the Devereux microfilm for research purposes. She is well versed in the pre-1865 history of the plantation.

Update: Patricia has spent the last six years in Washington watching national events unfold and, occasionally, intruding into her daily life. Her building is so close to the Capitol it was closed down on January 6, 2021; she had a difficult time getting to her home in Arlington, Virginia. Pat is an activist and has participated in all the major marches and gatherings of recent years.

HER ANCESTORS

I know with myself, I do not have an issue with being the descendant of slaves. That means that I know where I came from, and I know their names. I know how they lived, and I know some of the struggles, which helps me to get through my struggles today. I look at what my ancestors had to do to survive in terms of slavery. It was a struggle, it wasn't easy, but they did what they had to do in order to make it to the point where I am now. I know with their traditions, and what they learned, it was passed down to family members. They [Tabby and Scott] have great-great-great-great-grandchildren, and they are still in touch with one another and with all the descendants that Scott and Tabby had. We know one another, what we have turned out to be. From teachers to maids to lawyers to doctors. They would be very proud that what they went through paid off.

I talk to coworkers, they have no clue who they [their ancestors] were, what they did or even a name. They don't even know where they came from. So I feel that I am blessed to have that as part of my legacy and I can pass it on to my children so they, too, know. If you know a little about your family, even though it was slavery time, you have to know they did what they had to do to survive. Surviving meant a lot of things, and if you know what they had to go through, that took a lot of fortitude to go through what they did.

I believe that some of the slave owners treated some of their people as servants, and so they looked at themselves as servants. [Like] he [Jesse] was always there with Julien. It was almost like two white men. I know that sounds crazy but two men. Like they are two men in Austin, and it's like Julien looks around and there are all these other men. And Julien thinks, "Jesse is the person I go back to the room with, and have a conversation with, and eat with and not the politicians." He really wanted to go back home. The only person he has comfort in talking to is Jesse. It just goes to show you the humanity they had for each other and how Julien was with Jesse. It's very interesting.

If they treated them like slaves, then they looked at themselves as slaves. And when I look at my ancestors: to be able to have coins; to be able to have responsibilities; to be able to go to Shreveport; and to be able to transact business. To be able to carry money in your pocket when you know there was a time when that was unspeakable. They didn't take that for granted. Then I think that Scott and Tabby, the two of them, kept their family together. They could have said, "Okay this is the white man, the first chance you get kill him in his sleep, run off with his cows, kill the hogs," or whatever. But they did not do that and, in turn, I believe, that's how they were able to look at themselves in a different way. Now I'm not saying that everyone who was on that Devereux Plantation was the same, or they walked away feeling the same way.

DEVEREUX SLAVEOWNERS

I am sure they knew what would happen to them and their families if they rebelled. And being that they were from Monte Verdi which was the largest plantation there, they looked around and saw other farms and plantations and how they were treated. So in turn they did what it took to get by and to survive. And I also think that they were given a little incentive to do that, to learn. They could raise their crops, to grow cotton, to be able to sell it to Charles Vinzent and other owners in the area and that, too, I find very interesting. You have other slave owners who didn't do what Julien did. That was still in the time when you weren't supposed to do that. But I think that was the only reason that Charles Vinzent and others did that was because they saw the work of my Anthony and other members that were on that plantation. They saw what they could do, and they in turn wanted to work with them. And I think that was why they were paid for their crops and the work.

When you look at Julien's father, John W. Devereux, how he felt about slavery and owning humans. At age sixteen when he was given the responsibility of being an overseer by his father, Charles, he couldn't do that. He didn't believe in doing it. With the blessings of his mother, he left. With the way John was, even when he married, and as a gift his wife's father gave them the slaves. But after the wife died, he gave the slaves back to the father-in-law. And, I think the family he ended up with, he just could not do that, and bad as Julien could be sometimes—a womanizer, and a shrewd businessman, and trying to buy land from Indians and all, I think he learned something.

What caused Julien to be the plantation owner he was? I think the father was an influence on the son. When the father did not want to [break up] his family of slaves with Tabby and Scott, he wanted to keep them together [so] in his will he gave them all to Julien. I think he thought that Julien would do the job of keeping them together the way he wanted, but if something was to happen and he had to get rid of the slaves, that he wanted to keep Tabby and Scott together. Unfortunately, when the sister found out what was going on [Julien couldn't do what his father wanted], and I think a lot of it had to do with her husband, Mr. Holcombe.

ON HISTORIANS

An historian doesn't see black or white. Historians see facts. When you take anybody, regardless of what the color, and you go into the history, you do your research and you deal with that. You evaluate facts. I think that too many times people look at the color of the writer, rather than what the writer is saying. Because you are a white writer, you can walk into any library, any repository, and get whatever information you want. I might have a difficult time doing

Patricia Bowens Scott. *Courtesy of Patricia Bowens Scott.*

that, because what I ask for they might feel that I don't know what I need, and it might not be given to me. But when I find it, it might be a matter of evaluating that information that you get. And that is really all a writer is, but a historian deals with facts. It is either black or white. Every now and then you might have to deal with a gray area. But who's to say what color that person is to write that information. The only problem that I have is when you have someone that doesn't do their research. They don't cross their *t*s and dot their *i*s. They take a little information, and they sit there and they write it like they're writing a storybook. No, that's where I have a problem. But when you sit there and you can write the actual facts then I don't have a problem with that.

And you know when you get wrapped up in the everyday lives of the goings and comings on the slavery plantation or person you are working on you can easily lose yourself in them. Being a human, you don't see the color of their face. When I sit there and look at reel after reel, frame after frame after frame and I'm saying, "Oh, my gosh, how did they make it, how did they survive? Why can't I be that strong? Why is it that every little thing bothers me? Where else were they going to go? What else did they know to do on somebody else's plantation?" So you had to figure this out. I'm sure they had to teach the male slaves, "Now look, whatever you do, it is a reflection on us. We have to survive. We have to get to the next chapter." And I can see it being hard to do. You are a young buck on a plantation; you're strong but you just have to sit there and listen to whatever a person says about you and then get up the next morning and get in the field and still produce.

PART III

Chapter Ten
Cotton, Cotton, and More Cotton

'Why, all we have is cotton and slaves and arrogance.'[1]

RHETT BUTLER IN MARGARET MITCHELL'S *GONE WITH THE WIND*

In the hallowed halls of academia, it is surprising that no ambitious professor of economics or history has yet to carve out a department to determine precisely how much of the American economy in 1860 was dependent on the institution of slavery. It is one of those topics that could be a lifelong career. Graduate students would have spin-off dissertation topics for decades. A large part of the study would involve determining exactly how the value of slavery was to be calculated. From 1619, when slaves were brought into the first English colony in Virginia, to the ratification of the Thirteenth Amendment that ended slavery, the institution was an essential and integral part of American life, culture, politics, society, and economics.

Julien Devereux probably understood he was an integral part of a much larger enterprise, but it is doubtful he understood or appreciated just how big that larger enterprise was. In the Western world, cotton linked the Old South to the bankers and mill owners of the northeastern United States and England in a triangle of transatlantic trade, commerce, and intricate monetary dealings. Even though agricultural production of the fiber was centered in the American South while industrial processing was located largely in England, southern cotton found its way to nearly every continent in the world. It was so ubiquitous it became the first commodity to be traded worldwide and was a major source of international wealth.[2]

According to *Agriculture in the United States* produced by the United States Census Bureau in 1860, America produced over 2.1 billion pounds of raw cotton, defined as cotton fiber that has been through the ginning process and packed into bales.[3] Nearly all that cotton was raised in the South by slave laborers just like Tabby, Scott, their children, and neighbors in the quarters at Monte Verdi. The amount of money that their work represented in the economy could be found in the *Manufactures in the United States* produced the same year.[4] "The rapid development of the cotton husbandry and manufacture of the United States, and the still more extraordinary extension of the manufacture in Great Britain, are among the most remarkable correlated and concurrent events of the nineteenth century."[5] In essence, cotton manufacturing drove the Industrial Revolution for nearly a century in the Western world. Most southern cotton, however, found its way not to New England, but to mills in Liverpool, England.

Page after page of statistics and data contained in government reports of 1860 and earlier made it easy to understand why "cotton was king" in the South. In the slave-holding states, the white, fluffy bolls made a few select men and women fabulously rich. It supported lavish lifestyles, funded lengthy journeys to Europe and beyond, and afforded influence and power of national and international proportions. The importance of cotton to America's economy in the nineteenth century cannot be overestimated.

It was the old Southern slave aristocracies of Virginia and South Carolina and the planter classes rising out of the fertile Delta lands of the lower South in Alabama, Mississippi, and Louisiana that dominated plantation culture in terms of slaves owned, cotton grown, and wealth accumulated. While Texas slaveholders were no match for those true kings of cotton, they "had all the characteristics of an advanced slaveholding society," according to Randolph B. Campbell in *An Empire for Slavery*. "Slaveholders dominated the state's economy, controlled its politics, and occupied the top rung on the social ladder."[6]

Julien Devereux and other white enslavers in Texas may have been the beneficiaries of the cotton culture, but the indisputable fact is that the human beings they owned produced the cotton that placed them in the ranks of the southern and Texas elite. Without the labor and abilities of the men, women, and children who slaved day in and day out for a lifetime on plantations and farms across the South, none of the planters, including the Devereux family, would have enjoyed the prestige, influence, wealth, and power they did.

Planters, large and small, were businessmen and women. Most of them subscribed to magazines, journals, and newspapers written for planters that contained detailed instructions on running a plantation, managing slave

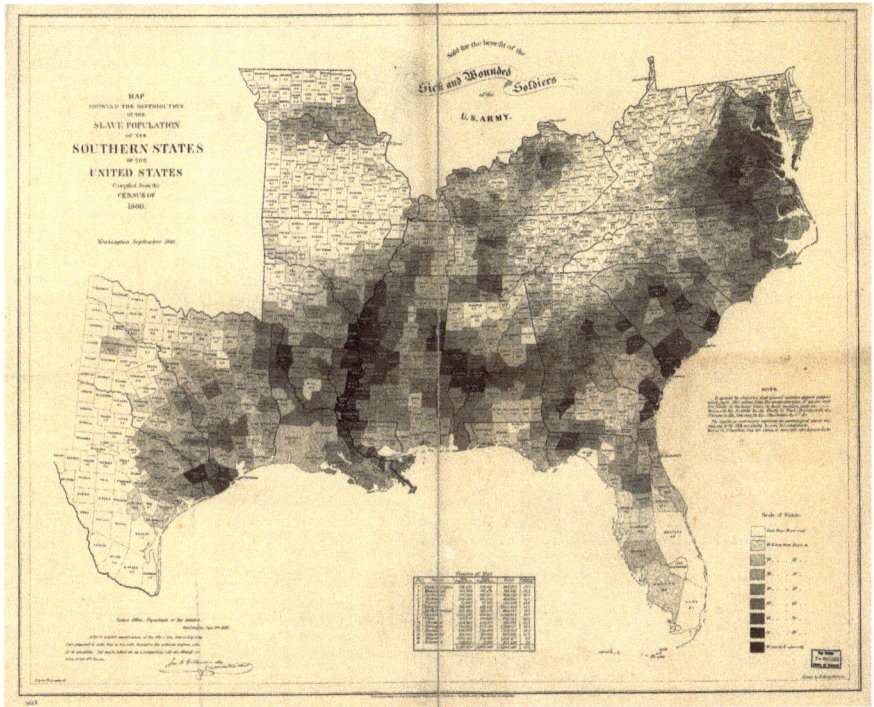

The economic and political clout of the cotton-growing South had begun to concern the North and East by 1845. This map, done in 1860, documents that growth leading up to the Civil War.
Courtesy of Library of Congress, Geography and Map Division.

labor, following prices and availability of supplies and products, and practicing the newest agricultural theories and advancements. Devereux was no exception. His household orders on October 6, 1851, listed no less than twelve such publications: *"Advertiser, Southern Press, Chrystal Fount, New Orleans Delta, Graham's Magazine, Debows Review, Ancient City, Democrat & Texas Register, Marshall Republican, Godies Ladies Book, Advocates Gazate [Gazette], Shreveport Review."*[7] *Godey's Lady's Book* was a must for Southern women of culture and position. Of the publications to which Devereux subscribed, *DeBow's Review* was the most influential.

DeBow's Review, published almost continuously from 1846 to 1880, in South Carolina by J. D. B. DeBow, was about as close to the planter's "bible" as possible. Writers and readers of history owe DeBow a debt of gratitude for instructing planters and would-be planters to keep careful records. In the Devereux family, the best recordkeeper was not Julien, but his father, John.

Like most large planters, John and Julien Devereux employed an overseer to manage plantation affairs and deal with the enslaved labor force. For the most part, the overseer was the conduit between the slaves and their masters. However, when slaves were displeased with the treatment and management of an overseer, they sometimes went directly to the master with their complaint. Overseers who lost the confidence, obedience, and cooperation of the workforce were also likely to lose their jobs. The beginning of 1846 found the Devereux Slave Community working under two different overseers and split between the plantation in Montgomery County and the new plantation in Rusk County.

When the new year arrived at Monte Verdi in Rusk County, there was no overseer. A young man named Reed had served as overseer until the end of 1845, and for the next two weeks, the slaves worked under Scott's supervision. On January 14, "Julien agreed with AC Heard to oversee & work 6 months for 80 dollars."[8] Heard was a demanding overseer. Just twelve days later, John wrote that Heard was pushing hard: "all hands busy and Heard continues to rush ahead with their work & all cheerful."[9] On Wednesday, February 18, "Heard out plowing with his hunting shirt wet and the hands ploughing in a cut of the dryest land—weather too bad to be out but I don't control him in pushing ahead as he wants to plant next week—they finished the cut at dark—heavy rain."[10] At least Heard was not asking the workforce to do something he would not do; however, it was a grueling day for the workers. Heard had the option to quit the fields; the slave force did not.

In Montgomery County William Howerton had signed on as overseer for Julien in early 1846.[11] Julien wrote his father about Howerton's progress shortly thereafter: "Howerton is getting on very well. there is altogether a different movement in every thing about the plantation since he has got underway. the negroes like him very well and appear much more cheerful and lively than they did under Fields administration."[12] Julien commented on Howerton's management of the Devereux Slave force: "[H]e is always in a good humor but exacts strict obedience from the negroes and thus far they render it cheerfully."[13] However, when Julien was evaluating Howerton's performance, the overseer and the slaves did not know their boss and master was moving his entire operation to East Texas.[14] Howerton and his family moved to Rusk County with Julien Devereux in 1846.

On Friday, March 20, 1846, at "about 12 OClock Howerton arriv'd with three waggons and the Negroes from Montgomery."[15] Howerton's initial arrival to East Texas was four months before A. C. Heard finished his overseer contract on the East Texas plantation. The men worked at separate tasks when they were both there. Having two overseers on the plantation may have been uncomfortable for all, but it was temporary. On Wednesday, March 25, Heard was "with the women grubbing and Howerton and the men cutting and hauling logs for Negroe houses and getting boards."[16] Howerton had the more important and demanding job it appears, while Heard was stuck with the women grubbing out weeds with hoes. However, Howerton's stay in Rusk County did not last long; on March 31, 1846, he "started after breakfast for Lake Creek [Montgomery County] to move up the remainder of Juliens concerns."[17] Julien, Sarah, and their infant remained in Rusk County.

One of the few episodes of punishment recorded on the Devereux plantation occurred on Tuesday, May 19, and it involved Heard. John Devereux wrote, "Fracas with Negroes and Heard–he gave July and Flora and Leven a good thrashing which they well deserv'd for impudence."[18] Impudence usually meant expressing an opinion not popular with the overseer or any white person, for that matter. Considering the pace at which Heard worked his enslaved crews, three of the most outspoken members may have registered their disagreement and were punished with a whipping. Julien was at the Monte Verdi Plantation at that time but there is no evidence he was involved. Heard was due to leave in just five days; he had served about four and a half months of his six month term as Julien's overseer. The Slave Community may not have been sad to see him leave early.

On Sunday May 24, 1846, John wrote, "Heard started on Kitty the mule on the expedition in the Rusk Company of mounted volunteer Rifle men ... to fight the Mexicans. [W]e shall be without an overseer until Howerton arrives."[19] (The Mexican War started in April 1846, and would last until February 1848.) It wasn't long before Howerton arrived to take up his position. On May 30, 1846, John recorded "Julien and Dan started to meet the wagons" bringing the last of the possessions and people to Monte Verdi.[20] On June 1, Julien returned to announce they "had met the wagons and found all well."[21] On Thursday, June 4, the "cattle and three boys arriv'd ... and before sun down the wagons with the rest of the movers"[22] rolled in to the plantation. Finally, the entire Slave Community was in Rusk County under Howerton as overseer.

Julien Devereux paid Howerton well for his services but did not pay him in a timely fashion. For the years from 1846 through 1852, Howerton's salary was between $250 and $350 a year for his services. It was February 7, 1850, when Julien paid Howerton $1,150 for work from 1846 through 1849.[23] The increase in Howerton's salary over the years probably had to do with the increase in the cotton-growing population moving into Texas. Howerton was highly employable, and Julien knew it. The Howertons were employees, neighbors, traveling companions, and friends for many years to come. He would serve as overseer for the Devereux Slave Community longer than anyone else would and returned after Julien's death to work for Sarah Devereux.

After Howerton left in the early 1850s, the overseers came and went on a regular basis. Viewed from the perspective of the Slave Community, it was difficult to deal with the persistent turnover. It was disconcerting for the slaves to get to know one overseer, judge their temperament, gauge when and how to approach them, and determine the best ways to manipulate and manage each individual overseer, only to have them leave. Just when the slaves had figured out how to cope with one overseer, along came another. It took time and patience on the part of the enslaved to learn how to cope with each new ruler. No doubt it was exhausting for the slaves.

Howerton quit in early 1853, and a man by the name of Fews came on board for the rest of the year. His contract with Julien does not survive, so presumably he was just a temporary hire. By October 6, 1853, Julien was in the market for another new overseer. He wrote Mr. Stroud asking about an overseer named Gilbert Julien had learned of. Gilbert had moved, so Stroud recommended Mr. McKnight; however, Stroud felt compelled to warn Julien about McKnight. "You would have to hold him back a little he pushes very tight but whips but little."[24] Julien hired McKnight but failed to heed Stroud's warning and came to regret it.

McKnight took up the position of overseer in 1854 and, along with his wife and family, worked for Julien for nearly two years. By the end of October 1855, McKnight and Mrs. McKnight were both *personae non gratae* at Monte Verdi. Mrs. McKnight had incurred Sarah's wrath when she proved herself a lazy, slovenly housewife. Sarah wanted the woman gone; Julien wanted the man gone.[25]

Before Julien left for Austin in late October 1855, he fired McKnight and hired S. S. Ramsey to be his overseer for the remainder of that year and the next.[26] On November 1, 1855, Julien wrote Sarah from Austin, "I am very much in hopes that Ramsey will come up to the standard of his own estimation of himself as our overseer and manager."²⁷ Even though he was an emergency hire, Ramsey took on the job with confidence in his abilities.

While in Austin as a legislator, Julien had opportunities to "converse with a great number of planters." He reported to Sarah he found "none of them spoil their overseers as I do."²⁸ Shortly thereafter, Julien learned, to his dismay, that McKnight and his family were still on the plantation and possibly sowing seeds of discord among the slaves. Julien wrote Sarah in the November 19 letter, "I was in hopes that Mac & Madame Moiselle . . . was off in a few days after I left."²⁹ He did not like the fact that they were "asking the negroes questions about their work."³⁰ The last line of the letter S. S. Ramsey wrote to Julien on November 21, 1855, stated "McKnight has not left yet he says he is going next week he has rented a place a bout ten miles off."³¹ Julien probably thought ten miles was not nearly far enough. The McKnight crew probably did not leave Monte Verdi until December 1, 1855. Julien had dismissed McKnight before he left for Austin in late October. Maybe Julien did spoil his overseers.

Julien had high hopes that Ramsey would turn things around on the plantation: "I feel very much in hopes that he [Ramsey] will get my plantation affairs in good order once more, for certainly things were getting into a very Shackling condition under McKnights management."³² Sarah reported to Julien on Ramsey's progress in just about every letter she wrote him while he was in Austin attending the state legislature.³³ Her reports pleased Julien. He wrote Sarah on November 19, 1855, that he was "pleased to learn that Ramsey is getting on with the plantation affairs and that the cotton crop is likely to reach 80 bales."³⁴ (Ramsey had overestimated the cotton crop—it barely hit sixty-five bales.) Julien was probably pleased when Ramsey wrote him in the same letter that Col. Landrum and Mr. Howerton had lent a hand and given advice on the pigs for slaughter.³⁵ The presence of Landrum, Julien's father-in-law, and Howerton on the plantation were signs of stability to both black enslaved workers and white owners.

On December 10, 1855, Julien was in Austin and had a head cold. He had time to think through the McKnight situation, and he communicated his thoughts on the subject to Sarah: "Since I have been here and have had time to reflect on the subject it is a matter of wonder with me that we have got through as well as we have in the management of our affairs [under McKnight] and more especially as relates to the plantation."³⁶

The inattention to details and the tolerance of sloppy operations and labor force management under McKnight seemed peculiar to Julien Devereux. It may have been his failing health, which would claim his life only four and a half months later, that rendered him less capable. Julien realized the problem was his fault: "When I reflect that my plantation and hands has been under the control of such a worthless, drunken, stubborn illnatured fellow as McKnight, I wonder things are no worse."[37] Certainly, Julien realized his close call with calamity. He wrote Sarah, "If McKnight had continued a year or two longer my plantation would have been broken up & we should have been compelled to sell our home or some of the negroes."[38]

The last quotation demands further analysis from the perspective of the Slave Community. Julien Devereux readily admitted to his wife that McKnight's poor management jeopardized his plantation. What Julien did not say was that his failure to stay up on things threatened the homes, lives, and families of his workforce—the seventy enslaved African Americans on his plantation. Just how much did the Devereux Slave Community have to do with McKnight's fall from grace? After all, they had more to lose if McKnight's tenure continued than Julien did.

There are no statements in the documents that firmly attested to the slaves' role in McKnight's departure; however, there is some room for supposition. It was the enslaved workers and their families who were in the best position to realize just how unsatisfactory McKnight's supervision was, and they knew they had some manipulative power in the situation. In Julien's December 10 letter to Sarah, Julien was far more explicit about McKnight's failings. In Austin and away from the plantation for several months, how had Julien come to learn so much information about McKnight?

The information may have come from Jesse. After all, Julien had moved Jesse into his room in Austin on a blanket pallet only ten days after he arrived in Austin to serve as a state legislator from Rusk County. Jesse was the lead plow driver on the plantation and would have had months and months to observe and work under McKnight. No doubt Jesse had the opportunity to hear all the stories of McKnight's failings from other slaves. Did Julien's expanded knowledge about McKnight's failings come from Jesse? They were living in the same room from early November until they returned to Rusk County in late January. They had to have something to talk about all those long hours in the evening in the boarding house. How else could Julien have learned so much more about McKnight while away from home if not from Jesse? There is no proof, but it is something that needs to be considered. In his book *Southern Honor: Ethics and Behavior in the Old South*, Bertram Wyatt-Brown defined what Jesse did as a personally and "subtly orchestrated ... self-protective accommodation ... suited to survival and even a degree of limited autonomy."[39] Call it what you like, it was a continuation of the dance they both danced.

Furthermore, how did the plantation get into such sad shape? After all, this was the same workforce that had been with the Devereux Plantation for decades. Some had grown old, others had passed; however, it was essentially the same people who worked well under Howerton and others for years. Were the slaves slacking off to make a point to their owner? It is certainly a possibility and something that historians of slavery need to be more attentive to in researching and interpreting records. If true, this demonstrates how enslaved communities have not been fully recognized for their influence in affairs that threatened them.

Chapter Eleven
Work, Work, and More Work

They finished picking cotton to day and came out of the field shouting and blowing their horns like there had been a democratic victory.[1]

SARAH LANDRUM DEVEREUX, DECEMBER 4, 1855

John Devereux spent the entire year of 1846 in Rusk County, watching over the establishment of the new place, while Julien worked to close down the Montgomery County plantation. John Devereux's memorandum book for 1846 survived intact and is a remarkable record of a year on a Texas plantation in the making. Because John missed very few days making a notation of some sort, it is possible to determine what chores the slaves performed, what the weather was like (for people who spent their entire lives in the elements, weather was important), what the health of the slaves was, and other personal details about slave life.

Simply knowing how many days slaves worked and how much time they had for their families and personal lives helps us understand slave lives. Devereux worked his slave crews every weekday and usually half a day on Saturday. Sunday was a day of rest for all. Well, sort of. Many chores were performed on Sundays, but they did not usually involve field work done for the master. The Devereux Slave Community worked their own fields on Sunday. The title of this book came from one such instance when Henry had postponed leaving for Rusk County because he wanted Sunday to attend to his own business.

John's memorandum book mentions the work for each day. The list of chores for 1846 is mindboggling. The activities listed below are those completed in 1846 alone. For the next decade, the slaves performed these tasks, as well as many new ones, every year for Julien Devereux. After Julien's death in

April 1856, for nine more years—until emancipation—they continued to do the same work for his widow, Sarah Devereux, and his four sons.

Work Routines for 1846 at Monte Verdi[2]
1. Grubbing weeds
2. Making trips (Special)
    a. to transport live swine
    b. to transport salted pork
    c. to get cotton seed
    d. to purchase tools
    e. to purchase corn
    f. to buy bacon
    g. to purchase iron
    h. to Shreveport
3. Making trips (Regular)
    a. to the blacksmith
    b. to bring home cows
    c. to purchase consumable supplies
    d. to mill for corn grinding
4. Driving wagons for trips to and from Montgomery County
5. Planting their own gardens and fields with corn and some cotton
6. Ridering (fencing done by women)
7. Cutting and hauling logs for building
    a. smoke house
    b. slave cabins
    c. kitchen house
    d. corn cribs
    e. new owner's house
8. Burning of fields and brush
9. Plowing
10. Planting
    a. field crops
        1. corn
        2. cotton
        3. field peas

   b. food crops
      1. sweet potatoes
      2. grapevines
      3. fruit trees
      4. Irish potatoes
      5. cabbage
      6. assorted vegetables
      7. assorted herbs
      8. tomatoes
11. Fencing-building and repairing (both genders)
12. Cutting firewood
13. Grinding corn by hand when mill broken or flooded
14. Laying out fields for planting
15. Building doors out of purchased planking
16. Hunting
17. Building with logs cut for the purpose
   a. smoke house
   b. corn cribs
   c. kitchen house
   d. new house for white family at Rock Springs
18. Cooking for both white and black families
19. Caring for the young
20. Caring for the sick
21. Making and mending clothing
22. Washing and ironing
23. General cleaning and upkeep

What an enslaved force was doing is only half the story. The hours, days, weeks, and months they worked mattered, too. Table 5: "Workdays for 1846" placed the work routines for the year into perspective. Some days listed as workdays were not entire days of field work. Inclement weather resulted in a morning or afternoon lost for outdoor work. For health and safety reasons, severe weather warranted taking slave hands out of the fields, but that didn't end the day's work. Even when it was too rainy, too muddy, or too something else, slaves were not free to employ their time as they pleased.

TABLE 5. WORKDAYS FOR 1846[3]

MONTHS	SUNDAYS	BAD WEATHER DAYS	OTHER OFF DAYS	DAYS WORKED
January	4	1 rain		26
February	4	3 rain		21
March	5	1 rain	2 family, 1 corn	22
April	4	5		21
May	5	1		25
June	4			26
July	4			27
August	5	5		21
September	4	4		22
October	4	2		25
November	5	1		24
December	4	1	holidays-3	23
Totals	52	24	6	283

Inclement weather meant more than just mills out of commission. Nobody who lived an agricultural life had leisure time—there were always things that needed doing. Bad weather gave time for maintaining tools, blacksmithing, performing household chores, taking care of children, cooking, sewing, etc. Such tasks did give the enslaved a break from field work, but to assume that rainy weather gave them the chance to sleep in and relax is erroneous.

Illnesses, childbirths, guests, trips, cooking, milking, washing, sewing, cleaning, caring for children, and nursing the sick all took hands out of the fields. The number of ill enslaved people during the summer and winter months was particularly high and placed extra strain on other workers. Like most plantations, the Devereux Plantation gave permanent assignments to slaves for milking, feeding, and caring for animals and other specific chores not associated with house servants. During periods of intense labor in the fields—planting and picking, mostly—all workers were called into the fields.

The newness of the Rusk County Plantation caused the work routines to be more varied and intensive than in later years. There is a lot of difference between building anew and maintaining and repairing. Certainly, there was more clearing, log cutting, breaking ground, fencing, and building than on a more established plantation. As shown, the hands worked 283 days of the year, with fifty-two Sundays off. Bad weather prohibited outdoor labor for twenty-four days, and there were six holidays or other off days. It was hardly a life of leisure; however, it was not the hard, long, killing work routines depicted on some plantations, especially those in the Mississippi Delta.

Traditionally, plantations gave a week off for the Christmas holiday. The Devereux Slave Community appeared to follow this tradition most of the time, but not in 1846, when labor demands on the new plantation were at their greatest. On Wednesday, December 23, 1846, the hands worked the entire day. On December 24, John mentioned "the family desir'd that I wou'd eat Christmas Dinner with them,"[4] so some of the slaves had the day off. That appeared not to have been a workday. However, someone prepared the holiday meal, set the table, tended the children, cleared the table, washed the dishes, cleaned the kitchen, and swept the dining room and kitchen. It is safe to wager it was not the white owners who did those chores. Christmas Day was on Friday that year, and certainly the hands who were not in house service had the entire day off.

John Devereux's entry for the next day, Saturday the twenty-sixth, was devoted to neighborhood gossip, so it was not likely a field workday. No doubt everyone on the Devereux Plantation got a charge out of the news that their often-inebriated neighbor, Billy Taylor, and some of his friends tied one on for the holiday and "were all Choctaw drunk yesterday & Sally said she had whip'd Bill & Worrell and Scroggins and had ran Vaughan off."[5] Unfortunately, alcoholism was rampant among American Indians, but liquor proved especially devastating to the Choctaw Nation. In the slang of the era, to be "Choctawed" meant to be very drunk. This was not the first time "Old Billy" had provided a few moments of mirth for the plantation.

So were the workdays for the Devereux slaves normal or an aberration? Without doing an in-depth study of virtually every set of plantation records in the Old South, it is difficult to say definitively one way or the other. These numbers, however, correlate well with those of a few professional scholars who have studied the issue with enhanced knowledge, tools, and data.

Calculations of such things as workdays are done by scholars called cliometricians. Basically, they are historians who crunch numbers. One of the early leaders in the field, Robert W. Fogel, coauthored *Time on the Cross* in 1974 with Stanley Engerman. The book nearly resulted in the excommunication of the two scholars from the field of history. To many, their contention that the conditions of slavery were not as horrendous as some had portrayed amounted to a justification and defense of slavery. However, while some of their methodology was flawed, the work has held up reasonably well over the years. Fogel and Engerman determined "the work year appears to have consisted of roughly 265-275 days."[6]

Fifteen years later, in 1989, Fogel, working solo, published *Without Consent or Contract* and revised the number of days worked in a year. He wrote, "Slaves on cotton plantations worked an average of about 2,800 hours per year. The number of work days per year averaged 281."[7] The number of workdays in 1846 on the Devereux Plantation averaged 283, only two days higher than Fogel's average of 281; in other words, these numbers are close enough to validate the numbers used in this study. It is reasonable to assume that workdays on a Southern plantation circa 1850 averaged around 280 a year.

Slaves worked in inclement weather—snow, sleet, wind, mud, rain, hot, and cold. The length of the typical workday was from sunup to sundown, but slaves worked late when needed. On Wednesday, February 11, 1846, John Devereux wrote, "All hands out at daylight tearing away with their ploughs."[8] A week later, on February 18, 1846, he recorded that "they finished the cut at dark—heavy rain."[9] On March 18, 1846, slaves continued working after dark. All were "busy planting late in the evening."[10] Even when the horns blew calling field hands in for the day, work was not over. Animals had to be fed, watered, and bedded down for the night. Cows had to be milked, chickens had to be fed and locked up for the night, and so did the dogs. Families had to be fed, clothing prepared for the next day, children put to bed, etc.

Additional chores involved construction of various structures and some long days to finish projects. Wednesday, January 21, 1846, was cold and cloudy. However, the "men" were "getting logs for smokhouse" while the women were "ridering."[11] "Ridering" was building a type of fence that women often constructed. Two days later, on Friday, January 23, 1846, the hands were "raising smokehouse today—finish'd all to covering and door shutter."[12] On Sunday, January 25, John Devereux wrote, "Finish'd smokehouse last night—3 days from the Stump—a prime one."[13] Later in 1846, the smokehouse was dragged to "the Springs" when the family moved to the new location on the Rusk County land.

Other building projects included their own homes. On March 1, John Devereux "stak'd off a line for the negroe houses that Sam Loftus might know where to build."[14] Sam Loftus was a slave from a neighboring farm and a skilled carpenter who married Eliza, the twenty-one-year-old daughter of Henry and Maria. John Devereux recorded the marriage on Sunday, January 25, 1846, the day after the smokehouse was completed. "A marriage between Sam Loftus and Eliza Henry Maria by consent of all parties—Sam brought a consent & good recommendation from his master."[15] It was rare in Texas for owners to allow their slaves to hire out their own time, so it is probable that the price paid for Sam Loftus's work was given to his owner. At least Sam and Eliza were able to spend more time together for a short while. Even now, in the twenty-first century, there are both black and white families with the surname of Loftus or Loftis in Rusk and Nacogdoches Counties.

Much of the work performed by slaves was dangerous. Handling sharpened hoes, axes, and other tools resulted in cuts that were slow to heal or became infected. Working large animals also had its dangers. Just the amount of construction done by the slaves carried a high level of possible injury. The gin and mill houses were the largest and most demanding of the buildings undertaken by the slave force. Julien had ordered his new gin parts in 1846 and noted that the "new gin stand had arrived in Shreveport"[16] on October 31, 1846. It would have been up to his slave force to make the long trip to Shreveport and cart the heavy, bulky equipment home.

In 1847, the slaves began construction on the large buildings designed to house the milling and cotton ginning equipment. On August 9, 1847, they began to cut the wood out of the forest for the new gin building. Then, "Friday and Saturday the 13th and 14th August," the slave crews "raised the Gin House."[17] On Monday, August 23, 1847, "hands commenced work on the screw and running gear timbers."[18] Seventeen days later, on Friday, September 10, 1847, Julien hired Mr. Rupel to assemble some of the mechanical parts of the gin.[19] Rupel and the enslaved "raised the Screw and all done well without difficulty or danger with about 20 hands."[20] On Monday, September 13, 1847, they "started the new Gin—performed well."[21] In addition to routine chores and picking the season's cotton, the slaves had spent over a month on the construction and setup of the new gin and mill.

Three years later, on April 5, 1850, Julien Devereux described, for insurance purposes, the gin and mill buildings constructed in 1847. The first structure was "one large frame building 41 feet square containing a 50 saw improved patent corn mill with cast iron Segments and running gear for Gin and mill."

That was a building of 1,681 square feet and possibly two stories. A smaller building was "36 feet square" and contained a "Pratts 45 saw gin. cast iron Segments and running gear complete." In addition, there was a "cotton press with a wall nut Screw."[22] Combined, they totaled nearly three thousand square feet of space full of heavy equipment. This description indicates what a major accomplishment building this gin and mill complex was.

Julien Devereux was aware of the danger certain work brought to the slaves. When they were not working on his plantation, sometimes risking life and limb, they were often wanted for labor on neighboring plantations. Julien was fairly generous about sending slave women to do domestic work on a short-term basis for a needy neighbor. He considered it his civic duty to offer up the appropriate number of slaves and white men for the annual county road work.[23] When he was requested to send workers for more dangerous undertakings, he was more cautious. He told the 1853 overseer, Mr. Few, to send five hands to Dr. Richardson's "Gin raising" because "he expects to be scarce of help." However, Julien told Few to "caution them about getting killed or crippled."[24] Dr. Richardson did not offer to treat an injured slave for free. Julien Devereux would probably have expected that.

Not all the work slaves performed was for the master; some of the time they worked for themselves. The Devereux owners allowed a select group of slaves in both Alabama and Texas to grow and sell corn. Six months before Julien came to Texas, he recorded a transaction: "to Negroes for corn etc. sold to Malone" for $70.00.[25] John Devereux recorded corn sales in his memorandum book. On Saturday, March 14, 1846, he wrote, "negroes planting their own corn."[26] That same day "travellers purchase their last year crop which makes them Sashes [he may have meant Pashas]."[27] John Devereux made several additional references to the slaves selling their corn crops in 1846.

In March 1846, the plantation had a run on the corn slaves still had for sale. It irritated John Devereux. He wrote about his "considerable annoyance with corn customers."[28] The slaves sold most of their previous year's corn crop that day. However, the new crop was in some jeopardy. The crows plucked out the seed corn and shoots about as fast as the slaves could plant them. On Friday, March 20, 1846, John wrote, "Razor eyed Jingles very ravenous to pull up our corn this morning."[29] John's statement left open the question of whether the "corn customers" who so vexed him were of the two-legged or winged variety. Likely both.

The business in corn was a year-round thing and repeatedly appeared in the records. Most of the corn transactions were for cash paid directly to the slaves, or the slaves were given credit of equal value at the merchant's store. Even Tabby made a bit of extra money. On July 10, 1848, A. C. Heard, who had been their overseer in 1846 for four and a half months, paid Julien $1.37 for "negro woman Tabby."[30] Tabby probably did some sewing for him.

In general, the enslaved had more association with money than many studies reveal. A look at just a small portion of the books for 1851 and 1852 shows slaves handling money on frequent occasions. Some amounts for reimbursement or plantation business purposes were hardly surprising. On January 13, 1851, Julien gave $10.00 "cash to Jesse" for expense money,[31] and then on May 23rd, he gave Tabby and Henry $4.00 as reimbursement for their trip to see family in Marshall, Texas.[32] A bit more unusual was a February 1853 loan of $8.00 to Jack.[33] On January 25, 1852, Devereux recorded "cash paid to the negroes money advanced by McLarty & Sons on 9 bales of cotton $205."[34] However, the most unique transaction involved Jesse. On January 20, 1852, Julien wrote, "Cash to Marion Dodson for negro man Jesse for crop of corn purchased by him from Dr. Dodson's negros" for $12.00.[35] It hardly seems likely that Jesse needed the corn. It appears Jesse was speculating in the corn market by purchasing from enslaved workers on another plantation with the intention of holding the corn until he could sell it for profit.

Additionally, Julien Devereux allowed select slaves to grow cotton in Texas and presumably Alabama, as well. Julien sold the slaves' cotton, purchased what the slaves wanted from his factors, and debited slave accounts. Sarah continued the practice when she was in charge. Charles Vinzent was Julien's factor in Mount Enterprise, Texas, but he also dealt with factors in Shreveport and New Orleans, Louisiana. Notations for items for the slaves and accounts for about a dozen slaves appeared in the plantation records year after year after year.

Table 6 details the money slaves earned and spent through Julien in the year 1850.[36] Cotton fetched ten and a half cents a pound that year. In the decade before the Civil War, it went higher, topping out at twelve to fifteen cents a pound. Devereux added money to the slave accounts when their bales were sold in the late fall or early winter. One account in the slave cotton records for 1854 is intriguing. In that year, Martha raised a bale that weighed 506 pounds;[37] it was the largest bale belonging to the slaves that year and the first time a female slave grew a bale. Julien settled the balance on the slaves'

TABLE 6. ACCOUNTS OF SLAVES' COTTON CROPS FOR 1850[38]

NAME	NO. OF BALES & WEIGHT (LBS.)	AMOUNT EARNED ($)	CASH RECEIVED ($)	AMOUNT SPENT ON ITEMS ($)	FINAL PAYMENT TO SLAVES ($ AND DATE)
Jesse	2 bales, 1158 lbs.	121.59	$65	1.30	55.29 7-12-1850
Jack & Scott	Jack 904 lbs., Scott 128 lbs.	Jack 94.92 Scott 13.44	Jack 25.00 Scott 5.00	Jack 27.33 Scott 1.56 2 plugs tobacco + other item	36.00 6-28-1850
July	1 bale, 422 lbs.	44.31	25.86	6.65	11.80 7-12-1850
Lewis	1 bale, 545 lbs.	57.22	2.00 tobacco 2.00	37.97	17.30
Daniel	1/2 bale, 545 lbs., Scott's	30.70	8.76	11.10 .75 to Lewis for Daniel	10.10
Bill	1 bale, 517 lbs.	55.12	25.00	17.35	12.77
Henry	1 bale, 540 lbs.	56.70	12.00	17.35	27.35
Martin	1 bale, 478 lbs.	50.19	40.49	9.70	0
Levin	1 bale, 385 lbs.	40.42	20.00	8.19	12.23
Stephen	1 bale, 600 lbs.	63.00	10.00	24.30	28.70
Scott	1/2 bale 297 lbs., 128 lbs. from Jack	44.15	20.00	15.68	8.47

accounts in the summer or fall with gold and/or silver. He loaned money to slaves between crops. Julien charged his slaves for cloth and twine for baling, but there is no record of charges for freight and insurance on stored bales.

Using this information, it is possible to estimate the amount of money slaves had available. Jesse regularly grew two bales. Julien balanced out the account on July 12, 1851, and gave Jesse the balance of $55.29.[39] Jesse did this for at least fifteen years. Ten cents a pound at five hundred pounds a bale was a good average. These numbers suggest that Jesse produced thirty bales of cotton weighing fifteen thousand pounds and earned $1,500 for himself in fifteen years. The 1850 records indicate he spent approximately half of the money that year.[40] If Jesse did something similar every year, when he became a free man in 1865, he likely had over $700 in gold and silver, assuming he managed to get through the Civil War with it.

The Devereux Family Papers contain numerous notes on slave business. On May 31, 1851, Charles Vinzent, the local merchant in Mount Enterprise, wrote Julien, "Your boys came this morning for a settlement and we have not got the money to settle with them but as soon as the money comes to hand I will send it down to you together with a full statement of the account of each."[41] Another transaction with Vinzent in 1853 involved even more money. Vinzent wrote Julien on April 6, 1853, to ask if Julien could "send some of Your negroes out next Saturday I suppose to have funds enough to pay them off."[42] Fifteen days later Vinzent wrote Julien the following: "I send you per Mr. Ray three hundred dollars in Gold, with the request to have the same distributed amongst those Negroes of yours who own the cotton which I bought of them."[43] Three hundred dollars in 1853 was about $911,400 in 2022 dollars.[44] And, note the phrase Vinzent used in respect to ownership of the cotton—the slaves "own the cotton." He recognized, and presumably others did as well, that African American slaves owned the cotton they raised.

So, what sort of money and method of paying his slaves did Julien have? By 1800, the US Mint was making a Gold Eagle ($10.00), a Half-Eagle ($5.00), and a Quarter Eagle ($2.50), and it made those gold coins, along with copper and silver coinage, until 1933, when the government recalled all gold coins. So Julien would have been paying the slaves in those gold coins, not gold nuggets or parts of bars or anything of the sort.

Information on Jesse's business acumen continued to accumulate. Jesse was the only slave who grew two bales of cotton year after year. Other slaves reached that level of productivity occasionally, but Jesse always did it. We also know Jesse bought corn in 1852 that he likely was holding until local corn demand and prices increased. Then, later in that same year, Jesse made arrangements to buy a team of oxen for himself. Late in 1852, Julien made a payment of $12 to James Thomas on behalf of Jesse, and on January 14, 1853, Julien recorded another payment of $5 to James Thomas for "balance due from Jess for oxen."[45] Obviously, Jesse bought a team of oxen with some of the money he earned.

Slaves had money and, like Jesse, became valuable consumers. The Devereux supply orders were strewn with things the slaves ordered for themselves. The amounts appeared on Julien's ledger sheets. In his April 21, 1853, letter to Julien, Charles Vinzent added that he "should be glad to have a chance to sell them [the slaves] any thing they want of such things as we have for sale. I would sell goods to them really very low."[46] It was apparent the enslaved were deeply ingrained into the market economy both as consumers and producers. Money does not see color.

Choppin. Artist Robert Jones

How common was this practice of allowing slaves to participate in the market economy? The way neighbors and acquaintances accepted the situation indicates it was quite common. The records suggest that locals were comfortable allowing slaves a place in the local economy, thus indicating slaves producing some crops for their own profit was common. Julien decided he spoiled his overseers after talking with other planters during his stay in Austin. Nowhere does he mention he spoiled his slaves. This one study is hardly proof of what might have been a widespread activity on farms and plantations; however, it certainly indicates an area in need of further research.

Whether slave owners admitted it or not, they owed much, if not all, of their success to their enslaved workforce. Julien Devereux had the expertise and experience he gained in his own lifetime. The cumulative knowledge, experience, talent, and skill of his combined workforce was staggering. If fifty of his slaves had thirty years of experience in agriculture, animal husbandry, and plantation management, plus the knowledge of meat preservation, food production, carpentry, blacksmithing, ginning, and assorted other tasks, they would have a total of 1,500 years of aggregate ability and knowledge. That is astonishing!

Chapter Twelve
Brogans, Lowells, and Log Cabins

Value of cotton goods manufactured annually in England is $164,560,000; 2,000,000 of persons are engaged directly in the cotton factories of England.[1]

JULIEN SIDNEY DEVEREUX'S NOTES, 1851

Provisioning a large plantation such as Monte Verdi was the other half of the business of raising cotton. In return for the cotton and the profits it earned them, owners supplied provisions for the people who produced the crop. This quid pro quo was one of the basic tenets of paternalism. Owners were in no way required to provide decent living conditions for their enslaved, but it is not a complicated concept that workers who were ill provisioned produced less than those who had adequate provisions.

The quality and quantity of the provisions made a huge difference in the lives of the enslaved. Julien Devereux provided a decent standard of living for his slaves: he fed them well, supplied adequate cloth for clothing, made certain they had cabins that protected them from the elements, and provided them with a home. Foodstuffs were fairly plentiful. The Devereux plantations maintained large amounts of pork—supplemented by beef, deer, bear, and fowl of all sorts. Vegetables, fruits, and dairy products were all grown on the plantation, and enslaved families had their own gardens for their personal use. In fact, the Devereux slaves had food that was probably above average for all groups across the south.

Julien Devereux did all those things for two reasons. First, he was by nature a caring man and an intelligent one. He was not oblivious to the fact that he participated in a system of human bondage, and he had appropriated—basically stolen—the fruits of the labor of those he owned. Therefore, paternalism taught that he owed his slaves decent provisions. That was what proper paternalistic slave owners of the Old South were expected to do. Second, Devereux provisioned his slaves well because they were very valuable. They were the means to the production of the cotton that made him successful. He was guided in this aspect by his business and practical side, not his altruistic or moral side. A planter simply did not get much productivity out of men, women, and children who were hungry, sick, beaten, heartbroken, cold, and ill clothed and housed.

The economic arrangements of how Devereux and others provided for their slave communities is the modern consumer method of credit. Planters, farmers, banks, mills, suppliers, slave traders, slave auction houses, and all the rest in the business gambled that cotton planted in the spring would get enough rain, but not too much. That the boll weevils, grasshoppers, and other insects would not destroy the crop, and the cotton would be worth more a year later than what had been invested. After the crop was harvested and ginned, Devereux and others insured their yield while it sat in warehouses in New Orleans awaiting sale and shipment to England. It wasn't until it actually sold that they reaped any money. So he borrowed on his credit. These are fairly standard conditions for agricultural businesses; however, the size of the investment on a large plantation and the lack of a second, or even a third, cash crop if the primary crop of cotton failed was one of the largest differences between what planters did and other, smaller farmers did.

Typical of most planters, Devereux's wealth lay in his slaves and his land, but he was by no means cash poor. There are few records of bank accounts or investment accounts; essentially, he lived daily with his investments of people and land. He did keep a considerable amount of cash on hand, however. In February 1851, he recorded, "Bank bills on the N O Bank 660, Gold in 2 leather purses 600, silver 500, Gold in my pocket purse 40 —$1800."[2] On May 6, 1853, Julien recorded, "Bank Bills 665, Amer Gold 795, Foreign Gold 212, Silver 90" for a total of $1571.00."[3] The conversion for $1,500 in 1850 to 2022 is about $56,200. The international nature of his finances is clear in the foreign coinage he mentioned in other accountings—francs, guilders, and pounds all made their way into his purse.

Just keeping his enslaved workforce in shoes was a year-round affair. Julien Devereux repeatedly placed orders for slaves' shoes, called "brogans" or "russets." One of the most puzzling aspects of the shoe orders is the lack of any mention of sizes. How would Devereux know if the shoes would fit anyone on the plantation? The answer emerges in the archives. On September 19, 1849, Julien ordered "39 Pair Russet Shoes–1.25."[4] Included in Julien's copy of the order is a long slip of paper. On one side someone had cut notches at intervals. The slip read, "measures for negro shoes."[5] Julien or someone had notched the paper to indicate the length of shoes needed. Apparently, such a strip was included in other orders, but rarely returned with the merchandise. This one made its way back into the records for some historian, like me, to find one hundred and fifty years later. That strip of paper with the notches struck me as utterly elegant in its simplicity and solution to the problem. It still does.

Brogans, or russets, were work shoes for slaves—heavy, cumbersome, and usually a reddish brown. They were neither comfortable nor stylish; however, they did protect the feet of a slave or anyone doing hard, manual labor, and they were very, very durable. The Devereux Slaves left no comments on the shoes; however, a formerly enslaved person interviewed by Works Progress Administration workers in the 1930s did. James W. Smith in Palestine, Texas, recalled, "Our shoes wasn't purty either. I has to laugh when I think of de shoes. There wasn't no careful work put on dem, but dey covered de feets and lasted near forever."[6] Brogans were destined to become the marching shoes of both the Confederate and Union armies in a decade or so. Today we call them hiking or work boots and the modern versions are comfortable, scientifically engineered, expensive shoes from Red Wing or REI. What began as a slave's work shoe is expensive and often considered high fashion.

Brogans were fairly cheap. In 1841, William Bond paid $20.00 for eleven pairs on the trip to Texas from Alabama.[7] In today's money, that is nearly $550. The fact that Bond was on the road caused the price to be a bit higher than what Julien could order. On September 23, 1846, Devereux ordered three pairs of Brogans and eight pairs of "boys shoes" plus "2 prs. of ladies Brogans."[8] His records over the years show a steady increase in the price of footwear but not drastically so. By 1856, the year Julien died, Sarah paid $1.65 each for "35 pr Ruset shoes" for a total of $57.75.[9] Assuming slave shoes were replaced once a year, then seventy enslaved individuals over a forty-year period required 2,800 pairs of shoes. An average of $1.50 a pair meant Julien Devereux spent $4,200 on shoes in four decades.

Most years, new shoes were ordered in the early fall on the Devereux Plantation. Many slaves shed the heavy work shoes in the warmer months and went barefoot part of the time. It is a safe bet that members of the Slave Community did what people always did with footwear that was painful—they modified the shoes by cutting the toes out, padding the soles, or doing whatever made them more comfortable. The Devereux records indicate that occasional orders consisting of a few shoes were made throughout the year, so Julien clearly saw fit to replace shoes that were damaged or worn beyond use when needed. Additionally, the records revealed that slaves sometimes bought shoes for themselves out of the money they earned. No doubt those shoes were more comfortable.

Just as there were shoes specifically meant for slaves, there were inexpensive fabrics called "slave cloth" or "Lowell's." It was produced in the mills of Lowell, Massachusetts, for slave clothing and was not unlike modern-day muslin, just cheaper and rougher. This is an item directly related to slavery that is readily traceable in an American production flow. First, slaves in the South grew the cotton. It was then transported, probably by water and/or train to the northern states. After it reached the north, the bales went to fiber manufacturers, where the cotton was cleaned and the fibers separated by mechanical carders. After that, mechanical spinners turned the fibers into thread. Then, the huge rolls of thread were transported to the mills. At the mills, the thread was loaded onto giant looms and woven into mighty bolts of fabric. The fabric was then transported to wholesalers or garment factories. Before Julien or his slaves ever saw any of the product, it was bought in smaller batches by wholesalers, who sold it to merchants like Charles Vinzent, with whom Julien dealt frequently. Of course, the cloth had to be transported again back to the plantation.

From when the slaves grew the cotton and turned it into bales until it came back to them as fabric for clothing, there were thirteen stages. Six of those stages were for transportation—wagon, ship, and/or rail. Two were for factory production. Three were for middle business purposes—brokers, suppliers, and wholesalers. Two stops were for warehousing. Then finally, the cloth was back in the control of merchants like Vinzent, to whom Julien could send Martin or Jesse with a wagon to either Shreveport or Mount Enterprise and, at long last, bring the finished cotton back to the plantation. Everyone added their profit to all thirteen stages, which raised the price of the product. There were a minimum of thirteen companies or businesses that employed or enslaved an unknown number of individuals who depended on those middle companies for their livelihood to do the work of their enterprise. Just tracing one bale of cotton exemplifies the economy and business of what one slave did. Doing this also makes it very plain why a slave was so valuable and vital to Southern agriculture, economy, politics, and society.

The raw cotton for the huge roll of 519 ½ yards Julien ordered in 1856 could conceivably have come from his own fields.[10] The yardage varied according to what the mills provided, but large rolls like this were ordered every year. The records from February 8, 1853, detail the distribution of cloth to the slaves. On average this included six yards for a woman, six and a half yards for a man, five yards for a girl child and five and a half yards for a boy child.[11]

This list only accounts for 284 yards of fabric, but the rolls Julien received were much larger. He must have provided fabric for other household uses. While this yardage per person seems standard, it was hardly enough to make more than two garments each, so possibly the Devereux Plantation did two cloth distributions a year.

TABLE 7. CLOTH RATIONS GIVEN TO DEVEREUX SLAVES IN 1853[12]

NAME	YARDS OF FABRIC
Lev Maria	31 yards
July	24
Mary	20
Katy	39
Henry Maria	33
Eliza	6
Judy	22
Levin	6 ½
Martha	27
Matilda	18
Jesse	18
Rhoda	6 ½
Jim	6 ½
Joanna	12 ½
Randal	6 ½
Bill	6 ½
Lucius (Frank)	6 ½

Clothing for slaves was made at home from yardage given out. The Lowell's fabric made shifts, aprons, teddies (undergarments), and nightwear for the women. Usually, shifts were the primary work clothing for women. Additionally, each woman had to have a collection of rags she washed out and used each month for her menstrual cycle. Those items were rarely mentioned in records, but logic dictates they were a factor for every woman. Gestation and lactation would have decreased the number of monthly cycles women had but would not have eliminated them. The Lowell's would have made shirts for the men, probably garments that were the short equivalent of shifts that the women wore. Until five years of age, boys wore shifts like those worn by girls, so the Community would have needed a large quantity of those. Certainly, the use of hand-me-downs was very common.

Records show that men's pants were ordered ready-made. A typical record of an order is from September 6, 1844, for "14 ps. B R. Osnabergs" for a total of $56.77.[13] Osnaburg fabric was made of linen and, later, jute fibers, and was heavier than Lowell's cloth. The sizes were listed as inseam numbers, ranging from 28 ½ to 29 ½. Those measurements would have been for men who were five feet eight or taller, except for one pair for a shorter man.

Nearly every woman of whatever color sewed by hand in the mid-nineteenth century. Isaac Singer patented a commercially applicable interlocking-stitch sewing machine for the home consumer market in 1851, but the treadle-powered machines did not become customary home items until the 1870s. White women had them long before women of color, but even the poor of both races managed to obtain treadle sewing machines by the beginning of the twentieth century.

Tabby was a seamstress for the Devereux family. Part of her duties included sewing for Sarah and the children and possibly making some items for Julien. The orders Julien made to his factors, including lace, ribbon, and calico, were clearly for Sarah. Tabby was still sewing for the family in 1855, when Sarah mentioned that Tabby's fall and injury to her wrist rendered her unable to sew. We know Tabby received a gift of cloth for herself from the man who bought the Alabama plantation in 1841. She made clothing for herself, Scott, and probably some of her extended family. Tabby had passed by 1861, but she lived through a ten-year period in which treadle sewing machines were available for home use, so it's possible that she used one of the new machines. This was an affluent family who kept up with the times, but no such machine is

Cotton cards and several bolls of cotton were essential tools to spinning, weaving, and making clothing. *Courtesy of Jo Snider.*

mentioned in the records. There is mention of at least one spinning wheel and several pairs of cards to prepare cotton fibers for spinning. Certainly some of the Slave Community also knitted and quilted—skills ubiquitous among women at that time and place.

Clothing was supplemented by the slaves with the profits they earned from selling their corn and cotton. One characteristic of communities such as the Devereux Slave Community was a sharing of resources. Money would have changed hands within the Community. Most of the orders that Julien made over the years for household supplies, clothing, and other sundries failed to identify for whom the items were ordered. One exception was a coat Henry bought one year. Also, slaves bought an unknown amount of clothing at stores such as Vinzent's in Mount Enterprise.

Another source of shopping that was off the consumer grid was the trade brought to the plantation by peddlers, the early version of traveling salesmen. The numerous lists of expenses for which Julien paid contained frequent small amounts to peddlers. Those purchases were likely for selections made by his wife and children, but if Sarah and the boys were buying small items, then it stands to reason that the enslaved were, as well. It has been determined they had money to spend. It is safe to assume the Devereux Slave Community supplemented their wardrobes beyond the clothing made from the cloth Julien furnished.

Members of the Slave Community had to have protection for their heads from the sun. Oddly, there were no orders for hats or bonnets other than one here and there, all of which were clearly for the mistress. The women probably wore bonnets, scarves, or turbans of their own making. Hats were not supplied by Julien Devereux for his male workers but were likely woven by those on the plantation out of straw and other fibers. Straw hats are standard headgear for Southern farmers and ranchers today.

There is every indication that the Devereux slave housing was on a par with, or a shade above, the slave housing on most plantations throughout the South. The documents state Devereux Slave Community housing was made of logs that were cut, dragged to the site, and assembled by the slaves. Planking to make doors was purchased locally. Only the slave housing that Sam Loftus built in early 1846 was done by someone other than the Devereux slaves. The slave cabins were situated a bit of a distance from the main houses occupied by the white families. On the Devereux Plantation, the location of the main house and the quarters—slave cabins—had spring-fed water sources. The quarters was the universal name for the slave housing area on any plantation. Today, nothing remains of the slave quarters on the Monte Verdi Plantation.

However, vestiges of this arrangement can still be seen today in small towns, hamlets, and villages across the rural South. Typically, a main street was common, with white residents living on one side of the street and black residents living on the other. Segregation and Jim Crow laws all reinforced this arrangement of space that had its beginnings on plantations. As railroads came into rural areas, the main street was often the route the rails took, giving rise to the adage of "being from the wrong side of the tracks." Even today, in small rural areas deep in Mississippi and Alabama, the black neighborhoods are still referred to as the quarters.

On the Devereux Plantation, houses and outbuildings of modest size were all moved when the location of the main house was moved in 1847, then moved again when the plantation house at Monte Verdi was established in 1855. Since there was no plumbing or wiring, a team of mules would drag a structure placed on wooden skids from one location to another in the course of a day or two. It took several more days to rebuild the fireplaces in each slave cabin. Most houses that had fireplaces sat on the ground due to fire hazards. Time and life welded those dirt floors together with cooking grease, water, mud, and food spills to make them almost adobelike. My grandmother told me how she sprinkled and swept the dirt floors in her first home in the early 1920s in rural north central Texas.

In 1855, Julien and Sarah Devereux started construction on Monte Verdi, the plantation's two-story, Greek Revival-style house that sits on a rise in the landscape and still exists today. Julien hired out a lot of the work, but slave builders and crews did their share of the work, too. On January 4, 1856, Sarah wrote Julien that she "had one room of our old house moved up on the hill for our kitchen. It is all neatly put up and Charles is laying the floors back in it."[14] It was probably the slave carpenters, maybe even Charles, who first built the room that became the new kitchen. It sounds as if the kitchen was dismantled and rebuilt at the new site, rather than dragged intact. It may have been too complicated to drag it, but more likely the terrain did not lend itself to dragging the structure. And, lo and behold, it had a wooden floor.

Julien left for Austin shortly after the work on the new house commenced. Workmen were already on site, and Sarah and her father oversaw the progress. Julien's concerns about debt led him to have Sarah stop most work on the house before he returned. He instructed her not to hire any more workmen and not to pay those who finished until he came home for fear they would overcharge her. Her father, John Landrum, did make partial settlement with some of the construction crews, however. While the bosses were white men, it appears from several of the letters of application for the work that most of the hired workmen were slave hands. For certain, the Devereux hands did a great deal of the work.

Late in the day on December 4, 1855, Sarah wrote Julien, "They came up this evening and extended the fence around the New house and helped to clean up the yard."[15] It is such a simple statement about a group cleaning up around a house. But it is not simple. The contrast between their lives as enslaved individuals and the beautiful new house could not have escaped them. How did the enslaved feel about this new structure? Did they see it as a symbol of their enslavement and denied liberty? These were intelligent people. They knew it was the fruits of their labors that paid for it. The reactions were likely different for each of them. But as they picked up the trash and tidied up around the big house that evening, under the oak and pecan trees, in the solitude and shadows of a winter evening in the Old South—what were they thinking?

Monte Verdi Plantation as it looks today is due to the careful restoration and continual upkeep of the current owners Joe and Cecilia Koch. The Kochs have graciously hosted descendants on several occasions and included the contributions of the enslaved population into the history of the property. The large cedar tree just visible in the far right-hand side of the photo was planted in May 1856 to memorialize Julien Devereux's death. *Courtesy of Paul Snider.*

Chapter Thirteen
Pork Chops and Potions

I try to make out something [a letter] twice a week. hog killing is all I can think of this time. they have killed 7160 pounds of pork out of the woods and say they can get a good deal more yet.[1]

SARAH LANDRUM DEVEREUX, 1855

Pork chops and doctors' visits linked together may seem odd; however, it makes excellent sense. Of course, food does not cure disease, but one of the strongest indicators of a person's ability to survive an illness or injury is adequate nutrition. Having body fat to spare can give a patient a greatly improved chance of surviving a major disease. This is especially true for older adults. Since infants and children are also vulnerable, maternal nourishment is vital. Research shows (CDC Breastfeeding website is the best) that the longer an infant nurses, the better their chances of surviving infancy. Good nourishment and longevity are inexorably linked.

Foodstuffs for the Devereux Slave Community came almost entirely from the plantation itself. Purchased food supplemented the supply when the pantry ran low. The first year on both the Montgomery and Rusk County plantations saw few food shortages. By the end of September 1846, John Devereux recorded "60 large wagon loads . . . measur'd upwards of 40 bushels making the corn crop 2400 bushels."[2] The basic southern diet centered around cornmeal breads or mushes and pork, mixed with a large supply of locally grown fruits and vegetables. Cornmeal, of which they had an abundance, was mixed with a liquid, usually water, milk, or oil, and seasoned with salt or molasses. Thick batter was shaped by hand and fried. It was served for breakfast with meat, molasses, and cornmeal mush. Harry Johnson, a formerly enslaved man, recalled this food when he was interviewed by WPA interviewers: "In dem days, we'd take cornmeal and mix it with water and call 'em corn dodgers and dey awful nice with plenty of butter."[3] Johnson failed to mention that the corn dodgers were fried before he added the butter, but otherwise his experience was probably akin to that of the Devereux Slaves. A more liquid version, like pancake batter, was poured out on a griddle and cooked. These flat "corn cakes" served as wraps for meat and were carried to the fields for lunch.

The amount and variety of meats on the Devereux Plantation was greater than expected, especially the amount of pork. Generally, slaves received the lesser cuts of meat; however, there was so much pork available the whites could not have eaten all the finer cuts. During the first year at Lake Creek, Montgomery County, and at Rusk County, the records indicate that the plantation bought pork and beef repeatedly throughout the year. By the second year, those living on the plantation started hunting more and had more of their own pork to preserve.

One of the first things John Devereux did in Rusk County was to buy breeding stock for a decent sounder (the proper name for a herd of swine). On Sunday, January 4, 1846, John "went to Smith's place and bought two sows and their 12 pigs mark'd and alter'd the 7 shoats—saw all the rest but the old & young black sows and John the boar."[4] The boar "was claim'd and taken away—Mr. Shivey told the man he was ours and he promis'd to bring him back."[5] Shoats were piglets and the seven neutered were males. That left the two sows and five female piglets as breeding stock and John the boar, assuming he found his way home. The new smokehouse was finished before the month was out, so the plantation was ready for pork curing and preserving.

By January 1848, the plantation was preserving meat for the year with both their own stock and some purchased animals. In total, the Slave Community killed and processed 10,531 pounds of pork for 1848.[6] For 1849, the plantation "killed pork for the year" that totaled 10,444 pounds.[7] The livestock was increasing according to Julien's taxable property declaration for 1849. He owned "150 head of cattle valued at $4 per head" and 400 hogs.[8] The same taxable property declaration listed sixty-two slaves in his ownership.

Pork was not the only meat eaten in the winter of 1848. Toward the end of November 1847, Julien recorded, "Mr. Seaborn Brewer came down from Henderson with a pack of Bear dogs," and "we hunted with him occasionally and killed six bear while he remained."[9] However, that was not the end of the bear hunts. "After he left we took up the business ourselves and killed 8 more making in all . . . 14 mostly large ones & very fat."[10] Bear meat was an excellent source of protein, a source the Lewis and Clark Expedition relied on during their 1804–06 expedition. Clearly, the Slave Community was sharing in the hunting and eating of the bears.

The pork supply continued to grow. By 1850, the total killed was 12,059 pounds,[11] and for 1851, the total was 12,307 pounds.[12] Julien, like most southerners, allowed some of their hogs to roam wild in the woods and fatten on the acorns, nuts, and berries available to them. Some of the prime hogs were fenced in midsummer and fattened on corn until the slaughter in the fall. Sarah Devereux mentioned to Julien on January 1, 1856, that "Jim and some of the other boys are here salting up our big corn fed hams this morning."[13] Those prime hams were probably reserved for the white table.

Sarah's reference to the "boys" salting the hams at the big house was a good reminder that all the meat meant a great deal of messy, vile, grueling work for the enslaved workers. Slaughtering, preparing, and preserving meat was not easy or pleasant work, and it was not just a pig or two—it was dozens. However, the work provided plenty of meat for the next year; a chance to score some big, meaty pork cuts for a few meals; and often, a party-like atmosphere to make the work go faster.

A careful study of the 1850 Federal Slave Schedule reveals a number of interesting things about the Slave Community related to food and caloric needs for agricultural work. In 1850, there were sixty-nine slaves on the plantation.[14] One female slave has no age listed, so the sixty-eight with ages included are the basis of this analysis. It is useful to have a general idea how these workers were employed on the plantation.

Gender does matter in this workforce because work was gendered. Women made a different kind of fencing while men cut the logs and built the structures. Woman were more in domestic service in the owner's home. Men clearly were the ones who left the plantation on their owner's business. Gendered work roles also translate into necessary caloric intake, as does age. Three individuals were over fifty and probably not doing heavy-duty work for a full day but were still contributing to the plantation. Among these three over fifty were Scott and Tabby, and they have been frequently mentioned and shown their contributions. Breaking down workers ages and roles makes it clear that the enslaved population on a plantation like the Devereux Plantation were productive and doing useful labor from childhood to near death.

There were twenty-seven slaves who were between infancy and ten years of age. Of this group, seventeen were five years of age or younger—not old enough or strong enough to do any work, but with high caloric needs for growth and protection against childhood illnesses. There were seven children between six and ten who could do some work that would have been helpful to the plantation. Enslaved children beyond the age of five did have chores and were expected to work. They were placed in groups to do such things as clean the yard, feed the chickens, gather fruits and vegetables, and run errands on the plantation.

Between the ages of eleven and nineteen, there were seventeen slaves who would have been capable of doing a considerable amount of work. They had the energy and strength, but they lacked the experience and knowledge to do many things. They would have been worked into gangs of older slaves who provided supervision and training. This is also the age range where marriages and children would have been common, so this group represented future increase of numbers and wealth to the owners. Due to pregnancy and gestation in this group, they would have had high caloric needs.

That left a fully capable workforce of twenty-one people between the ages of twenty and fifty. Of that twenty-one, eleven were women of childbearing years. At any given time, some of those women were pregnant or nursing an infant—both conditions which would have lessened their work time, but maintained their high calorie intake needs. That left ten men out of sixty-nine people of prime age and ability to do the heavy work on the plantation.

Let us use those numbers to discuss the consumption of all that pork. Add the white owners' family members and the overseer and his family, which takes our numbers up to eight. Those can be set aside for the moment. Of the sixty-nine slaves on the plantation, only twenty-one were fully grown men and women who would have had high calorie and protein needs. The twenty-seven children would have had varying nutritional needs. The third group, between the ages of eleven and nineteen, would have had high needs for calories and protein, but the three over fifty would have been on the downhill side of the curve on protein and caloric needs. Let's assume the equivalency of the thirty-five youngsters and oldsters was twenty adults. Thus, sixty adults shared in approximately twelve thousand pounds of pork, the basic meat of the South. That means that there were a little less than eight ounces a day for sixty adults, or about two and a half ounces of meat per meal for the year. The average would be a bit less for each slave once consumption by the enslaver's and overseer's families is factored out. However, those numbers would rise again when the additional fish, deer, duck, beef, and bear meat were added back to the totals. It appears the enslaved had sufficient protein to thrive. All in all, the Devereux slave diet is typical of the food that Millie Forward, a formerly enslaved woman, recalled on the plantation near Jasper, Texas, where she grew up: "Us never was knowed to be without mea[t]," said Forward, "'cause massa raise plenty pigs. Us have fish and possum and coon and deer and everything."[15] Millie Forward does not mention bear meat such as was eaten on the Devereux Plantation.

Proper protein allotments were crucial to people doing hard physical labor. Eaten with available fruits, vegetables, and various preparations of corn, the Devereux slaves had a good diet for the time, place, and conditions. The slaves grew their own gardens, and many of the larger plots were grown for the use of the entire plantation. Those crops included yams, Irish potatoes, peas, beans, squash, probably okra, cabbage, lettuce, spinach, beets, greens, peaches, apples, wild berries, and other fruits. On Saturday, April 10, 1847, as John Devereux was rapidly losing his hold on life, he wrote he "had half my garden planted yesterday—all culinary vegetable"[16] for the main kitchen, which no doubt the blacks enjoyed on a limited basis, as well. What a nice legacy for the future he left in his garden of herbs. Surely Tabby got all she wanted, and who's to say some of those herbs didn't find their way into the quarters? After all, who was going to miss a sprig or two of parsley or mint when the lush climate and nurturing rains replenished it in just a few days? East Texas is nothing if not verdant.

As mentioned, foodstuffs became most important in times of illness; malnourished individuals are at greater risk in a serious illness or injury, and pregnant and nursing mothers have special nutritional requirements for healthy babies. It is a good thing that ample food was available. Even though the Devereuxes were quick to call the doctor to treat ill and injured slaves, the state of medical training and practice was primitive, at best. Most of the doctors Julien employed may have started their careers treating animals and progressed to humans. That was a common way a doctor set himself up in practice, especially in the hinterlands like Texas. Few, if any of the physicians Julien retained, had any formal medical training. They probably relied on their experiences, input from colleagues, and what books and manuals they were able to order from urban book dealers.

To fully understand how one case of influenza could turn lethal for a slave and threaten an entire community, it is necessary to take a quick look at the state of medical care around 1850. The American Medical Association (AMA) was founded in 1847, but it was the carnage of the Civil War that moved medicine and surgery into new fields of discovery. One of the main lessons of the war was that going forward, professional medical schools and well-trained physicians were a necessity. The AMA began a long, slow slog of a campaign to require adequate training and licensing of physicians. It was not until the twentieth century that doctors went to well-equipped and professionally staffed medical schools. Even in the twenty-first century, licensing of doctors is not standardized by the federal government but conducted by the medical boards of fifty different states.[17]

Antibiotic drugs, which would have been so useful and lifesaving on the plantation, are modern medications of the twentieth century. Only iodine was used on the plantation to treat wounds. Later, sulfur was applied to wounds in World War I to fight infection, but the antibiotic sulfa was not developed from the element sulfur until 1935. Penicillin followed about five years later. Both were successfully used in World War II but not widely available to the public until the 1950s. Both drugs were among the first to fight bacterial infections, but many more were to follow, some extremely powerful agents to fight life-threatening infections. Drugs to fight viral infections have been more of a problem for researchers and drug developers because viruses mutate so efficiently. As microbes go, viruses are the super survivors of the lot; they change themselves into a version of what they were and render antiviral medications either totally useless or less effective. Thus, a few antiviral drugs have been widely available for only a few decades and they have severe limitations in fighting viruses. Viruses, like the COVID-19 epidemic of 2020-22, are better controlled with vaccinations.

How much illness could Julien have prevented if he'd had flu vaccinations for his enslaved? Interestingly, he did have some sort of a vaccine, probably for smallpox. The vaccine for smallpox was developed in the late 1790s, and its use spread across England and the United States in the first half of the nineteenth century. In 1855, Massachusetts mandated smallpox vaccinations for school children, the first such mandate.[18] On December 14, 1850, Julien received the following letter from S. W. March of Mount Enterprise: "I send you enough vaccine matter to vaccinate 10 or 15 subjects."[19] March gave no instructions on

RUSK COUNTY

Most travel to and from the Monte Verdi Plantation was confined to Rusk County. Daily runs were made to Anadarko and New Salem for mail and to Mount Enterprise for everything from groceries to nails. *Courtesy of Jeffrey Snider.*

the use of what he sent, nor was there any follow-up information on usage. It is doubtful Julien used the vaccine for any of his slave population. The number of doses would cover the white Devereux, Landrum, and Howerton families, and probably no others. However, Julien knew of the smallpox vaccine and may have vaccinated all or part of his enslaved population at a later time. There are no records of a smallpox outbreak on the plantation.

Medical care was fairly expensive—not as high as it is now, but still costly. It appeared that Julien Devereux kept copies of virtually every doctor's bill he ever received. He had the bills, but he rarely paid them on time. When he arrived in Montgomery County, he hired Dr. E. J. Arnold of Houston and retained him through 1842.[20] Julien hired Flora out for a month to Dr. Arnold for $10 credit on his medical bill.[21] In addition, he also sold Dr. Arnold a sorrel mare for $160 to reconcile some of his debt.[22] In that year, Arnold's bill was $114.75.[23] Another credit was arranged for $30 for Arnold in Houston.[24] Devereux had $85.25 credit on future bills.[25] A credit for Dr. Arnold was a first and a last for Julien. He never showed another credit in his records to any physician.

Interestingly, records indicate that there was no segregation in medical care—doctors routinely cared for white and black patients in the same trip to the plantation. Later medical bills listing patient, sometimes ailment, and treatment were more informative. In 1851, Dr. Elijah Dodson's invoices for January through April indicated a busy doctor (Table 8).

Extrapolating that amount to a year came to a potential total medical bill of $133.86. Further examination of the material indicates slightly more than half the visits by Dr. Dodson to the plantation were for the enslaved patients. Since there were around sixty-five slaves at the time and less than a dozen whites on the plantation, the ratio of medical personnel to patients was nowhere near equal. That may have been a good thing. This was likely the only case where inequality of care or attention might have proven beneficial to the slaves' health. Visits to pull a tooth, set a broken bone, close a wound, or other hands-on treatments were obviously useful, but the various medications used were likely more harmful than helpful. The notes at the end of the table of Dr. Dodson's four months of treating the inhabitants at Monte Verdi reveal the use of the most common drugs used in the nineteenth century. Quinine and iodine are the only ones administered that have some proven medical uses. The others are opiate concoctions, alcohol-based tonics, severe laxatives, or other potions laced with acids, dyes, and, of all things, mercury. In conversation, a microbiologist shared her reading of a 1900 medical treatment book. At the end of each chapter was the same sentence directing the physician to use leeches if the above-mentioned remedies did not work.[27] Thus was the state of medicine in the nineteenth century.

Julien must have stopped calling on Dodson for medical visits by June, because the invoices dwindled off in June and then ended. It was not at all uncommon to have several physicians treating the people on the plantation at the same time, however, and it is entirely possible that Julien juggled doctors

TABLE 8. DR. ELIJAH DODSON'S BILL FOR JANUARY THROUGH APRIL 1851[26]

MONTH	DAY	DUE ($)	CASE DESCRIPTION	MO. TOTAL ($)
Jan.	?	.50	"Bleeding his wife" (A)	
	14	.50	"givieing negro medicine in the night"	
	14	2.00	"medicine to his little son"	
	15	1.00	"visite and medicine to his little son"	
	31	.50	"Examining and giving negro woman medicine"	4.50
Feb.	2	5.00	"Case of Midwifery with your wife"	
	4	2.50	"one visit and medicine to negro man at the quarter"	
	6	5.00	"visit and medicine in the night to Mary and Delivering her of a child"	
	6	.50	"giveing his baby medicine and leaving 3 for it"	
	6	.50	"pulling a tooth for negro boye"	
	10	2.50	"visite and medicine in the night to mary's child"	
	16	2.00	"one visite and medicine to Mrs. Devereux"	
	16	1.00	"large dose of quinine" (B)	
	18	.25	"1 box of vegetable pills" (C)	
	18	.75	"giveing and leaving medicine for girl Eliza to take"	
	18	.37	"one viol of Elix of vitroll" (D)	
	28	.25	"one viol of paregorie" (E)	20.63
Mar.	1	.75	"one box of pills and one viol Tine of Iodine for Jack" (F)	
	1	.25	"one viol of paregorie" (E)	
	5	.75	"one box of pills and Loral for Jack" (G)	
	5	.37	"3 doses of medicine for negro child"	
	7	.50	"one visite and medicine to negro quarter"	
	7	.12	"Blue mass" (H)	
	7	.75	"6 doses of medicine for negro child"	
	18	2.50	"one visit and medicine to your quarter and to see martha"	
	21	2.00	"visite and medicine to see your child in the night and staying all night"	
	21	.50	"going from your Dwelling to your quarter and giving a little negro medicine"	

MONTH	DAY	DUE ($)	CASE DESCRIPTION	MO. TOTAL ($)
	?	.50	"medicine sent to your child by Mr. Howerton"	
	?	.75	"medicine sent to martha"	10.74
Apr.	6	.25	"one Box of Blue mass"	
	12	2.00	"one visit and medicine to your child"	
	13	2.00	"one visit and medicine to your child"	
	14	2.00	"one visit and medicine to your child"	
	22	2.00	"one visit and medicine to your child"	
	24	.25	"to powders for child"	
	26	.25	"one box of ointment"	8.75
			Total for Four Months	44.62
			Total Number Visits or Medicines to patients	28
			Total Number of Medicines unspecified patient	7
			Treatment to Slaves	15
			Treatment to White Family	13
			Extrapolated out for Year	133.86

A. Bleeding patients to get the body's "humors" (fluids) back into balance is as old as 500 BCE. It was mostly discontinued in the Western world by 1900.

B. Quinine is the standard and highly effective treatment for malaria.

C. Vegetable pills were made by several patent medicine companies, including Wright's Indian Vegetable Pills which were popular during the Civil War. The primary ingredient was borage, a vegetable dye with cathartic properties.

D. Elixir of vitriol was a mixture of sulfuric acid and alcohol which was used for scurvy.

E. Paregoric is morphine derived from opium. It was, and still is, used as an antidiarrheal and pain medication. It is a class III narcotic.

F. Iodine was used as a disinfectant and antibacterial. Since Jack was a "mechanic"—a blacksmith with manufacturing skills—it seems logical he may have needed the iodine to treat a wound. Iodine is widely used as a tracer in modern scanning x-ray technology.

G. No amount of research turned up this old medication.

H. Blue mass was widely used to treat patients for everything from tuberculosis to toothache. About a third of its composition was mercury.

like he did other creditors to delay paying them. Nevertheless it appeared that Dodson still had some connection to patients at Monte Verdi. In January 1852, eight months later, when Dodson reminded Julien he still had not been paid, Dodson mentioned that his latest invoices were still outstanding, and on "the first of January . . . we have a negro woman that will be Expecting to have a little one bout that time and other cases of the same kind depending on me to attend to them."[28] Dodson appeared reluctant to attend to the woman unless Julien paid him for his prior services. Dodson was still petitioning Julien for payment on January 10, 1852.[29] On March 4, 1852, Dodson once again beseeched Devereux to pay him so he could purchase a new supply of medicines from Philadelphia.[30]

It is entirely possible that Julien Devereux terminated his patient/physician relationship with Dodson because he could not pay Dodson and he knew it. Devereux had a history of refusing to pay debts to others and several of his other creditors were doctors, as well. This is just another case of the master's failures to honor his responsibilities, causing harm to those he enslaved. Had the need for medical care reached critical levels, the situation could have had catastrophic consequences. As it turned out, by reducing the amount of medicine given on the plantation, Julien may have been doing the Slave Community a favor, but he certainly did not do what he did on their behalf. By this time, he had been in Texas for ten years, which was more than enough time to have regained his position and financial standing. If he had ceased buying so much land, he likely could have paid his bills.

Medical care for the year 1856 was beyond the scope of the usual treatment and activity. Julien Devereux came home from his legislative duty in serious medical distress. He struggled through the winter and early spring, and passed on May 1, 1856.[31] The records indicate that a number of doctors came and went to attend to Julien's health. Dr. P. T. Richardson appeared as the plantation's primary-care physician. Others were consulting physicians to Julien's case but also treated the members of the Slave Community while they were there.

The 1856 and 1857 medical bills from Dr. P. T. Richardson for treatment at Monte Verdi are informative. From May through November of 1856, Richardson made forty-five visits to the plantation to attend patients.[32] On June 12, 1856, he made three trips to the plantation, two of which were at night.[33] He must have barely reached home and settled in his bed when someone rode up to summon him back to the plantation. On November 2, 1856, he traveled through the rain at night to visit an enslaved man named Dan with a prescription and medicines; he saw Dan the next morning, as well. Richardson charged $8 for his attendance upon Dan.[34]

Dr. Richardson's bills continued to accrue through 1857. Richardson was finally paid in full—$163.71—by Sarah Devereux on May 11, 1858. The doctor had included interest charged on the debt of $5.96. Richardson's invoice read, "Received pay in full of the above Acct of Mrs. Sarah Devereux." Richardson added, "Paid by Note."[35] In other words, she gave him an IOU. Richardson was free to sell the note for whatever he could get to someone who was willing to gamble on Sarah eventually paying the full amount in specie. So actually, Sarah did not pay him in cash he could use.

The routine sick season always hit plantations hard, because the people on them lived in close contact with each other and nursed each other when sickness struck. They shared their germs. Malaria, yellow fever, and cholera could decimate a plantation. The Devereuxes were lucky they did not incur huge losses to epidemics of deadly diseases. However, bouts of winter-weather influenza and summer-weather gastrointestinal illnesses and fevers brought all work on the plantation to a halt while victims recovered. It could take weeks to get all hands back to work. One such epidemic hit the plantation in summer 1846, and John Devereux once again provided a daily description of events. It first presented in early August and did not abate completely until cooler weather arrived in October. It was a highly contagious, probably viral, infection that caused a high fever. The first cases presented on August 3, and John wrote of "several cases of fever among the negroes."[36] All of John's memorandum book entries between August 3 and August 13 contain new cases in both the black and white families. By August 13, John reported "negroes half of them sick and convalescent—the rest nursing the sick."[37] By August 21, "negroes nearly all sick and convalescent."[38] By Tuesday, the twenty-fifth of August, things appeared to have improved and "most of the sick on foot but cant do much."[39] John reported further progress on the next day when he wrote, "Negroes mending that are sick."[40] By mid-September, the worst of the epidemic was over. Still, it would be October before full crews would be back to work on the plantation.

All things considered, the provisions and care provided to the Devereux slaves were probably better than most for the time, place, and condition of people held in bondage. Provisions such as those the Devereux Slave Community received have become subjects in an ongoing argument about slave treatment. Starvation rations, inadequate to wretched clothing and housing, and lack of medical care have been used by some scholars to prove the evils of slavery. Provisions should be evaluated for what they were, not what point they can prove. Good provisions, adequate provisions, inadequate provisions, or terrible provisions are just that—good, tolerable, or bad. Knowledge of provisions tells us more about the lives slaves lived, and that is the value of the knowledge. Provisions neither justify nor condemn the system of slavery. All the pork chops in the world cannot excuse a system that imprisoned people because they were of African heritage.

PART IV

Chapter Fourteen
Descendants All, 2021

You can never be as tired as they were.

DR. JOI SPENCER, 2021

When this all started, few of the interviewees had met me. In the first set, most of them had not even heard about me, but we became acquainted when I did the 2014 interviews in person. By 2018, I had met some of those interviewed personally and talked with others. Most of the 2021 interviewees had read the first edition of the book or at least heard about it; three of the people I had met personally; and one was a close friend. In this set of interviews, each person I contacted was happy to contribute their thoughts and opinions, and each one became special to me and gave me more than I had hoped. Here I was, probing some of the most sensitive areas of their lives as African Americans, and there was nothing coming back my way but warmth, honesty, and friendship.

By this point, I was seeing more and more connections between the ancestors on the Devereux Plantation and the present-day descendants. I had only scratched a small spot on the surface of this extended family's history. There could easily be thousands of descendants of the Devereux Slave Community, and there were days I thought all of them knew each other. Everyone I interviewed addressed the survivability and adaptability of their ancestors and credited those traits as the main reasons the ancestors were able to build this remarkable family. Actually, I think their determination to build and maintain the family is what may have honed their abilities to adapt and survive to the levels exhibited in the records.

Just as the ancestors had to find ways to adapt and survive in slavery, the modern-day descendants to whom I was talking had to find ways to cope, adapt, and survive modern-day racism and prejudice. It is obvious the descendants reached back into their past, to their ancestors on that plantation in East

Texas more than one hundred and fifty years ago, for support and comfort. Here came William Faulkner's ghost once again to remind me how much of the past is still with us in the present.

GERALD FREENY INTERVIEW

Gerald Freeny is a native Californian. He spent his professional career in law enforcement. In 2019, he was the first African American to be president of the Tournament of Roses in Pasadena, California. During his year as president, he had over 182 speaking engagements; on New Year's Day 2020 he led the Rose Parade as Grand Marshal, and tossed the coin to start the Rose Bowl Game.

ON HIS ANCESTORS AS SLAVES

It's part of something that we were taught growing up so it's just something that we accept and it's something that we have been taught from early ages. I know my grandparents from both sides taught me about it. And, you know, I really don't have a feeling. I don't feel it was right, but they survived. And they showed us how to survive and how to get through the struggles.

I look at some of our features. Like all Freeny men have a certain type of hand. We all have a hand thing. We all have an eyebrow and eyes that are alike. You can see it in our faces. Our noses are different and our faces. And I see a resemblance definitely in my grandfather and my great-grandfather. And I know they went through a lot when they worked but they made it better for us grandkids.

I think it put drive in all of us grandkids to make something of ourselves and to do something positive in our life. Not all of us have done that but the majority, most of us, you know, have worked, went to school, did something with our lives. So, we saw the drive, I would say, from the fact—I saw my grandfather. He worked at a trucking company for over thirty-plus years. It's about stability as far as "Take care of your family. Make sure you provide for your family. Make sure you have a home for your family." I can remember talking to my own dad. He's deceased. I think I was in college and I was talking to him about some problems I was having. And he said, "Just remember son, there's somebody out there that's worse off than you so stop complaining." And I think that's something that we have garnered from our family was the fact that there's always somebody worse off than you. Be appreciative and be grateful for what you have.

The only thing I would say, Jo, is that the Freenys are a loving family. We're all very caring and very protective of each other. I saw that from all my aunts and uncles. A lot of them have passed. But when I was little, even with my parents being divorced, my dad took me around to most of my uncles here, and a lot of my aunts.

Gerald Freeny.
Courtesy of Gerald Freeny.

HIS CAREER IN LAW ENFORCEMENT

I was in law enforcement for roughly twenty-eight years. We were taught to talk to people. I worked gangs; they knew when I said something I meant it. I gave them a break sometimes. I didn't always arrest them. It's all how you talk to people. And these guys nowadays are not trained like we are. And some of them don't need to be carrying a gun. They don't need to be on the streets because they don't know how to talk to people. It's all about how you approach somebody and how you talk to them. You can diffuse the situation very easily.

Let's face it, seeing George Floyd die on TV and all the videos, it's angered a lot of people, not just African Americans and, you know, minorities. You have a lot of people that are upset by it. And when you look at those Black Lives Matter, you know, marches and protests, there are a lot of Caucasians, not all minorities.

I probably would have pulled [Derek] Chauvin off his [George Floyd's] neck. And I probably would have talked to him first of all before they even had an issue. Tell him to relax, get in the car, let's see what's going on, and find out what we need to do. And maybe we don't need to arrest you. Let's see what's going on here. You know, sometimes it's how you approach people, like I say, how you talk to them, and you reckon with them. It's a way to ease the tension.

I think the thing that worked—community policing. You've got to know the people out in your community. Know the families. You've got to know the moms, the dads, the neighbors. That way they know when you come into the neighborhood you're there for a reason. You talk to them, and you treat them with respect. It's all about respect. And I think community policing definitely needs to be something that is addressed.

I was a supervisor too, so I would address people. And I could tell you all the time when we would go out and do search warrants, I would tell people, "Hey, we might be videotaped. Watch what you say. Watch what you do. Be careful. And realize how you talk to people and how you come across." We always had that in our briefings before we did search warrants.

ON THE TOURNAMENT OF ROSES

I was sponsored by one of my Cal State LA professors and a friend of his to get in the Tournament in 1988. Back then, you had to be sponsored by members that were in the association and there was no guarantee. Some people waited up to two to three years to get in. I was blessed. I got in my first year because one of the individuals on the executive committee, I think he was the secretary, I worked for him when I was in college part time at Bell & Howell. So that's how I got involved. They grade you every year on how well you do your job. You go from an aide to a vice-chair, to a chair, to a director, and then you're in line to be considered to become the executive committee. And it takes eight years to become president; that way you learn every committee that's in the association. That way when you're president, you can make a decision about everything.

It was thirty-one years before I became president. I was very humbled and very honored to receive that because there was a lot of competition to get to that position. In about another seven years we will have our second African American president. Him and I are very close. And, you know, I have to tell you, I just had a lot of mentors in the association that helped me through the association. Not only that, they helped me in business and life on making decisions. And I'm still very close to several of them today.

DR. JOI SPENCER INTERVIEW

Dr. Joi Spencer was raised in South Los Angeles, just a few blocks from the site of the Rodney King attack. She has degrees from Stanford University and UCLA. Dr. Spencer is the incoming Dean of Education at University of California, Riverside, in January 2023.

ON HER ANCESTORS

A lot of my own wholeness is because I have taken the time to learn my history. I think that is a huge cultural principle. So as blacks, as African Americans, we can't hate ourselves to life, we have to love ourselves to life. So if you want to improve as a community, if you want to see your community elevate, then you do it by letting them see how worthy they are of love, not shaking your finger at people. No, these folks have already been traumatized and hurt enough. The way you grow is by you teaching people how much love has been there, how much people have sacrificed, and how great the history is. I think for us as blacks, there's got to be a lot of that because there is so much around us in black communities to tell us that "there's something wrong with you."

So that's the first thing. We've got to learn how to recover. We have to love ourselves to life. And I think for the rest of us moving forward I think it is finding the truth. You have to find the truth of how you arrived. I just feel astounded at my heritage. I feel like there's a strength that my ancestors have given me because it's hard for me to give up when I say, you know, "Oh, God. I'm really tired." Yeah, I'm tired. But I can always say, "You can never be as tired as they were." And so it's something that strengthens me. And I'm really proud. I'm very proud to be a descendant. And I use the term "I'm a descendant of enslaved Africans in America." People went and got my ancestors because they were strong, and they were intelligent, and

Dr. Joi Spencer.
Courtesy of Joi Spencer.

they were skilled. And that's how, that's how Africans were chosen from the continent. And I descended from those folks. And so I feel incredibly honored, to be honest with you, to be a descendant.

IMPACT OF TRAVELING IN AFRICA

I do a lot of work with educators in Africa: Ghana, Liberia, and sometimes Ethiopia. When I first spent a good amount of time in Ghana and then came back to the United States, it was really hard for me to come back home. "Oh my God, this is so hard. What's going on here?" And what I realized is that for the first time, when I was in Ghana, I was culturally centered. It was the first time in my life that I was in a place where being black did not subject me to pain or this notion of inferiority. When you turn on the TV in Ghana, everyone looks like you. Blackness did not denote something that you were going to have to struggle through. People are not going to see me differently. And when I opened up magazines, I saw me. And I was psychologically centered so deeply so it didn't hit me. When I came back to San Diego and I was just so deeply affected. "Oh, here you are. Here it is again. Here you are back in this situation where everything points to the fact that you're not the center. You are not fully accepted in this place."

BEING BLACK IN AMERICA

I remember walking my dog in my little community. If she pooped and I didn't pick it up quickly somebody would swoop out, like educating me, and say "You know, when your dog poops you have to pick it up." You know basically, what they're really saying is, "You don't belong in this neighborhood." So that's when I realized the psychological violence that happens in a place where you're under surveillance and it's a quiet, unspoken—that's really what would happen on the plantations. You don't have to—the idea that another person does not have freedom in and of themselves to think, to dream fully, to leave if I want to leave, to mess up if I want to mess up. Let's say today I just want to mess up.

When I look at what has happened with George Floyd, it has been so traumatizing and re-traumatizing because that's what we lived with. And I don't think it's different. I think that maybe the outrage across non-African Americans is different. So that's good. I'm happy that my students are insulted almost. I mean my non-black students. For them this is an affront for who they think America is. And so they don't necessarily know the real America because they're young. They're a little naïve. But at least in their mind, in their consciousness this is an affront. And so maybe that has changed. And maybe people have more of a love, and understanding for black culture. African American culture is much more internationalized. But it's so heartbreaking because, Derek Chauvin, so much of what he was doing was about domination. It was about "Here is this big, strong, black man and in my mind, I need to dominate him to show him he's not that big. I'm still, I'm still stronger. I still have domination over you." And, it's frightening. And once George Floyd is gone, that's it. He's not coming back. That's precious. That's a life that's gone.

ON CRITICAL RACE THEORY

I use it as a frame so my students can conduct research. And one of the things that it requires of us is to center the voice of the marginalized. So methodologically I think I'm even infatuated with a critical race theory or a critical Latinx theory because it basically says to my students, "If you're going to conduct research about someone you have to center their voice and their experience. You can't sort of look at it from your voice and your vantage point and work to interpret it, but they have to get centered." And a second precept is that you have to assume that the story you've been told historically is one that's been altered. You have to in a critical race frame. And if you don't do that, then you're sort of missing the message. And so it acknowledges that power is this historical lever and that over time, power has determined the kind of story that we hear. It's determined the opportunities that people have. So in that way, critical race theory is absolutely essential.

This idea that folks can't perhaps get outside of themselves enough—so like somehow a white person can't be anti-racist or that a white person cannot do anti-racist work? I reject it because there's always been whites in America who have been anti-racist. In their mind they knew that they could not accept this idea that half people could be free and half people could be enslaved and that somehow, they retain their humanity. They knew that our humanity is wrapped up in one another's but when a system keeps benefitting you, the hardest thing to do is to question that system. In your mind you might lose out but the truth is you don't lose. You don't lose when you question a system that favors you because you basically get to a more honest place when you even question your own privilege. When you're able to say, "You know what? I don't deserve—this is an unearned privilege. And I'm giving it back. I'm giving it back even though it might harm me in the moment." Over time, the fact that we get to speak eye to eye, we get to speak as human beings to one another, that is way more beneficial than any privilege that you could ever gain by being white in a white-dominant society.

UNDERSTANDING BLACK AMERICA

If you really want to understand black people and you want to understand racism, you have to understand the ways in which people get subjected because racism has all these ugly, ugly parts of it. Go to the doctor that most black people have to go to. Like, go sit in the county hospital. Don't go to your fancy HMO [Health Maintenance Organization] or PPO [Preferred Provider Organization]. Go to the doctor that the folks of color have to go to. Like, that's how you understand racism, the big "R" like on that larger scale.

Get to know black people. Go to dinner. If you don't have one black friend or someone you can call on, then you can't really understand people. And that makes sense anywhere, right? Like, that's just common knowledge. Like if I want to know about someone, get to know them, not in an artificial way, not to study them as a science experiment, but get to know them, walk in love. What happens when a black elder passes away? I don't think you can really know black culture if you don't understand black experience around death, or life. What happens when a new baby is born in a black family? Or how do folks say grace over pizza versus how do they say grace over Sunday dinner? All part of any culture. And the only way to get to know it is to embed yourself in their life. But also, not just the individuals. Embed yourself in their communities, and in their experience. And learn about what they face, and how they face it, and experience that as well.

GEORGE EDWARD FREENEY, II INTERVIEW

George Freeney (with the extra *e*) has what he calls a "diverse past." He served in the United States Army as a police officer in the K9 force. Following that, he had a career in high tech. Now he is a talented artist, photographer, and genealogist. He only discovered recently that he was descended from the Devereux Slave Community.

HIS ANCESTORS

The difficult part for me was not knowing that they were slaves, it was not knowing who they were, right? I knew they were slaves but I had no idea who they were. I couldn't know who my grandfather was, or great-grandfather was, or anything past that. But I knew I came from slaves.

I'm a generation that was fortunate enough to be exposed to watch *Roots*. They were brought over as slaves, but they never got back home. So, that's where I'm at now. I've got a lot of ancestors to discover and find through the efforts I'm doing. I have a tree that's seven thousand folks strong.

Home as far as where I raise my right hand and defend a country for the democracy that I live in, then yeah, I can truly say I'm an African American at that point, right? Because I raised my right hand, and I actually defended the country to prove that I am that American. So, this is my home. I know where I'm from. I know where I was born. But that heritage home is the part that's been missing.

I have a great-great-grandfather, third great-grandfather, Alfred Spencer, that fought in the Civil War but he was on the Union side. And then as I follow my history all the way down, I descend from a long history of World War I, World War II, every conflict. My father, my father himself, my biological father, is a Vietnam vet. So, I'm next generation right after that. And remember I didn't realize that. I just discovered that I was a Freeney not too long ago.

RACISM IN AMERICA

I think we need to slow ourselves down. Instead of hating each other, I think we need to slow ourselves down and say we're more closely related than one would want to think. If you start thinking about separatism and racism, those are man-made. It's a choice. It's an absolute choice of a philosophy you want to believe in. You can change your mind. You're a rational being. We're the only rational being that walks on two legs on the planet with the largest brain. So, we can change that choice, but it's a choice to change. And if you don't want to change, then nothing changes. So we have to understand why we're changing. You have to understand and educate before we can change. So if we could have those conversations without fear, without fear of being judged that you're gonna call me "racist" if I ask this stupid question, right, 'cause some questions just might be stupid. They still might sound racist but then the other side has to understand that, hey, there was no racist intent with that. It was an education intent and also change.

BEING BLACK IN AMERICA

I caught the Spidey sense—the privilege of not being black. That's what privilege is. So, I'm black all the time so it's always gonna be there is the way I look at it unfortunately. Honestly—personally from my point of view, it's four hundred years of PTSD [Post Traumatic Stress Disorder]. That's passed down generationally. My mom told me her mom's stories. So, we kind of have to deal with that four hundred years of PTSD where you comply. The compliance when you're stopped by a police officer, which, knock on wood, I never have been, just for that vigilance. But my guard's never down. I mean, I was explaining to somebody the other day that was asking me at a retreat that I was at, I said, "It's exhausting being a black man." And I say that a lot of times in humor. Most of the things I say is in humor. But it's the truth. It's truthful humor. It's tiring. I'll say it this way, "White privilege is the privilege of not being black." I said, "You can walk into anywhere you want without a concern of anything. You can breathe. No nerves. You don't get butterflies in your stomach. You don't have to stop and say, 'Who's on the other side of that door?' A black man can go to those same places. We have those rights, right? But we have to be vigilant. We have to be speculative of who's asking those questions, why they're asking those questions. "Are they accusing me of something? Are they not?" And those are a lot of decisions to make a lot of the time, all the time. It's exhausting. That's the privilege that I see, the privilege of not being black.

LIVING IN THE SOUTH

I don't understand the Confederate flag because of me raising that right hand, and knowing what it means. Stand for one flag and one flag only. I don't think that flag should stand for anything. It should not be flown. Why? Because it's a traitor's flag. They lost a war.

If they want to keep their statues and they want to keep their history, they should be able to bring them indoors and close their doors so that way I can choose not to go in. Walking by it outside, I don't think they need to be out there. That way the history's not gone. There's still an audience that wants to go see it but this audience chooses not to. But if it's outside, I have to.

I made a choice that I would probably never go to a slave state as I would call it. These are slave states and the slave states tend to fly that Confederate flag. So, to kind of go back to summing up that fear, it's a fear of these states. And why put yourself in what you probably know is gonna happen in the first place so just avoid it, right? So now I can say as of probably two weeks ago, I have hit every one of them just on a nice little journey and trip trying to trace my ancestry. I learned a lot. I learned just that statement was ignorant itself.

Devereux, Georgia—I just assumed everybody there because it's Deep South Georgia, was gonna be all white so I refused to get out of the car. I sent Susan [Susan is George's wife; she is white] in. She comes back twice and says, "George, that's the second time that everybody that's gone in there is black." And I just talked to a convenience attendant and just told her I was from out of town and I was doing my genealogy research and I'm a Freeney. She'd never heard of the name Freeney and she said, "No, not Freeney." I'm like, Oh, I'm at a dead end. I said, "Okay, we're in Devereux. This is gonna be a dumb question but what about Devereuxes?" She said, "Which one?" I was like, "Oh, wow. Do they all look like us?" She said, "Well, here comes another one, oh here comes another one, and another." So a longer story short, we discovered through our DNA connections and her recognizing some through trees, we are related. I'm actually at the source of where my ancestors are coming from. The Georgia trek.

PART IV

ANTHONY (TONY) SOLOMON HENRY INTERVIEW

Anthony (Tony) Solomon Henry works in education and lives in Houston. He is a team leader for about sixty schools across the state's high school curriculum. Tony is a Henry and a Scott. He calls Florida home, but Houston and Texas are growing on him.

HIS ANCESTRY

I don't know if you've read the book *Invisible Man* by Ralph Ellison, but there's a part of that book where it said, "I used to be ashamed that I was a descendant of slaves and now I'm ashamed of myself for ever feeling ashamed." I feel so incredibly proud because they were survivors. They resisted in ways that they knew how to resist. They built this country. They got through what they could or tried their best to get through those things so that their descendants could have a better life. So that's—yeah, I'm really, really proud of it.

Anthony Solomon Henry.
Courtesy of Anthony Solomon Henry.

BEING BLACK IN AMERICA

It's always difficult to be black in this country. But there's a lot of joy that comes with being black in this country. And one of the factors that influenced joy is really me diving into this research. And there's just a lot of power in being able to piece together a story even when you don't have the answers. And sometimes—this is going to sound stupid—but sometimes I feel like when I'm researching, it's like, man, I feel like they're sitting there with me, you know? It's really, really, something.

I appreciate [people] want to do something. I tell them I feel like there's not much for me to say because, to be honest, that's a lot of mental labor for me to think, for me to navigate this system. Plus, you are seeking me out to find out what to do. And so it's one of those things where I get it, right? But you're like seeking guidance. I think that sometimes they don't always realize how exhausting it is. It is mentally exhausting even just to engage in conversations around race and equity because a lot of times some people who look like me choose not to speak up. I'm the person who if there's an elephant in the room I'm going to say it. But it is really, really, exhausting and you have to, like, decompress afterwards. And after awhile, you know, it takes a toll on you.

But I made a statement about how so often as a black person I'm forced to navigate a white-dominant world. But white people don't have to navigate, you know, my communities. You know what I'm saying? They don't have to know the ins and outs to be quote unquote successful. They don't understand that. They're like, "That's not true. When I went to college, I knew a lot of black people," or something like that, you know? And they couldn't understand why I said that. People really haven't internalized just how much whiteness dominates our society.

There is one thing that sticks out to me, and this is from a different lesson, but related. She [his professor] was covering civil rights. And she was so passionate about, like, Martin Luther King. And I remember it was time to go and she just wanted to keep teaching. She didn't want to let us go. And I remember typically when people are really invested in something, they stick around. They stick around and listen. And, you know, she was playing this speech. And I remember being the only one that stuck around. The only black kid. I was the only one in the class and everybody else is like, "Well, gotta go." And the way our classes were scheduled, you couldn't schedule a class back to back. So, nobody had another class they had to run to. But for me that felt very telling. It would have been nice to see other people stick around and, like, want to see that, but, you know. . .

ISSUES OF RACIAL JUSTICE

I'd like us to move toward action on repairing the harm that's been done for hundreds of years. I'll be honest with you, I'm not super optimistic about it. And one of the reasons I'm not is because I see the ways it still operates in stealth form. I see the people on social media saying all the right things, whether it's in meetings or out in public, around "black lives matter," and "I'm a fighter, I believe in racial equity"—but privately being anti-black. And I think those are the things that have allowed all of this to continue for so long. King talked about "Watch out for the white moderate." But, you know, nowadays we even see that with people that are even labeled "progressive." And so I think that's really dangerous to the cause of justice. And what I've noticed is even just how easy it is to weaponize blackness. It doesn't just come from Trump supporters, you know. We live in a society where people are like, "Well, I'm not racist. I'm not a neo-Nazi. I'm not a Klansman." It's like, "No, it's so much deeper than that." And I don't know that people have fully grasped what it means to be racist. And on top of that just how normalized anti-blackness is in our society.

SLAVERY

I think that we don't really emphasize enough the impact that enslaved people had on this entire country. We don't teach that they were engineers and mathematicians. But you had to be an engineer and a mathematician to do some of the things that they did. I think part of that is part of this hierarchical system. I think part of that is to maintain some of these privileged systems.

So, I think that what we have to do is take a really disruptive approach to white supremacist systems. And I think that a lot of our policies in schools, the way that we teach history, the way we teach a lot of classes are driven by this need to maintain the status quo. And that status quo was historically anti-black.

I've absolutely run into people who are just like, "Oh, I'm not comfortable teaching slavery because I don't want the kids to look at me a certain way" or "I don't want students to be angry at me" and things like that. That's why so many people, like myself growing up just feel this weird thing in your body when they start talking about slavery. And even when I was in college—like I said, I went to Marquette and there weren't many black folks there. We all knew each other. But even sitting in a history class there, you know, and they would bring up slavery, and I remember just locking eyes with the professor, and you could just feel the eyes on you all the time.

I was always comfortable discussing it. It was just uncomfortable in the classroom. And I think that just really speaks to the culture of some of our schools and some of our classrooms growing up. I also am a lot more comfortable discussing it now that, you know, I'm older—I just know more about it because when I was getting my K-12 education I had to do a lot of that research on my own. It's definitely easier. I do have a lot of friends though who aren't as comfortable. And I think that some of that is them kind of feeling tired of always seeing that. But I think it's also grounded in either not fully understanding the institution or just having that condition of feeling ashamed.

CARVELL BOWENS INTERVIEW
Carvell Bowens is a native of East Texas. He holds a BA in political science from Texas A&M University-Commerce and works in Dallas as a community organizer with an emphasis on inequalities in the judicial system for the Texas Organizing Project.

ON HIS FAMILY

I think that my family—we've always been a loving family. And never have been taught to be racist at all. Nothing like where I was ever taught to hate white people. Quite the opposite. I think I did take on that southern hospitality type, just being very, very nice to people, especially white people. Not wanting to ruffle feathers, not wanting to say anything that would bring discomfort at all. I do see it as more overt, especially in East Texas.

I had to battle with some elders in my own family. You know, my great-grandmother being born in 1914. She somewhat had some thinkings that she went through that her brain is inferior to the white people's brains. Those were the type of things that were being taught in the education system itself. And so, this is ingrained not only in white people but also it was ingrained in those people that were seen as "inferior" as well. And, you know, that's the sad part about it.

I saw Jesse and Martin as being almost like community organizers at Monte Verdi. A lot of people, especially black people, might give them different labels but if you have an enslaved person who's built a relationship with their master or owner, then they're pretty much seen as an "Uncle Tom." But, you know, the whole thing about building these relationships is to be able to have some sort of sphere of influence with that person who holds that power. Jesse being the body servant of Julien Devereux and actually being able to go with him down to the legislature and being able to just be there and having personal conversations with him.

Julien actually [arranged for] Jesse to be in the same room with him and not in a separate type of quarters. Just that right there will kind of maybe help break down—somebody who holds power—break down their view a little bit on how this power structure should look like and how we should be treating other people, and can bring about better living conditions for someone's people or something like that. It helped me get more grounded in community organizing by just knowing that.

Carvell Bowens.
Courtesy of Carvell Bowens.

BLACK COMMUNITIES

Seems like since slavery we have seen a decline, and not to the fault of black people themselves, but a decline in the black community, in the tight-knit structure of the black community. There are some smaller communities that have maintained that today but most people dispersed from communities during the Great Migration. And then you just have all these overtly racist practices and policies that broke down black communities.

We have another ism that we're suffering with here in America—individualism. That often takes away from the community tightness that we were used to back in the day. And when you have people just thinking about themselves and their family and that's it, there's a lot of loss of community and then just a lot of loss of connection with other people, period. Communities that still want to be there for each other as human beings, as people, together.

That's ultimately what I'm scared about the most. So I'm hoping we can kind of keep a community structure. So going back to what's in the book, you know, that's the one thing I felt like—especially black people—had working for them in slavery was somewhat trying to maintain a sense of community. And so I feel like if we can get some equity in place that we can at least have these oases in place where people can feel like they're part of a community whether it's you being down there in San Marcos or whether it's me being here in Dallas. It's "Okay, I'll have a chance to thrive in this community over here." We have a sense of community and I feel a sense of belonging even though it's not my home region where I grew up and where my family is from. I still have family in Dallas. And I can make family and friends, like you were saying, of people by being in a community with them. My hope is just maintaining community, honestly.

HIS WORK IN COMMUNITY ORGANIZING
I feel like I did experience racism growing up at the level—you know, me growing up in the '80s, I felt like I did have experiences like most people had in the '60s. East Texas has a history and just a culture of its own to where it resembles more a lot of the Deep South areas.

I think East Texas is like the edge of the Deep South. I was kind of polarized even going back to Trayvon Martin back in 2012, but these other accounts really, really brought me in to wanting to work and get connected to my community more and work on issues we all faced as a people—black people. It was very clear to me that American institutions, even capitalism itself, was rooted in racism.

When I started doing community organizing, when I was actually working on issues of policy and things like that, that were trying to overturn some of these policies that were rooted in racism, I had a lot of my white friends from East Texas, just various white acquaintances that I maybe had known from previous work or something like that—a lot of them felt like I turned into this racist by trying to fight for these issues. I'm like, "Well, why does it have to be racist? Even if I'm seen as pro-black, why does it have to be seen as racist?" I'm not out here wanting to lower the standards of how white people live or anything like that. I'm not out here fussing about communism or anything like that. It's just about elevating the way of life for black people, for people of color, you know, and just making sure they have a fair chance.

We just gotta come to a place where we don't feel like somebody is better because they're over somebody else. That's the whole premise I think where it came from. Just wanting to be over someone, wanting to be the leader of other peoples. That's what we're dealing with. And unfortunately, going back to earlier, what you see in East Texas, which is a particular story of its own here in Texas—you see that Deep South heritage in that region. The Confederacy shall rise again, you know, like, that's very much part of that heritage.

RACISM IN AMERICA

When you have black people standing up and speaking out on issues, then you get a lot of this backlash and it's evident where it's coming from. It's coming from a sense of white supremacy and just racist thinking. Period. And, yeah, East Texas—and I have to say, Texas overall—I hate to say it, but I feel like it does exhibit a lot of this overall.

I don't even know if we can really reach a point of "equal" but we're damn sure trying to fight for equity at least to have access to the things that people with power consider "good quality of life." Even some semblance of that, like not even the same level. But it's hard. It's hard to fight a power structure that's in place and holding that power right now.

JERI MILLS INTERVIEW

Jeri Mills comes with a story that must be told. In 2002, I wrote a paper about the Devereux Slave Community that was accepted by the East Texas Historical Association for their spring meeting in Galveston, Texas. When the time came for the meeting, I was unwell so I reworked the paper as a letter and asked the chair of the session to read it for me. In the audience was an African American woman who had noticed the title of my paper in her bulletin about the meeting. She packed up her husband and her aging mother, and they drove to Galveston. In the conclusion to my paper was a statement about how connecting with some of the descendants would enhance my work.

When the only African American in attendance stood up, the room began to quiet. She is a beautiful woman with a certain presence about her, so that is not surprising. She asked for my contact information. Then she identified herself as one of those descendants. I received three letters about what happened next. The silence was complete and total. Then a few people clapped, a few others gave a soft cheer, and others just sat there and stared.

Historians are mostly teachers and scholars. Get them all together at a conference, and they can be a pretty jaded lot. It takes something special to render them speechless and immobile. Jeri Mills did it, though. It is she who has been my conduit and connection to all the descendants.

Today she lives with her husband, Adell, in Nacogdoches, Texas, where they both work to make the world a better, more equitable place.

HER ANCESTORS AND FAMILY

I think a lot of Helen is in me. I think a lot of Tabby is in me. And I remember the first time I went to Monte Verdi—and I learned more about Tabby after I read some of your works than I did initially with family history until I started doing my own family history. But I feel that those ancestors left part of themselves in all of us. We're street people. We're ghetto people. That's different terms than for white people. We are doctors, lawyers. We have them in all faiths, and you've met a lot of them. Very intelligent. Women. Men. And I think some of the things that Tabby and Scott—heaven knows who some of our fathers are—I don't think Scott was the father of all of us, I mean all of that generation. And the truth may never be told about that. But I think that each generation from leaving Africa to the present day—in each generation, they've left a little bit of themselves in the rest of us.

And people physically—someone who physically knew Helen, who was my great-grandmother, they've looked at my sister Lynnda and they've said, "You look like Helen." No one's ever told me I look like either one of them because at my age now it's very few of us around that even knew of anybody

Jeri Mills.
Courtesy of Paul Snider.

that knew anybody beyond my great-grandparents. But, yes, I feel Tabby in me. I feel Amy in me. But I feel more of Tabby and Helen than Amy, which was Helen's mother. And I don't think as a black woman I'm alone. I think a lot of other blacks feel that way, too.

PART IV

BEING BLACK IN AMERICA

I recall an incident when I was a child growing up. I think I was about eight years old and my father had picked me up from my grandparents' house and I was in the back seat asleep. And my dad got pulled over by a policeman. And when I woke up, I heard my dad and the policeman at the back of the car engaged in a conversation. And I thought, "Is that my daddy talking?" My daddy was talking so soft, so humble. That was not in his character. That was not in his personality to be humble and submissive to no one. But he was trying to survive. And one of the things that stood out with me, he told this policeman, obviously a white policeman, he said, "Well, I have my daughter in the back seat. I'm trying to get her home." But he said it in a very soft, humbling way. And I'd never heard my father speak that way. But my father was trying to stay alive, keep me alive, and keep down trouble that he had grown up with. And that stayed with me.

I didn't hear about the *Green Book* [*The Negro Motorist Green Book*] until I grew up. But I'll tell you what, my daddy had a sense of—when we drove from Tyler to Houston our stopping point was in Lufkin, Texas. My daddy, like other black men who were on the highway, he knew a place in Lufkin owned by a black man where he could buy soda pop out of a tub with ice in it. And it was a little outhouse in the back where you could use the bathroom. And from Tyler to Lufkin, we'd stop. And then from Lufkin we'd drive on into Houston because we couldn't dare use the bathroom on the highway. And I think my daddy was like so many black men. I didn't personally know about the *Green Book* until probably about twenty years ago. And, again, like the black inventions, I was shocked. It was necessary.

RACISM IN AMERICA

You've got bad people on both sides. You have black men that are capable of violent crimes. You have whites, too. But to hear many whites tell it, we're the worst people in the world 'cause we're black. That's just the way we are. But, unless you've lived that, unless you've had to tell that story, or tell your son—like my mother told me that day. She said, "You can't sit at that counter 'cause you're a little black girl." And my husband had to tell his son like his dad had told him. He said, "Son, you be careful when you're driving a car. If the white policemen stop you, show them your license. Be calm. Do whatever he tell you because many black men have lost their lives because they didn't comply with the police."

When you hear your white neighbor, or your white friend, or your white family member say things that are racially incorrect or fundamentally goes against what you think is wrong—and I think racism on a white side or a black side is wrong—then you should tell your neighbor, or your friend, or your family member, "No, you're wrong. Let's look at this this way" because people take your silence to mean consent. And if you don't say something to them, then they'll feel that you're in total agreement and they will continue to feel that their racist attitude is accepted by everyone. That would be my advice is you stop it by expressing to a person what you feel is the right thing to do. Some will respond in a positive way; some will be negative. Silence means consent sometimes, too. If you don't speak up and you say nothing, then people will think that you're in total agreement with it.

And one of the ministers that I admire in this city, his name is Kyle Childress. I think it was MLK Day, at a rally. And he said to the few white people that were there after the march, "You know what, white folks? We've got to sit down and listen." He said, "We don't listen. We've got to sit down and hear these stories and listen."

IMPORTANCE OF BLACK HISTORY

I discovered probably it was in my thirties or maybe forties before this really hit home with me. And after I realized it, I became angry. And I was putting together a Black History program and I can't remember if it was at the university where I worked or if it was in high school where I worked. But I was putting this program together. And I was pretty clear what the program was going to be about. And then a young student comes up and gave me a typed piece of paper and it had Negro inventions. I couldn't put it down. And all of a sudden it was revealed to me that black men had discovered things like a lawn mower, or whatever they represented cutting grass then. They had discovered something with electricity, something they used on the train for brakes. And I could just go on and on naming things from this list. At first, I was just amazed. I was appalled. Why didn't I know this? And then the students came back later and we were supposed to be rehearsing over what I was going to do. But now it was no longer clear what the program contents would be. Black history should be a learning experience. And I wanted all my students, black and white, to know this. I didn't even know. And I was angry that I didn't know, Jo. It wasn't taught to me in school. We integrated the "black inventions" they were called. And I got more comments on that because there were other blacks in the audience who'd never heard of that, too.

I became aware that we did this out of necessity! We were the ones doing the physical labor and we wanted to find an easier way to do it and we did. They modified the way we physically worked in the house, the way we used ironing boards, all of that. But the thing was, black people didn't get credit for those inventions. We did it out of necessity. We wanted to make an easier way to do the work we had to do. But later on, white people actually got paid for the invention. And I always found something wrong with that. But Jo, that never sat well with me.

And now it upsets me to think that the state of Texas—the state in which I reside, the state in which I was born, grew up in 'til I finished college—is going to be changing the curriculum and teaching a false history, as I call it. Now, I know it took me a long time to answer that question, but somehow, I want my children and grandchildren, and all other children to know what happened with their people and the truth about it. And I want them to know that their parents, grandparents, ancestors, and my ancestors, we were smart, intelligent people and we invented things. And you read something from that book a few minutes ago that talked about how we built so many things in this country. And I want those stories told. Because not only does it help me to feel good about myself, but it also helps the little white boy and girl and other white people to know that our knowledge went way beyond being a slave. And those are the stories I want told.

Chapter Fifteen
The Dance

Henry has delayed a day or two on account of the rainy weather and he rather claims to day (Sunday) to attend to his individual affairs—and in the mean time...[1]

JULIEN DEVEREUX TO JOHN DEVEREUX, 1846

Slaves constantly danced the dance of slavery—a new step here, a quick turn there. It was a neverending, subtle, nuanced dance of the powerless against the powerful to gain, exert, and control some aspects of their lives. The dance was a constant give-and-take on the part of both slave and master. The master's dance part walked a fine line between permissiveness and severity. Owners seemed to believe too much generosity encouraged slaves to be less controllable, while too much severity might cause slaves to rebel in subtle ways that were very damaging to the work routines and attitudes of other slaves and, thus, the overall productivity of the plantation.

The dance role of the slave was designed to constantly push and shove at the system of slavery, trying all the while not to endanger themselves or their families. One wrong step brought disaster for all, but, properly performed, a slave's steps could achieve additional advantage on the side of the badly unbalanced equation that constituted their lives. The enslaved had to be the more astute partner in this constant routine. They had to know when to resist and when not to resist. They had to recognize an opening and know when to take advantage of it, pushing at the boundaries of the system, and when not to do so. They had to learn how to subtly take advantage of privileges and convert them into rights. Henry, the slave who is quoted in the chapter epigraph and who gave *Claiming Sunday* its name, was one of those. At some point, Henry was allowed the privilege of having his own affairs. He saw an opening and slowly converted it into a right he later claimed.

Both sides danced the dance of slavery according to precise but unwritten and unspoken rules. It was likely that both master and slave knew what the other was doing, but only up to a point. The ultimate power unquestionably belonged to the master or mistress. Owners could beat, kill, buy, and/or sell slaves or their families on a whim. However, owners who went to those extremes of cruelty and depravity got little production out of their slaves and limited increase of numbers. Many slave masters, including Julien, cautioned their overseers never to punish a slave in anger, and there was a good reason for that. It gave the enslaver time to calm down, so that if common humanity did not cause an owner or overseer to pull back from doing a slave everlasting harm, then the importance of the almighty dollar would.

However, to believe that slaves were devoid of any control in the dance would be a serious mistake. The enslaved generally knew more about their white owners than the white owners knew about them. This equation is true in most relationships involving those of unequal power. The actions or reactions of those with lesser power are often calculating and even a bit deceptive. They have to be; it is the safest and most effective way the powerless can control some aspects of their lives. For example, women have been accused for centuries of being manipulative. That is because they often had to be if they were to achieve some modicum of self-determination. In terms of the possession of power, women and slaves had a lot in common.

Slaves did not survive nearly 250 years of enslavement by being totally passive instruments of their enslavers' wills. Slaves were masterful at slowing down work routines, breaking or hiding tools, feigning illness, starting fires, or simply playing ignorant. The stereotype of the intellectually disabled, indolent, happy-go-lucky black individual dancing in the yard is etched deeply in the myths of the Old South. The image carried forward into freedom, became an icon of Jim Crow segregation, and even crops up in today's racial stereotypes. To what degree whites actually bought into the ruse is debatable, but enslaved black laborers knew better.

African American groups contain people of superior intelligence in the same proportion as any other population group. Slaves used their intelligence to gain whatever individual and community advantage they could. They had generations of experience in slavery and used it to their advantage in their constant struggle to gain some control over their own existence. Such knowledge was one of the crucial lessons older slaves like Tabby and Scott could pass down to the members of the Devereux Slave Community. Even though slaves had been deprived of any formal education, many had earned advanced degrees from the "university of street smarts"—an institution of higher learning with a formidable and robust curriculum.

Among the many things taught in the quarters were the methods and reasons to go directly to the master with a complaint or request. Those encounters—negotiations, actually—were usually for personal reasons. Complaints, which had to be carefully made, about work conditions or routines always went to the overseer first. Only when treatment or performance of an overseer reached massive proportions of cruelty or mismanagement was it acceptable to go directly to the owner. Although it was after the fact, Jesse probably reinforced Julien's decision to fire the overseer, McKnight, by telling his master all about the recently departed McKnight.

One incident of a slave appealing to the master for assistance concerned Julien's blacksmith, Jack. On May 13, 1850, Julien related to the sheriff that Andrew Jourdan Sr. had accosted his slave Jack "on the road and without any provocation or Justification 'did cruelly, unreasonably treat and abuse said negro man slave' contrary to act Approved February 14th 1848." It is amusing that Julien was quoting the law to the sheriff; however, Julien wanted action out of the sheriff. "You will greatly oblige the citizens of this neighborhood & myself by causing an indictment to be prepared against said Andrew Jourdan, Sr." Then Julien fulfilled his role as paternalistic community leader by adding, "This man Jourdan is a nuisance and a terror to the people of this settlement having recently come from the Cherokee portion of Arkansas and having no fixed place of abode, he visits dram shops and when drunk is truly a desperate character."[2]

Jack visited his master again in September of that same year to appeal to Julien for his assistance. On September 26, 1850, Julien wrote the minister J. B. Renfro "at the request of my man Jack who believes that he has some religious impressions and is very desirous to make his feelings known[?] to you." Julien added Jack thought "he can be relieved and comforted by a conference with you."[3] Julien gave his opinion of the situation and, in so doing, told us more about Jack. Julien wrote, "I have no slave who needs or who has needed a change of reformation more than Jack, and I would be well pleased if he shall become reformed."[4] Jack was not a happy man and probably with good reason. He was sold to Julien by Henry Holcombe in 1840; taken to Montgomery

County, Texas, in 1841; and in 1846, moved to Rusk County with the Devereux slaves. There is no way to know how many family and friends he may have left along the way. All of this must have affected his behavior, leading Jack to telegraph his pain and loss to his master.

All in all, the Devereux slaves had considerable access to their owner. Julien gave men money and instructions before they left for trips and errands. He ordered merchandise for them. He extended cash to them from their accounts on his books. He related information to them that was sent by others concerning their families and friends. And clearly he supervised a considerable amount of the work on the plantation. The encounters with the master that resulted allowed for the more nuanced, subtle forms of communication with which slaves were well versed and highly adept. Bertram Wyatt-Brown in *Southern Honor* recognized the techniques the slaves used: "Tolerant masters watched impotently as each new privilege begged for and granted, at once became plantation tradition and the precedent for further requests."[5] Julien knew the dance well enough to realize that on some occasions, he was simply outplayed.

One of the privileges that became tradition was Julien Devereux's allowance for slaves to possess weapons. Slaves in Texas could own guns with the permission of the slave owner. Generally, it was assumed that slaves were not allowed firearms. Neighboring states Louisiana and Alabama, specifically, did not allow slaves to have guns under any circumstances. Most Southern states did the same. Texas, the most western of the Southern states and the only slave state in 1860 with a hostile Native population in its borders, allowed slaves to carry firearms with the owner's permission. There was ample evidence that the Devereux Slaves owned and used firearms. Jesse certainly had a gun; most likely so did others.

John Devereux recorded in 1846 and 1847 that Julien and his men hunted both bear and wildcat those years. On Sunday, January 25, 1847, "Julien went with the Negro men Wild Catting."[6] They were hunting panthers (the nineteenth-century Texas term for "mountain lion"): another animal, like the bears, no one wanted to face without a gun. If not for the protection of the black men themselves, Julien would have allowed his men to have guns for his own protection. However, Julien was sensitive to the issue of his slaves with guns when they were hunting without him. In 1855, when Julien was in Austin as a representative to the Texas legislature and was not home to hunt hogs with his slaves, he instructed Sarah "whenever it becomes necessary to kill any [hogs] in the woods, I want some one of our neighbors to be certain to be with our people in killing them."[7] Clearly there were limits to circumstances when the slaves could use weapons. Julien allowed his men to hunt with guns when they were with him, but wanted a white neighbor with them if he was gone from home. Slaves with guns as well as passes, transportation, and money were a problematic issue for most white Southerners, and Devereux Slaves had all four of those things. Julien Devereux may have been trying to maintain community norms and not cause concern among his neighbors. In many instances white supervision was probably as much for the slaves' protection as the white community's peace of mind.

However, Julien's men certainly had guns when they traveled for him, but that was a small and privileged group which included Martin or Jesse on every long trip. It was required by law in southern states that slaves have passes to be off their home grounds, but handwritten passes could be destroyed easily by robbers and slave kidnappers. It was common knowledge that slaves with wagons loaded with bales of cotton headed to a shipping or sale point had money for expenses. Thieves knew those same wagons would be on that road again in a few days loaded with goods for the farm or plantation where they were enslaved. Since highway robbers plagued rural areas of the South, it was unthinkable to send slaves on multiday trips unprotected against thieves. Not only were the oxen and wagonloads of cotton or goods subject to capture, so were the slaves themselves. There was a lively black market in slaves throughout the South. On trips for their master, it made sense his workers were armed.

The following episode at a river crossing confirms that Jesse had a gun and illustrates just how artfully a slave could deal with a situation that might otherwise be to his detriment. On July 16, 1845, John Landrum, Julien's father-in-law, wrote to him from Montgomery County. Apparently, Landrum's younger son, Wells, had accompanied Julien, Sarah, and John, along with some of the slaves and supplies, to Rusk County in June 1845, and was returning to Montgomery County with some of Julien's slaves and his wagon. In crossing the Trinity River, the group had a mishap. Several of the slaves were unhitching the wagon from the oxen in order to take them across the river. The wagon was ferried and the animals swam across. Landrum reported that somehow "the oxens wagon and all went into the river to gether." He added, "They saved the wagon and oxens without ingerry but nearly all that was in the wageon was lost. Jesses gun was lost with all the negroes bed clothes."[8] Jesse had a gun, and his master knew it.

It was clear Jesse had influenced Landrum in the writing of this letter. "Jes is verry uneasy for fear you may attach some blame to him but the boys seemes to excuse him and blame Anderson with all of it."[9] In the last line of the letter, it appears Jesse claimed the lead in this set and asserted some control. In a postscript, Landrum wrote, "Jess says he left a pair of pantaloons there and he wants you if you pleas to get Mr. Gaff [Goffe] to bring them down when he comes."[10]

Jesse managed to accomplish several things in this situation: he absolved himself of any fault in the misadventure at the river, and he did so by having one white man tell another. Therefore, he was not responsible for explaining what happened to his master. Then, Jesse asked his master to round up his pants and send them along to him with the overseer Goffe. If this seems inconsequential and the interpretation speculative, then consider: if Jesse needed his pants, he could have requested Julien to ask any of the other slaves with him to find and send the pants, but he asked Julien. We have no way of knowing what was going on in Jesse's mind, however, such instances as this that appear in white records should be looked at carefully and from the perspective of all involved. Not only did Jesse assign his owner the menial chore of hunting down the slaves' clothing, but take note of the item of clothing—a pair of men's pants. Jesse wanted his master to find and send the piece of clothing which covered maleness. This could have been a very subtle message to Julien from Jesse: "I am a man, too, and I know how to manage these things. This time things got out of control. However, this does not diminish my ability in the future."

It is also possible that Jesse just needed his trousers, but to assume the obvious interpretation is to overlook the potential of the message from the person who didn't leave any records. Enslaved individuals often used coded messages to get their points across. The overt, obvious method could get them into serious trouble. The interpretation of this quote is open to question and challenge, but to ignore the possibilities is to miss the message Jesse may have been sending. It behooves the historical profession to recall as they do their work lessons learned as children—look both ways at all the players before crossing the historical street. Here, the lead in the dance may have shifted to Jesse, and we need to be open to that possibility.

Jesse was one of the valued slaves on the plantation and one of the most astute at the dance of slavery. Julien's time in the Texas legislature highlighted the relationship between the two men. In late October 1855, Jesse drove the carriage that carried Julien to perform his civil duty as a representative to the Texas legislature in Austin. Julien wrote Sarah, who was back home at Monte Verdi with the other slaves and children, that on October 31, 1855, the "carriage broke down within a few miles of this place."[11] Julien went on ahead, and Jesse was left to deal with the broken vehicle. "Jesse succeeded in getting the carriage in Town,"[12] where it went straight to the blacksmith's repair shop.

Julien boarded at Mr. Haralson's boarding house, paying $50 a month for himself and $7 a month for Jesse.[13] Then, Julien hired Jesse out to Haralson to defray costs of Jesse's board. On November 9, 1855, just ten days after their arrival in Austin, Julien wrote Sarah that he had "obtained leave from Col Harralson [his landlord] for Jesse to sleep in our room [he had a roommate] and I have bought him two good heavy blankets, which with the lodging furnished him by the house is amply sufficient."[14]

It is interesting that one of the few references to slave religion in the Devereux family collection occurred during the Austin sojourn. Certainly, their religious beliefs were as central to the lives of the members of the Slave Community as they were to most of the enslaved in the American South. The fact that religion is not central in the Devereux papers doesn't mean it wasn't there. Many things that happened in the quarters did not make their way into white records. Julien was not a churchgoer, so he might not have thought it important to mention the slaves' religious activities. Alwyn Barr shed some light on the subject in his book *The African Texans*: "Slaves in some churches sat in separate pews from whites, more often different services were held on Sundays. Many heard sermons by white ministers."[15] Barr's statement fit the case with Jesse while he was in Austin with Julien Devereux, but may not have appealed to slaves on the plantation.

In the running dialogue Sarah and Julien maintained about their lives apart, they sent messages about the Slave Community. In one letter to Sarah, Julien wrote that Jesse "inquires every night if I have got any letters from Mistress."[16] He brought Sarah up to date on Jesse's spiritual health on November 30, 1855, when he wrote to Sarah, "you can tell Amy that Jesse continues very well and goes to the Baptist Church every Sunday."[17] One Sunday, Julien wrote that Jesse went to a special service to "hear Judge Baylor preach to the Negroes."[18] No such services were ever mentioned being held on the plantation.

Neither Julien Devereux nor Jesse were entirely healthy during their Austin stay. Jesse began suffering from recurring dental problems almost as soon as they arrived. On November 1, 1855, Julien wrote, "Jesse complains some this morning of his jaw being swelled again."[19] The problem did not improve. On November 9, 1855, Julien wrote, "Jesse has suffered a good deal with his jaw . . . and another small piece of bone came out the inside of his mouth."[20] By November 13, 1855, Julien wrote, "Jesse has been troubled a good deal with his Jaw and he has had to have one of his teeth pulled out and he thinks he will now get entirely well."[21] However, Julien was quick to add that Jesse's infirmities did not stop him from carrying out his duties, saying, "He has not lost any time in attending on my room."[22] The tooth extraction must have helped Jesse's health. On November 22, 1855, Julien wrote Sarah, "Jesse continues very well and makes so good a waiter that I don't know but you will have to take him from the ox wagon into the house."[23]

While there were no messages transmitted to Jesse from his wife, Amy, there were two from men in the Slave Community, and both involved work matters. And so the dance continued. It appears the men used Jesse to communicate messages to their owner. They wanted Julien to know they were keeping up with things back home. Lewis was the first to ask Sarah to add something to Jesse on his behalf in her letter to Julien. The letter was badly damaged with tears and holes, but the content was still clear. Sarah wrote, "Lewis has come in since I [missing] my letter and tell me to write to [missing] a manageing his Teem since he has been [gone] as well as they did when he left."[24] (Jesse owned his own team of oxen.) Then on January 1, 1856, Jim used the same technique Lewis had employed. Sarah wrote, "Jim tell me to say to Jesse that they are all well and heap of work ahead of them but thinks they are geting on finely and in a fair way to get through with it in good time."[25] With whom, exactly, were Lewis and Jim communicating? It seems unlikely they had a need to communicate work affairs to Jesse, but they wanted the master to know they were doing their duties; it seems both men were talking through Jesse to Julien. This technique turned up in the Devereux records several places. Lewis wanted Julien to know they were taking good care of animals and things, but Jim was communicating more to Julien. There is a good lesson in the rules of the dance built into Jim's message. He could not straightforwardly tell Julien he thought there was too much work to be done in the time allotted for completion, so he subtly tucked that information into a message for Jesse. It is important to note that Jim then ended on a note of optimism and commitment to the master's work, saying they were working diligently and making steady progress.

The stay in the capital of Texas revealed other interesting things about the relationship between the two men—one black, one white; one enslaved, one the enslaver; one servile, the other dominant. By December 10, 1855, both men complained of bad colds. However, Jesse's cold did not stop him "from his business any yet."[26] Part of Jesse's business was to care for Julien Devereux, but also to keep Julien company. Julien wrote Sarah that even when his roommate was there, which was not often, "he is not near as much company to me as Jesse is."[27]

The legislative session did not end until February 4, 1856; however, Julien had asked to be released on January 20, 1856.[28] Both men were unhealthy and eager to return home.[29] Devereux's health was much worse than Jesse's. Julien made it back to Rusk County only a short time before he died on May 1, 1856, after years of suffering from an enlarged spleen, severe chills, and severe digestive problems. The time between January 1 and the date they were liberated from Austin must have seemed an eternity. In his letter dated January 1, 1856, Julien told Sarah that Jesse was "almost crazy to start home."[30] Sarah responded on behalf of all the people back at Monte Verdi, "if we could know the day that you would reach home the whole plantation would be a half a day journey to meet you for there never was a set of people that want to see any body as much as we all want to see you and Jesse."[31]

The interactions between Julien and Jesse while in Austin highlighted one of the most intriguing aspects of the dance of slave and master. It was episodes such as these that detailed just how intimately the lives of the two races were intertwined. This sort of physical closeness combined with the differences between black and white was the occasion for comment by coauthors John Hope Franklin and Loren Schweninger in *In Search of the Promised Land: A Slave Family in the Old South*. They wrote that "the two races were inextricably bound, with slavery both bringing them together and driving them apart."[32]

Jesse and Julien lived together in the same room for three months. They were company for each other, shared news of home, pined for their families, and had intimate knowledge of each other's ailments and maladies. They were roommates and, in a sense, friends. Black and white people across the South lived together as did these two men and shared each other's lives amidst the violence, pain, heartache, and misery experienced by the enslaved. They each danced their own versions of the dance of slavery.

In the January 1, 1856, letter, Julien wrote that he would "stop Jesse as a hireling in a few day" even if "he had to pay his [Jesse's] board. He has had a tolerable hard lot of it lately."[33] The image of the two mature men, both ill and desperately homesick, bordered on poignant. Julien added, "Jesse has been quite unwell for several days and last night I gave him some of my cough medicine about mid night."[34] The dance partners had changed places; the enslaver was now attending the enslaved.

Martin, another slave with major responsibilities for the plantation's successful administration, held a post requiring finesse and discretion, so he knew the dance well. He was Gincy's son, and he may not have even belonged to Julien. Martin's marriage to Louisa was broken apart in the lawsuit separation initiated by Julien's sister, Louisiana Holcombe. Julien Devereux's records are full of information that reveals a profile of Martin. He was capable, honest, and trustworthy with his duties. Martin made many eighty-eight-mile trips from Monte Verdi to Shreveport, where the plantation bought all manner of things and consigned their cotton to be sent to markets in New Orleans. Julien wrote on April 10, 1852, that he "started Martin with the ox waggon to Shreveport for groceries."[35] On December 4, 1855, Sarah Devereux wrote to Julien in Austin, "Martin starts this morning to Shreveport after Rope and Baling"[36] for the cotton ginning and packing. Then on December 15, 1855, Sarah wrote, "Mart got home this evening from Shreveport makeing the trip in ten days and a half days."[37] Sarah wrote that they heard from Martin "the day he got to Town. River is up and large Boats having plenty of salt etc."[38] On his own initiative, Martin bought salt for the upcoming hog killing and preserving. Sarah continued, "We have not killed any hogs yet but will this week."[39] These are just two of the many trips Martin made in the plantation's behalf.

Certainly, Martin had some ability to read and do basic arithmetic. He handled receipts and needed to be able to read some of the words and the numbers to ensure his master was being fairly treated in the marketplace. Buying things for which the price was uncertain until the actual purchase meant Martin had to determine if he had enough money for what he was purchasing, make change, and obtain a valid bill of sale. It defies credibility to think that he did not understand some of what he was doing for his master.

Artist Robert Jones's painting titled *Claiming Sunday* was the cover of the first edition of this book. Jones depicted slave life from within the quarters in this wonderful piece painted from the perspective of the inside of a slave cabin. Artist Robert Jones.

While Julien was in Austin in fall 1855 and early 1856, Martin was handling the ginning on the plantation.[40] The gin mechanically removed the seeds from the bolls of cotton and then packed it into rectangular bales of approximately five hundred pounds. It was then wrapped in burlap and tied tightly with twine. The Devereux gin was powered by animals, and possibly water, but not steam. It was a big operation and carried a lot of responsibility for the individual in charge. Julien ginned cotton for those in the area, so his men processed more cotton than just the plantation's normal sixty-five to eighty bales. It was dangerous work, so the gin master had to be vigilant and careful. On November 11, 1855, Sarah wrote Julien, "I went to the gin House and plantation Saturday. As well as I can tell every thing is geting on very well."[41] Martin asked her to give his owner a message and, in doing so, left us with one of the more memorable quotes from the Devereux Family Papers: "Martin says they are trying to do their best."[42] This message, like the episode at the river with Jesse, is part of the coded material that is buried in white records. Those citations say so much more than the obvious. Clearly, Martin is looking out for his own interests, but assuming Sarah's memory is accurate, Martin is speaking for the community laboring to pick the cotton crop and get it ginned. It is subtle, but the message reminds Julien that Martin and the others were competent and working at the highest level of their ability. There is none of the indolent, careless, African American slave in the mythology of the old south in Martin's words. He sounds more like a manager of a company. And with that, our two dancers, Martin and Julien, twirl out of sight.

Henry was another slave who was accomplished in the dance of the subservient and the dominant. He was Tabby and Scott's firstborn, arriving into the world in 1808. John Devereux knew Tabby and Scott as young people and Henry as a child. In addition to running errands for the Devereux men, Henry was often John's body servant and companion in Rusk County. Both John Devereux and Henry knew their roles in the dance they had performed endless times.

Very early in 1846, John Devereux missed a step and left a fascinating record in his memorandum book. Henry was younger than John but afflicted with tuberculosis and often ill. Henry managed to outlive John Devereux by seven years, but both men were facing their mortality in 1846, and they knew it. John Devereux started the year off on January 1 commenting on Henry's condition, "I don't expect he will ever see another well day."[43] The next day

John recorded that all the slaves were "in good spirits & happy singing and carroling at their work except poor Henry who continues to suffer."[44] Then the master's mask dropped for a second, and he added Henry "will before long be emancipated from slavery to freedom."[45] It was unthinkable for John Devereux, master of slaves, to hint at freedom being a desirable condition for a slave, even if it meant death. Part of the dance of slavery was for the enslaver to maintain the constant, perpetual image that slavery was a positive good for slaves, that they were well provided for in return for their fealty and labor. No other such statement, or anything close to it, appeared anywhere else in the Devereux collection. John Devereux, probably, never expected that statement to see the light of day.

Sometimes the entire elaborate performance crashed. On some farms and plantations, those crashes came often and were ruinous. The missteps on the Devereux plantations, however, were few. A. C. Heard whipped three slaves in 1846 for impudence. It was not until 1850 that mention of another enslaved being punished or problematic in the view of the owner appeared in the records. In March, Julien paid William Reagan for a "clog made to put on negro man Ben." A clog was a weight attached to a slave's leg to keep him from running away. The iron weighed fifteen pounds, and Julien paid Reagan 25¢ a pound for a total of $3.75.[46] It appears that Julien Devereux sold Ben shortly thereafter, for Ben vanishes from all the records after that incident. Two years after Julien felt compelled to order a clog for Ben, he experienced his first runaway. On January 5, 1852, Julien recorded a transaction concerning July: "$10 Gold piece paid to Mr. Birdwell for bringing negro man . . . home when Runaway (the first occurrence of the kind that ever happened to me)."[47] Actually, Julien was incorrect—July was not his first runaway. On June 5, 1848, Julien recorded the following: "Old Jack runaway on the 5th June—returned home early in the morning of the 7th June."[48] There are no records of what punishment was administered to the two runaways.

Because Julien's management of his slave population appears to be largely benign, some of the Devereux descendants were under the impression that the white Devereux family gave land to some of their former slaves. That is highly unlikely. After slavery ended, there was little incentive on the part of former owners to engage in such generosity. The dance no longer required any acts of largesse. Additionally, white owners in the South had lost a fortune in slave property at the end of the war, and they would have been in no mood to give land to those whom they had previously owned and who represented capital and property lost. Besides, many white Southerners had no land to give. In 1869, Sarah Devereux married James Garrison. What the war hadn't taken, Garrison did. She was nearly destitute by the early 1870s and still responsible for her younger children. Garrison drank and gambled away what she had left. What property, stock, and businesses the formerly enslaved people acquired, they acquired on their own.

Despite Jim Crow and increasingly strict segregation laws, many African Americans and their families did very well as freedmen and women. How did the former slaves do so well? Assuming that many ex-slaves lived under similar circumstances as the Devereux Slaves, it seems reasonable that they learned skills as slaves that served them well as free people. Given the performance of Martin, Jesse, and others, it is no surprise many prospered.

For a case in point, consider the Greenwood District in Tulsa, Oklahoma. Until it was destroyed by racists in the 1921 Tulsa race massacre, the African American section of the city of Tulsa was a model thriving black community. Greenwood was home to most of the city's ten thousand blacks, many of whose ancestors had migrated from Texas. Known as the "Black Wall Street," it boasted two newspapers, a number of churches, a library, and dozens of prosperous locally owned black businesses and banks. During a twenty-four-hour period, the thirty-five square blocks of Greenwood were reduced to charred embers. The true death toll of the riot has never been determined. Estimates range from three hundred to three thousand. Combining the injured and missing with the confirmed dead has muddled the actual number of lives lost.

To question or doubt the ability of freed persons to prosper is a continuation of the racism of slavery. Such a position is based on a preconceived notion of black people under slavery that this study calls into question. Many of the Devereux slaves danced the dance of slavery brilliantly. They learned and applied that learning while in slavery and after slavery to improve their lives. They took pride in their families, their work, and their homes, and the failure to recognize that fact is to once again challenge their abilities. The question should not be, How did they manage to prosper? but rather, What could they have achieved had they not been subjected to the oppressive system of slavery and then the racism and segregation that followed?

Conclusion

You are going to be so lonely next week when you are done with this.

PAUL SNIDER, 2022

This edition of *Claiming Sunday: The Story of a Texas Slave Community* is a new book in more ways than I had envisioned when I began work on it. The two themes of the book stated in the introduction—to tell the story of the Devereux Slave Community and to relate that story to modern racial issues—wove themselves together as gracefully as I hoped they would. It is just about time to call this one done and let it go.

Before that, however, there are questions that need answers. What was accomplished? What was learned? Did the book contribute to the understanding of slavery? Does the work contribute anything new to the scholarship on Texas or American slavery? Is the work valuable and/or useful? What work remains to be done now? And, lastly, and most importantly, does this book, or any book for that matter, resolve the dilemma William Faulkner identified? Will our past as a nation of slaveholders ever truly be past us?

Dealing with American slavery records was, once again, sad and upsetting. I watched helplessly as huge impersonal systems of government, economics, and politics pushed dark-skinned people of African American descent around like toy figures in a game, with not the least concern for their families, connections, and futures. Nearly two centuries of distance and time have not eased that misery and pain. On the more uplifting side, encountering whatever it is in human beings that equips them to continue and endure in the face of unbelievably tragic sorrow and loss was encouraging. I remain in awe of the people I studied. My advice to writers of history is to find a way to center yourself in the lives of those you write about. This opens up the human story in remarkable ways. In my mind, good history is not fetched up from the cold marble slab of academia; it is the living story of human society and human interaction that makes good history.

The author with Jeri and Adell Mills at the 2018 Caddell Family Reunion in Oklahoma City, Oklahoma. *Courtesy of Paul Snider.*

It is that principle of concentrating on human beings that drove the new placement and format of the interviews. The nineteenth-century Devereux slaves were tied to the second decade of the twenty-first-century descendants so that they worked side by side to enhance and enrich the book. The two themes worked together so well from start to finish, it seems the descendants knew what part they were to play from the beginning. I was a bit embarrassed I hadn't thought of it sooner. All the credit for that success goes to the descendants. I may have done the presentation, but they gave me the content.

The methodology in *Claiming Sunday* is clearly different from that of many books on slavery. Traditionally, historians have used a number of primary sources where this book has used only the one set of records of the Devereux family of enslavers. I've studied those records closely and over many years. There is much to be gained by staring at the same thing for a long period of time. It takes concentration and time to decipher the records. Then, and only then, did the enslaved begin to step out of the shadows in which their lives were lived.

Readers were under the impression that what I had found about slave lives is unusual or rare. It is not. The American South is a rich, fertile land of records, like the ones that supplied the raw materials for *Claiming Sunday*, that tell us about slave lives. Those papers are buried in archives, personal collections, and libraries just waiting to be examined with new purpose and methodology.

However, it is imperative that scholars who research and write about non-elite groups be more willing to take some chances in their work. Sometimes we have to use circumstantial evidence because it is all we have. Be honest about it, but use it, interpret it, present it. Being wrong can be of as much value as being right. Younger scholars appear to have caught on to some of these new truths: They are on the cutting edge of new methodology and techniques, and they are bold and bright. I applaud them. Those of us who were trained what now seem to be eons ago need to listen to and learn from them.

All historians have to find the common ground that allows them to understand and connect with those whose lives are playing out in the records they are reading. That place lies in our shared humanity, and it must be the force that drives works such as this. One does not have to have been a slave or the descendant of slaves to feel the pain of Tabby as a Texas court gave half her children and grandchildren to Louisiana Holcombe. Tabby was a smart woman; she knew they would end up in Alabama at some point, and she would likely never see them again. I am a woman and a mother, and I can sense some of her pain in that moment when they left Monte Verdi in the wagon Louisiana's son-in-law sent to carry them away. It hurt just reading about it, but it also allowed me to identify and write about it. We all have to find that place that allows us as historians to understand the human side of what we do.

There is some information that is new in the second edition of *Claiming Sunday*. I added more information about medical care for the Devereux Slave Community, along with the fact that medicines given in the nineteenth century probably did more harm than good. The further I delved into the issues of illness and health on the plantation the more I realized how much has yet to be done on medical history in this country. If other sets of documents are even half as rich as the Devereux records, then there is ample material. Health, epidemics, bacteria, viruses, and medicine should not be solely the providence of scientists and medical personnel. There is good, useful, necessary history buried away on the subject across the country.

I repeat from the previous volume that the extent to which the Devereux slaves were involved in the market economy has been underappreciated, especially the information on Julien Devereux's system of allowing some of his slaves to grow and sell a crop for money of their own. Even more information on this topic surfaced with the second edition. How Jesse developed in his business acumen is striking. By the time Julien Devereux died in 1856, Jesse was growing two bales of cotton a year and a large amount of corn, owned a set of oxen, and was seizing opportunities to resell crops. A closer look at slave activity in the market economy is seriously needed. Attempting to learn more about this topic for the second edition did yield some new material, but not much. This is a fascinating topic and has great potential for more work, but the work suffers from what I have already mentioned—way too often the research materials are limited to what the ruling class of white capitalists have had to say. Historians have to be able to look beyond that, or the story will never change.

Recognizing the fact that a slave had money and might have been able to keep some of it until emancipation is another area of research that needs work. Texas was not taken over by the Union armies, so the Devereux slaves could have managed to maintain some of their earnings through the war years and until emancipation. New material on this subject will do much to illuminate and develop work on freed men and women, freedom colonies, and other subjects of the post emancipation era. Since John and Julien Devereux were exemplary for their group and time, there is a good possibility that many more slaves in the Old South may have experienced similar circumstances. That is ample reason to examine old records anew and new records for the first time.

Slaves in Texas with money ties into the theme of slaves in the market economy, but it hits on another theme that surfaced in the historiography I looked over. Texas is still treated as a backwater in writing on slavery; rather uninteresting and nonessential. Texas is ripe for some truly groundbreaking work on the issue. Slaves in Texas had more opportunities to escape than most anywhere in the South. Mexico was a free country right on the edge of slave Texas and not subject to the laws of states that bordered slave states. After the passage of the Fugitive Slave Act as part of the Compromise of 1850, true freedom for a runaway slave was all the way to Canada. Mexico was a nearby haven for escaped Texas slaves, but communities of escaped slaves in Mexico have had little historical attention.

The close proximity of the Native Americans also affected how slavery adapted and changed. It was partly the presence of Native tribes that accounted for slaves in Texas having weapons, but many general studies on slavery claim slaves never had access to weapons anywhere in the South. Some western heroes in Texas and Oklahoma were African Americans who were noted Indian fighters and whose abilities and exploits gave rise to the U.S. Army's creation of the Buffalo Soldiers. As another example of just how undertaught slavery in Texas is, consider this: I often have people tell me, "Oh, there was no slavery in Texas" or ask "was there slavery in Texas?" The absolute total lack of historical context some Texans operate with was demonstrated by the student who asked me, "Were you born before or after the Civil War?" The failure to teach the history of Texas as a Southern slave state needs to be remedied.

Certainly, the first edition of *Claiming Sunday* contributed to the knowledge of the Slave Community that lived under the ownership of the Devereux family. But there are good reasons to believe that much of what the Devereux slaves experienced was similar to the experience of many other slaves in the region. However, there is such a paucity of Texas materials that it is difficult to evaluate other works. The work of Randolph Campbell in *An Empire for Slavery* set a high bar for further work to be done, but what has been done since Campbell is included in the general histories of the state by Harrigan, Brands, and others. A call for more work on Texas slavery is not an unreasonable demand. New works on slavery in other former slave states appear regularly.

I hope I have communicated what a remarkable group of people the Devereux Slave Community was. Being immersed in their lives, day after day, was not a casual experience. Poring over a microfilm reader, alone in my study for hours, was mind-altering. I became so wrapped up in what was on my screen that it took serious effort to reorient myself back into my life and time. I had to mentally climb back through the layers of the past into the here and now. I thought it was just my imagination that I was identifying with these people from so long ago, but descendants share similar experiences with me. Recently I received the following from a descendant: "Sometimes when things get challenging I wonder what Tabby would do." It is difficult not to be impressed with such strength and character. The question for me was always, How did they survive it?

My answer to that question is basically the same as it was in the first edition but elevated a notch or two. Going back into the reels of microfilm, hunting specific quotes, gave me a crash course on the enslaved, and I believe even more firmly now that the enslaved lived the best way they knew how. They knew they deserved better than they got. They did not buy the platitudes, excuses, and white rationales about slavery that paternalism taught. They believed in themselves as no one else did, and they never accepted slavery as something that by nature was their lot. They, better than most people, knew enough about life, death, and unfairness. They lived with a system that treated them as unequal—as inferior, even subhuman. They could not escape that system, but they used their ability, knowledge, intelligence, and loyalty to survive and endure the system of dehumanization that held them captive.

This does not mean they accepted slavery. Far from it. They battled it daily in the only ways they could—by constantly pushing at the boundaries of slavery, by grabbing and holding onto privileges and rights when they saw an opening, and by understanding more about the power structure than the power structure understood about them. They managed to manipulate situations toward their best interests when they could and, by using the intuition and savvy developed over a lifetime of enslavement, managed to improve their environment and conditions. They passed their knowledge along to each generation.

The most important goal of *Claiming Sunday* is to present a picture of a slave community in sufficient detail that the individuals become real human beings to the reader, and to do so in a fashion that is readable and interesting. I cannot and should not assess the success of that goal. That is for the reader to determine.

The book's second goal is to tie the past of slavery to the problem of current racial issues and relations in America. In my mind, I have made that connection with the able assistance of the Devereux descendants. On the issue of racial harmony and disharmony, all the descendants spoke with one voice. That collective voice came out strong for open, frank, and knowledgeable conversations about slavery, about prejudice, about racial harmony, and about the future of this country.

The first edition of *Claiming Sunday* encouraged many descendants to learn their history and work on their family trees. By now, descendants number in the thousands, and many have connected with relatives from coast to coast. More will in time, and when that happens, the Devereux descendants will continue to grow their numbers, study their history, and rejoice in it. I hope the second edition adds to those involved in their family history.

This book, and the material in it, speaks for itself and welcomes discussion and reflection. It was written to inform and educate. If you are reading this, then you have been with me through this book, and you know the sadness and

CONCLUSION

The Texas State Historical Commission Marker dedicated to the slaves on the Monte Verdi Plantation in 1856. *Courtesy of Jo Snider.*

injustice of American slavery. But you have also seen the strength, intelligence and perseverance of the Devereux Slave Community and their descendants. That is cause for hope for the future of racial harmony and greater awareness of the subject of slavery. I elect to end on that more hopeful note.

As a writer it is difficult to end a book. There is always another document or source you would like to check or paragraph that you still aren't exactly happy with. In closing, allow me to end *Claiming Sunday: The Story of a Texas Slave Community* on a personal note by sharing what hung in Garrison Hall at the University of Texas on one history professor's office door for years back in the 1990s. In the first frame an older man is at his desk, and he is surrounded by tall stacks of books and papers. He is busily writing away. Second frame is his wife leaning up against the doorway of his office, and it is clear she is speaking to him. In the final frame, the man is looking up toward her, pen in hand, glasses pushed up on his forehead. He has a puzzled look on his face. The caption reads, "Finish it? Why would I want to finish it?"

Courtesy of Paul Snider.

appendix I
Slave Register

I compiled and organized all the information contained in the Slave Register from various places in the Julien Sidney Devereux Family Papers over a series of years. The original documents reside in the Briscoe Center for American History at the University of Texas in Austin, Texas. The microfilm from which this register was taken are Reels 36 through 42 of the *Records of the Ante-Bellum Southern Plantations from the Revolution through the Civil War*, ed. Kenneth Stampp, Series G, Part I.

SLAVE REGISTER LEGEND
LDH   Louisiana Devereux Holcombe
JSD   Julien Sidney Devereux
JWD   John William Devereux
SLD   Sarah Landrum Devereux
DSC   Devereux Slave Community

(O)   older
(M)   middle
(Y)   younger

AARON
    born October 1845 at Lake Creek
    mother was Katy

ADALINE (OLDER)
    born circa 1820
    mother was Betty
    purchased in Alabama July 15, 1833, w/mother & three siblings

ADALINE (YOUNGER)
    born May 1860 at Monte Verdi Plantation, Rusk County, Texas
    mother was Jane

ALBERT
    married to Elisa
    probably stayed in Montgomery County, no record in Rusk County

Aleck
  born February 1859
  mother was Martha

Alleck
  born March 1831
  brought to Texas 1841 with Bond
  mother was Kizzy
  originally named Albert
  was a twin to Allen

Allen (older)
  born March 1831
  mother was Kizzy
  originally named Alfred
  was a twin to Alleck
  brought to Texas 1841 with Bond
  bequeathed to Antoinette in probate

Allen (younger)
  born December 20, 1852
  mother was Judy

Amanda
  born 1862
  mother was Sarah

Amy (older)
  sometimes spelled Amey
  daughter of Scott & Tabby
  born June 6, 1819, in Conecuh County, Alabama
  left Alabama September 30, 1841, with Alfred Devereux
  mother of Charles, Mahala, Sam & Haney
  husband was Jesse (O)

Amy (younger)
  born February 9, 1852
  mother was Henry Maria

Amos
  born 1836 at Val Verdi, Macon County, Alabama
  son of Henry and Henry Maria
  left Alabama September 30, 1841, with Alfred Devereux

ANDERSON (OLDER)
born December 12, 1814
son of Tabby and Scott
left Alabama September 30, 1841, with Alfred Devereux
was involved in the disagreement between LDH and JSD over JWD's will

ANDERSON (YOUNGER)
born on October 17, 1848, in Rusk County, Texas
mother was Matilda

ANNA
born January 22, 1851, "p.m."
mother was Matilda

ANTHONY (OLDER)
born May 15, 1835
mother was Kizzy

ANTHONY (YOUNGER)
born 1839 in Macon County, Alabama
mother was Mary
after emancipation he went to Jacksonville, Texas, and worked for William Devereux who opened a pharmacy there

ARTHUR
born the latter part of 1842 at Lake Creek
mother was Katy

BEN (OLDER)
March 1850 JSD bought a clog to put on "negro man Ben"
may have been sold—does not appear in later records

BEN (YOUNGER)
was born April 1860
mother was Peninah
sister was Margaret
may have been named for Ben (the older)

BERRY
born August 13, 1833
son of Lucius and Sally
did not come to Texas

BETTY (OLDEST)
purchased by JSD in Alabama July 15, 1833, for $1,000
purchased with her four children—Henry (Y), Adaline (O), Kitt, and Mary (M)

Betty (Betsy) (middle)
born October 1845
was Cynthia's child who died about 1850

Betty (youngest)
born March 3, 1853
mother was Little Tabby

Bill (William)
was born Summer 1828
was bought with mother Kizzy and 3 siblings in 1833
brought to Texas 1841 with Bond
died April 1857 of typhoid fever

Caroline
born September 12, 1855, "a.m."
mother was Joanna

Celia
born December 3, 1863
mother was Mahala

Charity
was 10 years old
not mentioned after last sale date

Charles
son of Jesse and Amy
born on September 7, 1836, in Macon County, Alabama
left Alabama September 3, 1841, with Alfred Devereux

Charlotte
born August 3, 1851
mother was Peninah
married to Harrison

Collin (Colin)
born prior to 1841
mother was Flora
left Alabama September 30, 1841, with Alfred Devereux

Cynthia (older)
born on December 13, 1823
daughter of Scott & Tabby
left Alabama on September 30, 1841, with Alfred Devereux
went to LDH in 1849
mother of Betty (M)
married George (Gincy's son) in Alabama after the lawsuit

CYNTHIA (YOUNGER)
  born February 20, 1849, in Rusk County, Texas
  mother was Rhoda

CYRUS (OLDER)
  born prior to 1841
  mother was Polly
  left Alabama September 30, 1841, with Alfred Devereux
  selected by LDH in 1848 document

CYRUS (YOUNGER)
  born January 17, 1854
  mother was Peninah
  bequeathed to Sarah in probate of JSD's will

DANIEL (DAN) (OLDER)
  born September 10, 1825, in Covington County, Alabama
  son of Scott and Tabby
  brought to Texas September 30, 1841, with Alfred Devereux
  died November 19, 1855, at Monte Verdi

DANIEL (YOUNGER)
  born February 7, 1857
  mother was Rhody (Rhoda)

DENNIS
  born April 25, 1846
  son of Henry and Henry Maria

DIANA
  born October 8, 1827, in Covington County, Alabama
  mother was Mary
  came to Texas with Alfred Devereux September 30, 1841
  twin sons Jesse and Harrison born July 1845
  Harrison died September 10, 1845
  daughter Louisa born September 20, 1849, in Rusk County, Texas
  son Hal born January 22, 1851
  daughter Emelina born February 14, 1853
  daughter Milly born April 11, 1855
  Diana died August 1855

DICE
  daughter Mary born September 6, 1857
  son Hall born June 1862
  another child born December 1863

Elisa
married Albert sometime around mid-August 1845 in Lake Creek, Montgomery County, Texas
no record in Rusk County, Texas

Elisha
born December 14, 1849
mother was Mary
died February 27, 1850

Eliza (older)
born 1825 in Covington County, Alabama
daughter of Henry and Henry Maria
left Alabama September 30, 1841, with Alfred Devereux
married Sam Loftus (from neighboring plantation) Sunday, January 25, 1846
son John born November 3, 1853
boy child (no name listed) born March 19, 1856, "a.m."
died in October 185?

Eliza (Elizabeth) (younger)
born July 5, 1858
mother was Jane

Elmina (older)
born summer 1823 in Alabama
daughter of Mindah and Jerry
did not come to Texas

Elmina (younger)
born October 1845 at Lake Creek
mother was Katy

Emeline (Emilesa)
born February 14, 1853
mother was Diana
bequeathed to Antoinette in probate
various spellings of this woman's name

Flora
born January 6, 1822
daughter of Scott and Tabby
left Alabama on September 30, 1841, with Alfred Devereux
mother of Collin
married Richmond, son of Gincy (O), after lawsuit separation

Frances
born March 8, 1853
mother was Matilda

Frank (older)
   was 35 years old in 1854, so was born in 1819
   bought from Charles Vinzent in 1854

Frank (younger)
   born December 24, 186?
   mother was Sarah

Franklin
   born August 2, 1850, "p.m."
   mother was Little Tabby
   died July 12, 1853

George (older)
   born Spring 1852
   mother was Judy
   bequeathed to Antoinette in probate

George (younger)
   born November 24, 1856
   mother was Katy

Gincy
   born circa 1795
   belonged to LDH
   son Lucius (O) born 1811
   son Martin born 1813
   daughter Maria (Lev Maria) born 1815
   daughter Martha (O) born 1817

Green
   born December 1840 in Macon, Alabama
   mother was Lev Maria
   brought to Texas with Bond in 1841
   bequeathed to Sarah in probate

Hal
   born January 22, 1851, "p.m."
   mother was Diana
   died August 1853

Ham (older)
   born September 14, 1837
   mother was Mary (Scott and Tabby's daughter)
   left Alabama on September 30, 1841, with Alfred Devereux
   died August 1855

HAM (YOUNGER)
mother was Phebee

HANEY
born February 1859
mother was Amy (O)

HARRISON
born September 10, 1846
mother was Diana
married to Charlotte
listed on the 1848 list of the 27 slaves of JWD's estate
selected by LDH in 1848 document

HENRY (OLDEST)
born 1808 in Wilkes County, Georgia
first-born child of Tabby and Scott
married to Henry Maria
father of Dennis, Nelson, Walton, Amos, Peninah, and Eliza
left Alabama September 30, 1841, with Alfred Devereux
died February 10, 1854

HENRY (MIDDLE)
born circa 1820
mother was Betty
was purchased July 15, 1833, by JSD

HENRY (YOUNGEST)
born July 22, 1855, "a.m."
mother was Matilda

HUGH
bequeathed to Sarah in probate

ISAAC
born 1846
mother was Judy
in estate of JSD in 1856
bequeathed to Antoinette in probate

JACK
born 1836 in Macon, Alabama
mother was Lev Maria
brought to Texas with Bond in 1841

Jack (Shaw)
purchased in Alabama about 1840-41 for $1,280
bought from Henry B. Holcombe
was a blacksmith, "a machinist by trade"
brought to Texas October 1841 with Bond
was a runaway on June 5, 1848, returned home on his own
died June 9, 1855, with "Cholera Morbus or Cholera"

Jane
born July 10 or 11, 1840, in Alabama
mother was Katy
left Alabama on September 30, 1841, with Alfred Devereux
a daughter Elizabeth (Eliza) born July 5, 1858
a second unnamed child born December 1 or 12, 1863

Jerry
was married to Mindah
was the father of July, Jim, Stephen, Joe, and Rhody
stayed in Alabama, five children came to Texas

Jesse (older)
was husband to Amy (O)
left Alabama September 30, 1841, with Alfred Devereux

Jesse (younger)
born September 1845 in Rusk County, Texas
mother was Diana
transferred to LDH in 1848

Jim
born Spring 1827
son of Jerry and Mindah
brought to Texas Fall 1841 with Bond
bequeathed to Antoinette in probate

Jincy
born October 1847 in Rusk County, Texas
mother was Lev Maria
bequeathed to Sarah in probate
Jency (as "Jincey") in probate given to Sarah

Jinny
born the latter part of 1842 at Lake Creek, Texas
mother was Lev Maria
son Randle born January 23, 1860
had child (name not readable) June 1862

Jinney
born November 18, 1857
mother was Matilda

Joanna (older)
born September 12, 1837, at Val Verdi, Macon County, Alabama
mother was Martha (O)
probably the Joanna, who was brought to Texas with Bond in 1841
had girl child Caroline September 12, 1855, "a.m."
was given to Sidney Devereux in Julien's will along with Joe and Joanna's daughter Caroline

Joanna (younger)
born 1860
mother was Sarah
reference siblings Amanda & Frank

Joe (older)
born Summer 1830 in Covington County, Alabama
son of Jerry & Mindah
brought to Texas with Bond, Fall 1841
was given to Sidney Devereux February 28, 1857, along with Joanna and her child Caroline

Joe (younger)
son of Matilda but birth date is unreadable

John
born November 3, 1853, "p.m."
mother was Eliza

Juba
born on December 3, 1833, in Covington County, Alabama
mother was Lev Maria
brought to Texas in 1841 with Bond

Judy (Juda)
was born sometime in 1825 in Covington County, Alabama
brought to Texas in 1841 with Bond
son Peter born Spring 1843
had twin girls (Kizzy (Y) and Melissa) September 18, 1848
son Allen born 1852
bequeathed to Antoinette in probate

Julius
born January 6, 1862
mother was Little Tabby

July

born Winter 1825 in Covington County, Alabama
son of Jerry and Mindah
married to Diana
brought to Texas with Bond in Fall 1841
died June 1855

Katy

born in 1817
mother was Mindah
daughter Little Tabby born April 11, 1834
son Tom born November 18, 1837, in Macon County, Alabama
daughter Jane born July 11, 1840
left Alabama September 30, 1841, with Alfred Devereux
son Arthur born in the latter part of 1842
daughter Elmina (Y) born October 1845
son Aaron born April 1845
son Rolly (Rolla) born April 19, 1850, "a.m."
daughter Lucy Ann born in 1852
son Robert born July 1854
son George born November 24, 1856

Kitt (boy)

born circa 1820
mother was Betty
purchased July 15, 1833, in Alabama for $1,000 along with mother and 3 siblings

Kizzy (older)

Purchased by Julien Devereux in 1832
Children purchased:
Judy, daughter, born in 1825
William, son, born Summer 1828
Alfred, and Albert, twins, born in 1832
Alfred and Albert changed to Allen and Alleck because Alfred and Albert were Devereux family names
daughter Rose born February 1833
son Anthony born May 15, 1835

Kizzy (younger)

born September 18, 1848, in Rusk County, Texas
mother was Judy
twin sister was Melissa

Levin, Jr.

born Spring 1830 in Covington County, Alabama
mother was Lev Maria
married to Peninah

LEVIN, SR.
: was married to Lev Maria
father of Levin, Jr.
brought to Texas with Bond in 1841
was at Lake Creek Summer 1845
bequeathed to Sarah Devereux

LEWIS
: bequeathed to Sarah in probate
JSD exchanged his slave Limas for Loftus's slave Lewis in 1847
probably one or both slaves had family on the other's plantation

LIMAS
: born Summer 1828 in Covington County, Alabama
mother was Sally
brother to George and Elsey
was at Lake Creek in mid-Summer 1845
was "exchanged," traded "for negro man Lewis" in 1847

LORENZ
: born 1859
mother was Little Tabby

LOUISA (OLDER)
: born March 31, 1827
Scott and Tabby's daughter
left Alabama September 30, 1841, with Alfred Devereux
was married to Martin before the split
miscarried in 1846
went to LDH in 1849

LOUISA (YOUNGER)
: born September 20, 1849, in Rusk County, Texas
mother was Diana

LUCIUS (OLDER)
: born 1811 in Georgia
mother was Gincy (O)
wife and family left in Alabama
son Berry born August 13, 1833
brought to Texas October 1841 with Bond
married to Sally
died at Monte Verdi of pneumonia on February 3 or 5, in 1854 or 1857

LUCIUS (YOUNGER)
: born December 9, 1855, "p.m."
mother was Martha

Lucy
was born prior to 1848
mother was Polly
selected to go to LDH

Lucy Ann
born April 28, 1852
mother was Katy

Mahala (Mahaly, Helen)[1]
born 1838
mother was Amy
left Alabama September 30, 1841, with Alfred Devereux
son Ossian born July 19, 1856
daughter Mariah born May 1858
daughter Celia born December 3, 1863

Margaret
born August 1862
mother was Peninah

Maria (Henry Maria)
married to Henry
daughter Eliza born 1825
daughter Peninah born Summer 1832
son Amos born 1836
son Walton born July 1838
son Nelson born March 9, 1844
son Dennis born April 25, 1846
daughter Amy born February 9, 1852

Maria (Lev Maria)
born 1815 in Georgia
mother was Gincy (O)
married to Levin Sr.
son Levin Jr.
son Juba was born December 3, 1833
son Jack was born 1836 at Macon County, Alabama
son Green was born 1840 at Macon County, Alabama
brought to Texas with Bond in October 1841
died June 1856

Mariah
born May 1858
mother was Mahala

APPENDIX I

MARTHA
    born December 25, 1817, in Mobile, Alabama
    mother was Gincy (O)
    daughter Joanna born September 12, 1837, at Macon County, Alabama
    son Richmond born March 1, 1840
    listed as one of the ones with Bond in October 1841 trip to Texas
    daughter Sarah born Spring 1842, "first one in Texas"
    son Mason born September 1845 at Lake Creek, Texas
    son Lucius (Y) born December 9, 1853
    son Aleck born February 1859

MARTIN
    born in Georgia, 1813
    mother was Gincy (O)
    brought to Texas October 1841 with Bond
    married to Louisa who was transferred to LDH
    married Katy later
    judging from the symptoms Martin had malaria with recurring bouts of fever and chills

MARY (OLDEST)
    born 1811 in Baldwin County, Georgia
    daughter of Scott and Tabby
    left Alabama September 30, 1841, with Alfred Devereux
    daughter Diana born October 8, 1827
    son Ham born September 14, 1837
    son Anthony born 1839
    daughter Phebe born October 9, 1844
    son Elisha born December 4, 1849, and died February 27, 1850
    son (no name) on February 6, 1851, "a.m." who died March 10, 1851
    died November 9, 1853

MARY (MIDDLE)
    born circa 1820
    mother was Betty
    purchased in Alabama on July 15, 1833, for $1,000 along with mother and three siblings
    left Alabama on September 30, 1841, with Alfred Devereux

MARY (YOUNGEST)
    born November 6, 1857
    mother was Dice

Mason
born September 1845 at Lake Creek, Texas
mother was Martha
in JSD's 1848 list

Matilda
born 1829
daughter of Scott & Tabby
left Alabama September 30, 1841, with Alfred Devereux
son Anderson born October 17, 1848
daughter Anna born 1851
daughter Frances born March 8, 1853
son Henry born July 22, 1855, "a.m."
daughter Jinney born November 18, 1859
son named Joe (Y) but birthday is unreadable

Mats
married to Mary

Mellissa (Melissa)
born September 18, 1848, at Rusk County, Texas
mother was Judy
was twin to Kizzy

Milly
born April 11, 1855
mother was Diana

Mindah (older)
wife to Jerry
mother to Katy, born 1817
mother to Elmina, born summer 1823
mother to July, born winter 1825
mother to Jim, born spring 1827
mother to Stephen, born summer 1828
mother to Joe, born summer 1830
mother to Rhody, born fall 1831

Mindah (younger)
born September 6, 1850, p.m. at Rusk County, Texas
mother was Rhoda
Rhody's mother was Mindah

Nelson
born March 19, 1844, at Lake Creek, Texas
mother was Henry Maria

Appendix I

Newton
   born 1858
   mother was Sarah

Ossian (older)
   born July 1842
   mother was Polly
   went with LDH

Ossian (younger)
   born July 19, 1856, in Rusk County, Texas
   mother was Mahala

Patrick
   born April 13, 1850, "a.m." in Rusk County, Texas
   mother was Peninah
   died January 30, 1852

Peninah
   born summer 1832 in Covington County, Alabama
   daughter of Henry and Henry Maria
   married to Levin, Jr.
   left Alabama September 30, 1841, with Alfred Devereux
   son Patrick born April 13, 1850, "a.m." and died January 30, 1852
   daughter Charlotte born 1851
   son Cyrus born January 17, 1854, "p.m."
   boy child (unnamed) March 20, 1856, "p.m."
   son Richmond born April 19, 1858
   son Ben born April 1860
   daughter Margaret born August 1862

Peter
   born spring 1843 at Lake Creek, Texas
   mother was Judy
   bequeathed to Antoinette in probate

Phebee (Phoebe)
   born October 9, 1844, in Montgomery County, Texas
   mother was Mary
   son Ham (Y) born on April 19, but birth year is unreadable

Phillis
   born December 1854
   mother was Diana

Polly
born June 29, 1820
daughter of Scott and Tabby
mother of four children: Cyrus, Lucy, Ossian, & Little Scott—valued at $1,350
left Alabama September 30, 1841, with Alfred Devereux
son Little Scott born October 1846
was to be transferred with children to LDH but Polly died before the transfer
died circa 1848

Randle (Randal/Randall) (older)
born December 26, 1831, in Covington County, Alabama
son of Scott and Tabby
left Alabama on September 30, 1841, with Alfred Devereux
died May 1857

Randle (Randal/Randall) (younger)
was born January 23, 1860
mother was Jinny

Rhoda (Rhody, Rody)
was born fall 1831 in Covington County, Alabama
daughter of Jerry and Mindah
daughter Cynthia born February 20, 1849
daughter Mindah born September 6, 1850, "p.m."
son Daniel born February 7, 1857

Richmond (older)
was born in March 1840 at Val Verdi, Macon County, Alabama
mother was Martha

Richmond (younger)
born April 19, 1858
mother was Peninah

Robert
born July 18, 1854
mother was Katy

Rolly
born April 19, 1850, "p.m."
mother was Katy

Rose
born February 1833
mother was Kizzy

Sally[2]
was married to Lucius
son Berry born August 13, 1833
Lucius taken to Texas
Sally did not come to Texas

Sam
born May 15, 1843, in Montgomery County, Texas
mother was Amy (O)
grandson of Scott and Tabby

Sarah
born Spring 1842 at Lake Creek, Texas, "first one in Texas"
mother was Martha
son Newton born 1858
daughter Joana born 1860
daughter Amanda born June 16, 1862
son Frank born December 24, 186?

Scott (older)
born 1792 in Columbia County, Georgia
married to Tabby
father of:
son Henry born 1808
daughter Mary born 1811
son Anderson born December 12, 1814
daughter Amy born June 6, 1819
daughter Polly born June 29, 1820
daughter Flora born January 6, 1822
daughter Cynthia (O) born December 6, 1823
son Daniel born September 10, 1825
daughter Louisa (O) born March 31, 1827
daughter Matilda born 1829
son Randle (o) born December 26, 1831

Scott (younger)
born October 1846
mother was Polly
one of the slaves selected by LDH as "little Scott"

Simms
left Alabama September 30, 1841, with Alfred Devereux

Stephen
born summer 1828, in Covington County, Alabama
son of Jerry and Mindah
brought to Texas with Bond Fall 1841

Tabby (older)
born 1787 in Wilkes County, Georgia
married to Scott (O)
son Henry born 1808
daughter Mary born 1811
son Anderson born December 12, 1814
daughter Amy born June 6, 1819
daughter Polly born June 29, 1820
daughter Flora born January 6, 1822
daughter Cynthia (O) born December 6, 1823
son Daniel born September 10, 1825
daughter Louisa (O) born March 31, 1827
daughter Matilda born 1829
son Randle (o) born December 26, 1831
left Alabama September 30, 1841, with Alfred Devereux

Little Tabby (younger)
born April 11, 1834, in Macon County, Alabama
mother was Katy
left Alabama September 30, 1841, with Alfred Devereux
son Franklin born August 2, 1850, "p.m." and died July 12, 1853
daughter Betty born March 3, 1853
son Lorenz born 1859
son Julius born January 6, 1862

Tom
born November 18, 1837
mother was Katy
left Alabama September 30, 1841, with Alfred Devereux
in the 1850 list of JSD's slaves

Walton
born July 1838
son of Henry and Henry Maria
had son named Aaron Henry
left Alabama September 30, 1841, with Alfred Devereux

Willis
born December 9, 1855
mother was Little Tabby
bequeathed to Sarah in probate of will

Appendix II
Devereux Slave Community Family Trees

APPENDIX II

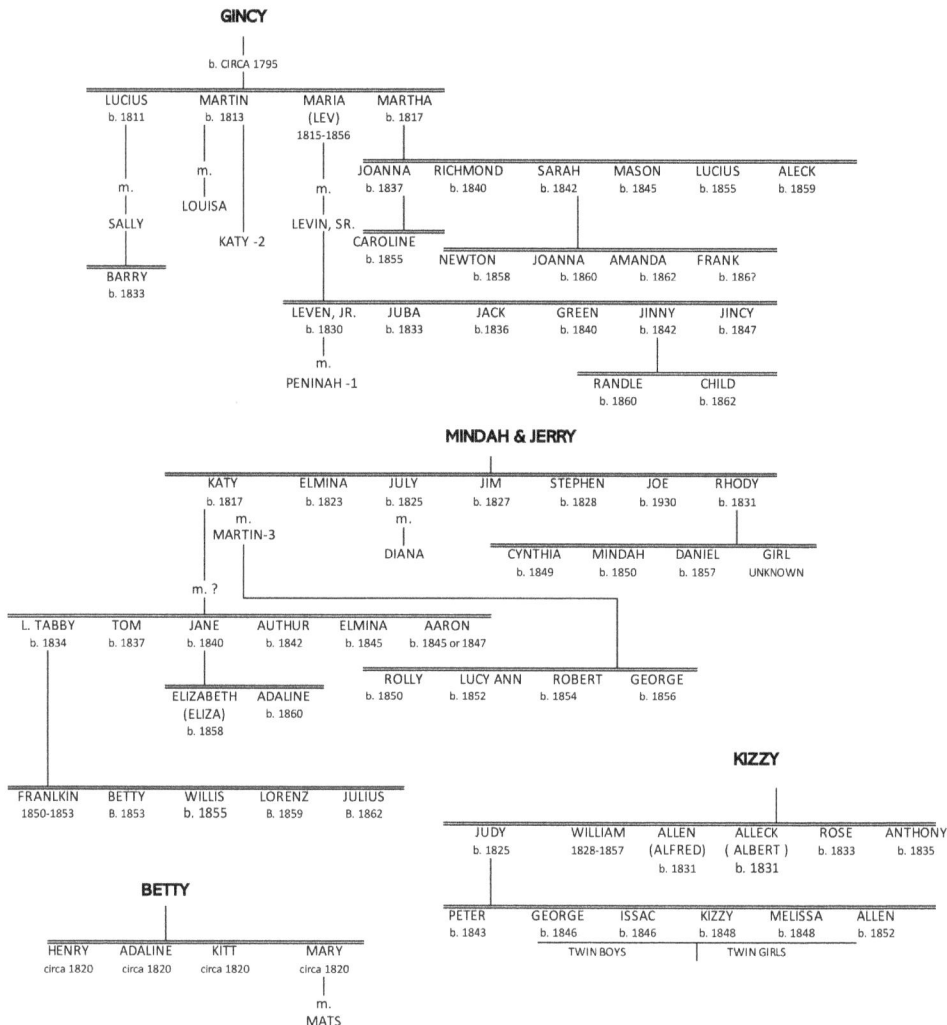

1 SEE TABBY & SCOTT
2 SEE MINDAH & JERRY
3 SEE GINCY

DEVEREUX SLAVE COMMUNITY FAMILY TREES

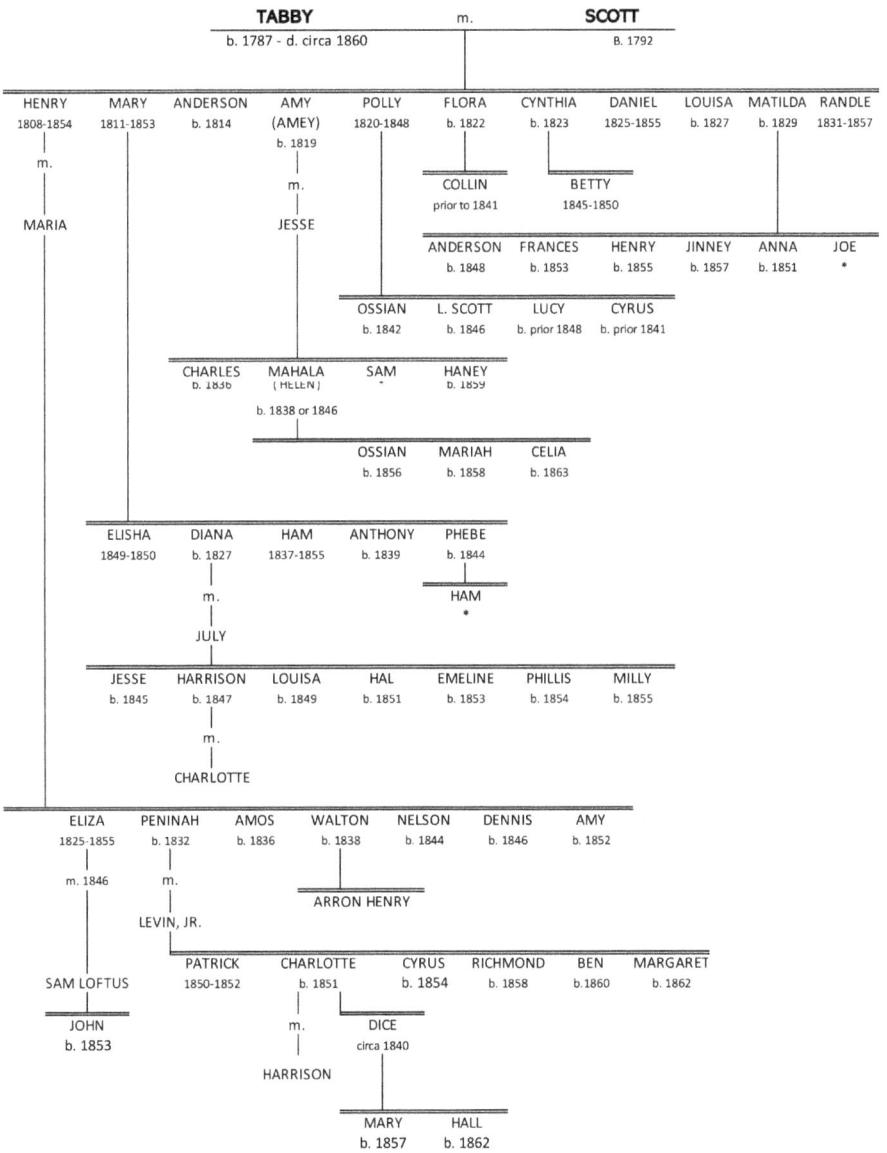

Notes

CHAPTER ONE

1. John Jay Chapman, *William Lloyd Garrison*, 2nd ed. (Boston: The Atlantic Monthly Press, 1920), Perseus Digital Library, accessed November 4, 2021, http://www.perseus.tufts.edu/hopper/.
2. Faulkner, *Requiem for a Nun*, 63.
3. Thomas, *The Slave Trade*, 804-5.
4. Statistics of Slaves, Section XIV, United States Census, accessed November 20, 2021, www2.census.gov.
5. Statistics of Slaves, Section XIV, United States Census.
6. Statistics of Slaves, Section XIV, United States Census.
7. Baptist, *The Half Has Never Been Told*, 147, Kindle.
8. Winkler, ed., *Journal of the Secession Convention of Texas*, 61-65.
9. Julien Sidney Devereux Family Papers, *Records of Ante-Bellum Southern Plantations from the Revolution through the Civil War*, Series G, Part 1, Reel 39, Frame 416, Briscoe Center for American History, The University of Texas at Austin.
10. Baptist, *The Half Has Never Been Told*, xxiii–xxiv.
11. "Academic Disciplines Where African Americans Received Few or No Doctorates in 2019," *Journal of Blacks in Higher Education* (January 4, 2021): accessed November 20, 2021, https://www.jbhe.com/2021/01/.
12. Frederick Douglass, as quoted Gregory, *Frederick Douglass the Orator*, 66. Douglass used the phrase quoted here in several of his speeches.

CHAPTER TWO

1. Julien Sidney Devereux Family Papers, *Records of Ante-Bellum Southern Plantations from the Revolution through the Civil War*, Series G, Part 1, Reel 36, Frame 979, Briscoe Center for American History, The University of Texas at Austin.
2. Winfrey, *Julien Sidney Devereux*, 15.
3. Winfrey, *Julien Sidney Devereux*, 18.
4. Devereux Family Papers, *Records of Ante-Bellum Southern Plantations*, Reel 36, Frame 501.
5. Devereux Family Papers, *Records of Ante-Bellum Southern Plantations*, Reel 36, Frame 533.
6. Devereux Family Papers, *Records of Ante-Bellum Southern Plantations*, Reel 36, Frame 559.
7. "Alabama, U.S., Marriages, Deaths, Wills, Court, and Other Records, 1784-1920" (database on-line), Ancestry, Ancestry.com Operations, Inc., 2010, accessed November 9, 2021, https://www.ancestry.com/discoveryui-content/view/.

8. "U. S. Census 1830, Julien Devereux" (database on-line), Ancestry, Ancestry.com Operations, Inc., 2010, accessed November 6, 2021, https://www.ancestry.com/search/collections/8058/.
9. "U. S. Census, 1840, Julien Devereux" (database on-line), Ancestry, Ancestry.com Operations, Inc., 2010, accessed November 6, 2021, https://www.ancestry.com/search/collections/8057/.
10. Dattel, *Cotton and Race*, 68, Kindle.
11. Roberts, *America's First Great Depression*, 33, Kindle.
12. Zinn, *A People's History*, Location 2749, Kindle.
13. Winfrey, *Julien Sidney Devereux*, 28.
14. Winfrey, *Julien Sidney Devereux*, 28.
15. Winfrey, *Julien Sidney Devereux*, 28.
16. Dattel, *Cotton and Race*, 63, Kindle.
17. Roberts, *America's First Great Depression*, 51, Kindle.
18. Roberts, *America's First Great Depression*, 52, Kindle.
19. Beckert, *Empire of Cotton*, Location 2387, Kindle.
20. Dattel, *Cotton and Race*, Location 1314, 66, Kindle.
21. Devereux Family Papers, *Records of Ante-Bellum Southern Plantations*, Reel 36, Frame 113.
22. Devereux Family Papers, *Records of Ante-Bellum Southern Plantations*, Reel 36, Frame 1103.
23. Baptist, *The Half Has Never Been Told*, 27.
24. Devereux Family Papers, *Records of Ante-Bellum Southern Plantations*, Reel 37, Frame 449.
25. Devereux Family Papers, *Records of Ante-Bellum Southern Plantations*, Reel 36, Frame 1064.
26. Devereux Family Papers, *Records of Ante-Bellum Southern Plantations*, Reel 36, Frame 1115.
27. Devereux Family Papers, *Records of Ante-Bellum Southern Plantations*, Reel 37, Frame 252.
28. Devereux Family Papers, *Records of Ante-Bellum Southern Plantations*, Reel 37, Frame 272.
29. Devereux Family Papers, *Records of Ante-Bellum Southern Plantations*, Reel 37, Frame 275.
30. Devereux Family Papers, *Records of Ante-Bellum Southern Plantations*, Reel 37, Frame 339.
31. Devereux Family Papers, *Records of Ante-Bellum Southern Plantations*, Reel 37, Frame 340.
32. Devereux Family Papers, *Records of Ante-Bellum Southern Plantations*, Reel 37, Frame 329.
33. Devereux Family Papers, *Records of Ante-Bellum Southern Plantations*, Reel 36, Frame 1091.
34. Winfrey, *Julien Sidney Devereux*, 41.

NOTES

35. Winfrey, *Julien Sidney Devereux*, 98–99.
36. Devereux Family Papers, *Records of Ante-Bellum Southern Plantations*, Reel 37, Frame 775.
37. Devereux Family Papers, *Records of Ante-Bellum Southern Plantations*, Reel 42, Frame 005.
38. "Texas, U.S. Marriage Index, 1824–2017" (database on-line), Ancestry, Ancestry.com Operations, Inc., 2010, accessed November 6, 2021, https://www.ancestry.com/discoveryui-content/view/.
39. "Find a Grave Index, 1600s–Current" (database on-line), Ancestry, Ancestry.com Operations, Inc., 2010, accessed November 6, 2021, https://www.ancestry.com/discoveryui-content/view/.

CHAPTER THREE

1. Julien Sidney Devereux Family Papers, *Records of Ante-Bellum Southern Plantations from the Revolution through the Civil War*, Series G, Part 1, Reel 37, Frame 329, Briscoe Center for American History, The University of Texas at Austin.
2. Kennedy, *Population of The United States in 1860*, 486, accessed November 6, 2021, https://www.census.gov/library/publications/1864/dec/1860a.html.
3. Kennedy, *Population of The United States in 1860*, 515.
4. Campbell, *An Empire for Slavery*, 36.
5. For those wanting to know more about the background to the Texas Revolution and Mexico and Texas during the period leading up to the Texas Revolution, Chapter Two in Randolph Campbell's *An Empire for Slavery* is a well-done presentation of that material.
6. Campbell, *Gone to Texas*, 207.
7. Devereux Family Papers, *Records of Ante-Bellum Southern Plantations*, Reel 36, Frame 1064.
8. Devereux Family Papers, *Records of Ante-Bellum Southern Plantations*, Reel 41, Frame 214.
9. Devereux Family Papers, *Records of Ante-Bellum Southern Plantations*, Reel 37, Frame 351.
10. The contract between Bond and Devereux to make the trip to Texas was dated October 22, 1841, and appears on Reel 37, Frame 349 in the microfilm. However, the earlier date of September 30, 1841, coincides with the recollections of John Devereux in his journal entry of the departure. Bond and Alfred Devereux left the same day.
11. Devereux Family Papers, *Records of Ante-Bellum Southern Plantations*, Reel 37, Frame 349.
12. Devereux Family Papers, *Records of Ante-Bellum Southern Plantations*, Reel 37, Frame 339.
13. Devereux Family Papers, *Records of Ante-Bellum Southern Plantations*, Reel 41, Frame 988.
14. Devereux Family Papers, *Records of Ante-Bellum Southern Plantations*, Reel 41, Frame 1001.
15. Devereux Family Papers, *Records of Ante-Bellum Southern Plantations*, Reel 41, Frame 210.

16. Devereux Family Papers, *Records of Ante-Bellum Southern Plantations*, Reel 41, Frame 210.
17. Montgomery County, Texas, *Records of the District Court* Book, Spring 1846, Book (B57-65 & 268-270); Book (B2), 348-349, 383-384, 482-483, 489; and Book (C2), 145-161, Clayton Library, Houston, Texas. Information and citation provided by Terrance A. Garnett via Patricia Bowens Scott, email message to author, October 15, 2011.
18. Winfrey, *Julien Sidney Devereux*, 30.
19. Devereux Family Papers, *Records of Ante-Bellum Southern Plantations*, Reel 41, Frame 210.
20. Devereux Family Papers, *Records of Ante-Bellum Southern Plantations*, Reel 37, Frame 723.
21. Devereux Family Papers, *Records of Ante-Bellum Southern Plantations*, Reel 37, Frame 723.
22. Devereux Family Papers, *Records of Ante-Bellum Southern Plantations*, Reel 41, Frame 210.
23. Devereux Family Papers, *Records of Ante-Bellum Southern Plantations*, Reel 41, Frame 210.
24. Devereux Family Papers, *Records of Ante-Bellum Southern Plantations*, Reel 41, Frame 211.
25. Devereux Family Papers, *Records of Ante-Bellum Southern Plantations*, Reel 37, Frame 353.
26. Devereux Family Papers, *Records of Ante-Bellum Southern Plantations*, Reel 37, Frame 333.
27. Devereux Family Papers, *Records of Ante-Bellum Southern Plantations*, Reel 36, Frame 333.
28. Deyle, *Carry Me Back*, Location 76, Kindle.
29. Baptist, *The Half Has Never Been Told*, 394, Location 11935, Kindle.
30. Devereux Family Papers, *Records of Ante-Bellum Southern Plantations*, Reel 37, Frame 353.
31. Devereux Family Papers, *Records of Ante-Bellum Southern Plantations*, Reel 37, Frame 353.
32. Devereux Family Papers, *Records of Ante-Bellum Southern Plantations*, Reel 37, Frame 353.
33. Devereux Family Papers, *Records of Ante-Bellum Southern Plantations*, Reel 37, Frame 449.

CHAPTER FOUR

1. Julien Sidney Devereux Family Papers, *Records of Ante-Bellum Southern Plantations from the Revolution through the Civil War*, Series G, Part 1, Reel 39, Frame 58, Briscoe Center for American History, The University of Texas at Austin.
2. Robert Fogel, *Without Consent or Contract*, 152.
3. Baptist, *The Half Has Never Been Told*, 181.
4. Devereux Family Papers, *Records of Ante-Bellum Southern Plantations*, Reel 41, Frame 989.

NOTES

5. Devereux Family Papers, *Records of Ante-Bellum Southern Plantations*, Reel 41, Frame 989.
6. Genovese, *Roll, Jordan, Roll*, 475.
7. Crouch, *The Freedmen's Bureau*, 58.
8. Devereux Family Papers, *Records of Ante-Bellum Southern Plantations*, Reel 40, Frame 547.
9. Author's calculations.
10. Ancestry, *1840 United States Federal Census* [database on-line] Provo, UT, USA: Ancestry.com Operations, Inc., 2010, accessed November 6, 2021, https://www.ancestry.com/search/collections/7668/.
11. Devereux Family Papers, *Records of Ante-Bellum Southern Plantations*, Reel 41, Frame 214.
12. Devereux Family Papers, *Records of Ante-Bellum Southern Plantations*, Reel 41, Frame 214.
13. Devereux Family Papers, *Records of Ante-Bellum Southern Plantations*, Reel 41, Frame 214.
14. Devereux Family Papers, *Records of Ante-Bellum Southern Plantations*, Reel 41, Frame 214.
15. Devereux Family Papers, *Records of Ante-Bellum Southern Plantations*, Reel 41, Frame 214.
16. Devereux Family Papers, *Records of Ante-Bellum Southern Plantations*, Reel 41, Frame 214.
17. Devereux Family Papers, *Records of Ante-Bellum Southern Plantations*, Reel 37, Frame 060.
18. Devereux Family Papers, *Records of Ante-Bellum Southern Plantations*, Reel 39, Frame 986.
19. Devereux Family Papers, *Records of Ante-Bellum Southern Plantations*, Reel 39, Frame 58.
20. Devereux Family Papers, *Records of Ante-Bellum Southern Plantations*, Reel 39, Frame 58.
21. Devereux Family Papers, *Records of Ante-Bellum Southern Plantations*, Reel 39, Frame 1030.
22. Devereux Family Papers, *Records of Ante-Bellum Southern Plantations*, Reel 41, Frame 216.
23. Devereux Family Papers, *Records of Ante-Bellum Southern Plantations*, Reel 41, Frame 215.
24. Devereux Family Papers, *Records of Ante-Bellum Southern Plantations*, Reel 39, Frame 788.
25. Devereux Family Papers, *Records of Ante-Bellum Southern Plantations*, Reel 39, Frame 964.
26. Blassingame, *The Slave Community*, 41.
27. Herbert G. Gutman, *The Black Family in Slavery and Freedom, 1750–1925*.
28. Devereux Family Papers, *Records of Ante-Bellum Southern Plantations*, Reel 39, Frame 416.

29. Devereux Family Papers, *Records of Ante-Bellum Southern Plantations*, Reel 40, Frame 547.
30. Winfrey, *Julien Sidney Devereux*, 37.
31. Devereux Family Papers, *Records of Ante-Bellum Southern Plantations*, Reel 37, Frame 384.
32. Devereux Family Papers, *Records of Ante-Bellum Southern Plantations*, Reel 37, Frame 379.
33. Devereux Family Papers, *Records of Ante-Bellum Southern Plantations*, Reel 37, Frame 408.
34. Devereux Family Papers, *Records of Ante-Bellum Southern Plantations*, Reel 37, Frame 408.
35. Devereux Family Papers, *Records of Ante-Bellum Southern Plantations*, Reel 37, Frame 419.
36. John William Devereux, as quoted in Winfrey, *Julien Sidney Devereux*, 48.
37. Devereux Family Papers, *Records of Ante-Bellum Southern Plantations*, Reel 37, Frame 621.
38. Devereux Family Papers, *Records of Ante-Bellum Southern Plantations*, Reel 37, Frame 621.
39. Devereux Family Papers, *Records of Ante-Bellum Southern Plantations*, Reel 37, Frame 621.
40. Devereux Family Papers, *Records of Ante-Bellum Southern Plantations*, Reel 37, Frame 626.
41. Devereux Family Papers, *Records of Ante-Bellum Southern Plantations*, Reel 37, Frame 626.
42. Julien Devereux to John Devereux, Julien Devereux Papers, Box 2N209, File 3, Briscoe Center, Austin, Texas.

CHAPTER SIX

1. Julien Sidney Devereux Family Papers, *Records of Ante-Bellum Southern Plantations from the Revolution through the Civil War*, Series G, Part 1, Reel 37, Frame 343, Briscoe Center for American History, The University of Texas at Austin.
2. Devereux Family Papers, *Records of Ante-Bellum Southern Plantations*, Reel 41, Frame 227.
3. Devereux Family Papers, *Records of Ante-Bellum Southern Plantations*, Reel 41, Frame 245.
4. Devereux Family Papers, *Records of Ante-Bellum Southern Plantations*, Reel 41, Frame 247.
5. Devereux Family Papers, *Records of Ante-Bellum Southern Plantations*, Reel 41, Frame 220.
6. Devereux Family Papers, *Records of Ante-Bellum Southern Plantations*, Reel 41, Frame 215.
7. Devereux Family Papers, *Records of Ante-Bellum Southern Plantations*, Reel 41, Frame 216.

8. Devereux Family Papers, *Records of Ante-Bellum Southern Plantations*, Reel 41, Frame 242.
9. Devereux Family Papers, *Records of Ante-Bellum Southern Plantations*, Reel 37, Frame 261.
10. Devereux Family Papers, *Records of Ante-Bellum Southern Plantations*, Reel 37, Frame 263.
11. Devereux Family Papers, *Records of Ante-Bellum Southern Plantations*, Reel 37, Frame 264.
12. Devereux Family Papers, *Records of Ante-Bellum Southern Plantations*, Reel 41, Frame 220.
13. Devereux Family Papers, *Records of Ante-Bellum Southern Plantations*, Reel 41, Frame 222.
14. Devereux Family Papers, *Records of Ante-Bellum Southern Plantations*, Reel 41, Frame 224.
15. Devereux Family Papers, *Records of Ante-Bellum Southern Plantations*, Reel 41, Frame 223.
16. Devereux Family Papers, *Records of Ante-Bellum Southern Plantations*, Reel 41, Frame 235.
17. Devereux Family Papers, *Records of Ante-Bellum Southern Plantations*, Reel 41, Frame 242.
18. Devereux Family Papers, *Records of Ante-Bellum Southern Plantations*, Reel 41, Frame 244.
19. Devereux Family Papers, *Records of Ante-Bellum Southern Plantations*, Reel 41, Frame 252.
20. Devereux Family Papers, *Records of Ante-Bellum Southern Plantations*, Reel 41, Frame 252.
21. Devereux Family Papers, *Records of Ante-Bellum Southern Plantations*, Reel 41, Frame 252.
22. Devereux Family Papers, *Records of Ante-Bellum Southern Plantations*, Reel 41, Frame 252.
23. Devereux Family Papers, *Records of Ante-Bellum Southern Plantations*, Reel 41, Frame 252.
24. Devereux Family Papers, *Records of Ante-Bellum Southern Plantations*, Reel 41, Frame 253.
25. Devereux Family Papers, *Records of Ante-Bellum Southern Plantations*, Reel 41, Frame 253.
26. Devereux Family Papers, *Records of Ante-Bellum Southern Plantations*, Reel 41, Frame 253.
27. Devereux Family Papers, *Records of Ante-Bellum Southern Plantations*, Reel 41, Frame 253.
28. Devereux Family Papers, *Records of Ante-Bellum Southern Plantations*, Reel 41, Frame 253.
29. Devereux Family Papers, *Records of Ante-Bellum Southern Plantations*, Reel 41, Frame 253.

30. Devereux Family Papers, *Records of Ante-Bellum Southern Plantations*, Reel 37, Frame 786.
31. Devereux Family Papers, *Records of Ante-Bellum Southern Plantations*, Reel 37, Frame 786.
32. Devereux Family Papers, *Records of Ante-Bellum Southern Plantations*, Reel 37, Frame 442.
33. Devereux Family Papers, *Records of Ante-Bellum Southern Plantations*, Reel 37, Frame 441.
34. Devereux Family Papers, *Records of Ante-Bellum Southern Plantations*, Reel 37, Frame 442.
35. Devereux Family Papers, *Records of Ante-Bellum Southern Plantations*, Reel 37, Frame 442.
36. Devereux Family Papers, *Records of Ante-Bellum Southern Plantations*, Reel 37, Frame 442.
37. Devereux Family Papers, *Records of Ante-Bellum Southern Plantations*, Reel 37, Frame 442.
38. Devereux Family Papers, *Records of Ante-Bellum Southern Plantations*, Reel 37, Frame 442.
39. Devereux Family Papers, *Records of Ante-Bellum Southern Plantations*, Reel 37, Frame 442.
40. Devereux Family Papers, *Records of Ante-Bellum Southern Plantations*, Reel 37, Frame 987.
41. Devereux Family Papers, *Records of Ante-Bellum Southern Plantations*, Reel 37, Frame 987.
42. Devereux Family Papers, *Records of Ante-Bellum Southern Plantations*, Reel 37, Frames 987-88.
43. Devereux Family Papers, *Records of Ante-Bellum Southern Plantations*, Reel 37, Frame 443.
44. Devereux Family Papers, *Records of Ante-Bellum Southern Plantations*, Reel 41, Frame 379.
45. Devereux Family Papers, *Records of Ante-Bellum Southern Plantations*, Reel 41, Frame 337.
46. Devereux Family Papers, *Records of Ante-Bellum Southern Plantations*, Reel 41, Frame 337.
47. Devereux Family Papers, *Records of Ante-Bellum Southern Plantations*, Reel 41, Frame 339.
48. Devereux Family Papers, *Records of Ante-Bellum Southern Plantations*, Reel 41, Frame 340.
49. John W. Devereux, June 10, 1847, Box 2N214, File 5, Devereux Papers, Briscoe Center, Austin, Texas.
50. "U.S., Find a Grave Index, 1600s–Current" (database on-line), Ancestry, Ancestry.com Operations, Inc., accessed November 26, 2021, https://www.ancestry.com/discoveryui-content/view/.

NOTES

CHAPTER SEVEN

1. Julien Sidney Devereux Family Papers, *Records of Ante-Bellum Southern Plantations from the Revolution through the Civil War*, Series G, Part 1, Reel 37, Frame 349, Briscoe Center for American History, The University of Texas at Austin.
2. Devereux Family Papers, *Records of Ante-Bellum Southern Plantations*, Reel 37, Frame 441.
3. Devereux Family Papers, *Records of Ante-Bellum Southern Plantations*, Reel 37, Frame 784.
4. Devereux Family Papers, *Records of Ante-Bellum Southern Plantations*, Reel 37, Frame 784.
5. Devereux Family Papers, *Records of Ante-Bellum Southern Plantations*, Reel 37, Frame 784.
6. Devereux Family Papers, *Records of Ante-Bellum Southern Plantations*, Reel 37, Frame 785.
7. Devereux Family Papers, *Records of Ante-Bellum Southern Plantations*, Reel 37, Frame 985.
8. Devereux Family Papers, *Records of Ante-Bellum Southern Plantations*, Reel 37, Frame 884.
9. Devereux Family Papers, *Records of Ante-Bellum Southern Plantations*, Reel 43, Frame 742.
10. Devereux Family Papers, *Records of Ante-Bellum Southern Plantations*, Reel 43, Frame 742.
11. Devereux Family Papers, *Records of Ante-Bellum Southern Plantations*, Reel 43, Frame 742.
12. Measuring Worth, "Purchasing Power Today-US$," The Measuring Worth Foundation, accessed November 18, 2021, https://www.measuringworth.com/calculators/uscompare/.
13. Devereux Family Papers, *Records of Ante-Bellum Southern Plantations*, Reel 37, Frame 884.
14. Devereux Family Papers, *Records of Ante-Bellum Southern Plantations*, Reel 37, Frame 985.
15. Devereux Family Papers, *Records of Ante-Bellum Southern Plantations*, Reel 37, Frame 974.
16. Devereux Family Papers, *Records of Ante-Bellum Southern Plantations*, Reel 37, Frame 974.
17. Devereux Family Papers, *Records of Ante-Bellum Southern Plantations*, Reel 37, Frame 975.
18. Devereux Family Papers, *Records of Ante-Bellum Southern Plantations*, Reel 37, Frame 975.
19. Devereux Family Papers, *Records of Ante-Bellum Southern Plantations*, Reel 37, Frame 975.
20. Devereux Family Papers, *Records of Ante-Bellum Southern Plantations*, Reel 38, Frame 54.
21. Devereux Family Papers, *Records of Ante-Bellum Southern Plantations*, Reel 38, Frame 54.

NOTES

22. Devereux Family Papers, *Records of Ante-Bellum Southern Plantations*, Reel 38, Frame 54.
23. Devereux Family Papers, *Records of Ante-Bellum Southern Plantations*, Reel 38, Frame 54.
24. Devereux Family Papers, *Records of Ante-Bellum Southern Plantations*, Reel 37, Frame 785.
25. Devereux Family Papers, *Records of Ante-Bellum Southern Plantations*, Reel 37, Frame 785.
26. Devereux Family Papers, *Records of Ante-Bellum Southern Plantations*, Reel 37, Frame 785.
27. Devereux Family Papers, *Records of Ante-Bellum Southern Plantations*, Reel 37, Frame 785.
28. Devereux Family Papers, *Records of Ante-Bellum Southern Plantations*, Reel 37, Frame 785.
29. Devereux Family Papers, *Records of Ante-Bellum Southern Plantations*, Reel 39, Frame 507.
30. Devereux Family Papers, *Records of Ante-Bellum Southern Plantations*, Reel 39, Frame 344.
31. Devereux Family Papers, *Records of Ante-Bellum Southern Plantations*, Reel 39, Frame 345.
32. Devereux Family Papers, *Records of Ante-Bellum Southern Plantations*, Reel 39, Frame 345.
33. Devereux Family Papers, *Records of Ante-Bellum Southern Plantations*, Reel 39, Frame 345.
34. Devereux Family Papers, *Records of Ante-Bellum Southern Plantations*, Reel 39, Frame 504.
35. Devereux Family Papers, *Records of Ante-Bellum Southern Plantations*, Reel 39, Frame 505.
36. Devereux Family Papers, *Records of Ante-Bellum Southern Plantations*, Reel 39, Frame 507.
37. Devereux Family Papers, *Records of Ante-Bellum Southern Plantations*, Reel 39, Frame 660.
38. Devereux Family Papers, *Records of Ante-Bellum Southern Plantations*, Reel 39, Frame 660.
39. Devereux Family Papers, *Records of Ante-Bellum Southern Plantations*, Reel 39, Frame 893.
40. Devereux Family Papers, *Records of Ante-Bellum Southern Plantations*, Reel 39, Frame 893.
41. Devereux Family Papers, *Records of Ante-Bellum Southern Plantations*, Reel 39, Frame 895.
42. Devereux Family Papers, *Records of Ante-Bellum Southern Plantations*, Reel 39, Frame 895.
43. Devereux Family Papers, *Records of Ante-Bellum Southern Plantations*, Reel 40, Frame 093.

NOTES

44. Devereux Family Papers, *Records of Ante-Bellum Southern Plantations*, Reel 40, Frame 093.
45. Devereux Family Papers, *Records of Ante-Bellum Southern Plantations*, Reel 40, Frame 156-57.
46. Wikipedia contributors, "Timeline of women's legal rights in the United States (other than voting)," Wikipedia, The Free Encyclopedia, accessed September 24, 2021, https://en.wikipedia.org/w/.
47. "1850 U.S. Federal Census—Slave Schedules," Ancestry, Ancestry.com Operations, Inc., accessed November 11, 2021, https://www.ancestry.com/search/collections/8055/.
48. "1860 U. S. Federal Census—Slave Schedules," Ancestry, Ancestry.com Operations, Inc., accessed November 11, 2021, https://www.ancestry.com/search/collections/7668/.
49. "1860 U. S. Federal Census—Slave Schedules," Ancestry, Ancestry.com Operations, Inc., accessed November 11, 2021, https://www.ancestry.com/search/collections/7668/.
50. "1860 U. S. Federal Census—Slave Schedules," Ancestry, Ancestry.com Operations, Inc., accessed November 11, 2021, https://www.ancestry.com/search/collections/7668/.
51. Devereux Family Papers, *Records of Ante-Bellum Southern Plantations*, Reel 37, Frame 443.

CHAPTER EIGHT

1. Sheila Spencer, Association for the Study of African American Life and History, Annual Conference, Atlanta, Georgia, 2015.
2. Genovese and Fox-Genovese, *Fatal Self-Deception*, Location 390, Kindle.
3. Genovese and Fox-Genovese, *Fatal Self-Deception*, Location 1121, Kindle.
4. Julien Sidney Devereux Family Papers, *Records of Ante-Bellum Southern Plantations from the Revolution through the Civil War*, Series G, Part 1, Reel 37, Frame 441, Briscoe Center for American History, The University of Texas at Austin.
5. Devereux Family Papers, *Records of Ante-Bellum Southern Plantations*, Reel 37, Frame 931.
6. Devereux Family Papers, *Records of Ante-Bellum Southern Plantations*, Reel 37, Frame 931.
7. Devereux Family Papers, *Records of Ante-Bellum Southern Plantations*, Reel 37, Frame 931.
8. Devereux Family Papers, *Records of Ante-Bellum Southern Plantations*, Reel 37, Frame 931.
9. Devereux Family Papers, *Records of Ante-Bellum Southern Plantations*, Reel 37, Frame 949.
10. Devereux Family Papers, *Records of Ante-Bellum Southern Plantations*, Reel 36, Frame 501.
11. Devereux Family Papers, *Records of Ante-Bellum Southern Plantations*, Reel 36, Frame 501.
12. Devereux Family Papers, *Records of Ante-Bellum Southern Plantations*, Reel 36, Frame 501.
13. Devereux Family Papers, *Records of Ante-Bellum Southern Plantations*, Reel 36, Frame 502.

NOTES

14. Devereux Family Papers, *Records of Ante-Bellum Southern Plantations*, Reel 41, Frame 587.
15. Devereux Family Papers, *Records of Ante-Bellum Southern Plantations*, Reel 41, Frame 587.
16. Devereux Family Papers, *Records of Ante-Bellum Southern Plantations*, Reel 41, Frame 987.
17. Devereux Family Papers, *Records of Ante-Bellum Southern Plantations*, Reel 41, Frame 987.
18. Devereux Family Papers, *Records of Ante-Bellum Southern Plantations*, Reel 37, Frame 473.
19. Devereux Family Papers, *Records of Ante-Bellum Southern Plantations*, Reel 37, Frame 505.
20. Devereux Family Papers, *Records of Ante-Bellum Southern Plantations*, Reel 37, Frame 505.
21. Julien Devereux's letters, Box 2N209, File 2, Devereux Papers, Briscoe Center, Austin, Texas.
22. Devereux Family Papers, *Records of Ante-Bellum Southern Plantations*, Reel 39, Frame 680.
23. Devereux Family Papers, *Records of Ante-Bellum Southern Plantations*, Reel 39, Frame 680.
24. Devereux Family Papers, *Records of Ante-Bellum Southern Plantations*, Reel 41, Frame 756.
25. Devereux Family Papers, *Records of Ante-Bellum Southern Plantations*, Reel 41, Frame 756.
26. Mary Boykin Chesnut, Quote.org, accessed November 13, 2021, https://quote.org/quote/.
27. "1850 U.S. Federal Census—Slave Schedules," Ancestry, Ancestry.com Operations, Inc., accessed November 11, 2021, https://www.ancestry.com/search/collections/8055/.
28. "1860 U. S. Federal Census—Slave Schedules," Ancestry, Ancestry.com Operations, Inc., accessed November 11, 2021, https://www.ancestry.com/search/collections/7668/.
29. Gincy to Julien Sidney Devereux, Letter, Box 2N209, File 2, Devereux Papers, Briscoe Center, Austin, Texas.
30. Devereux Family Papers, *Records of Ante-Bellum Southern Plantations*, Reel 41, Frame 756.
31. Barr, *The African Texans*, 23.
32. Gutman, *The Black Family in Slavery and Freedom*, 31.

CHAPTER TEN

1. "Gone with the Wind (movie)," *Wikiquote*, accessed November 12, 2021, https://en.wikiquote.org/w/index.php?title=Gone_with_the_Wind_(novel)&oldid=3012182.
2. Dattel, *Cotton and Race in America*, 28.
3. https://www2.census.gov/library/publications/decennial/1860/agriculture/1860b-02.pdf, accessed November 20, 2021.
4. https://www.census.gov/library/publications/1865/dec/1860c.html, accessed November 20, 2021.

NOTES

5. https://www.census.gov/library/publications/1865/dec/1860c.html, xiv, accessed November 20, 2021.
6. Campbell, *Empire for Slavery*, 209.
7. Julien Sidney Devereux Family Papers, *Records of Ante-Bellum Southern Plantations from the Revolution through the Civil War*, Series G, Part 1, Reel 39, Frame 44, Briscoe Center for American History, The University of Texas at Austin.
8. Devereux Family Papers, *Records of Ante-Bellum Southern Plantations*, Reel 37, Frame 217.
9. Devereux Family Papers, *Records of Ante-Bellum Southern Plantations*, Reel 37, Frame 219.
10. Devereux Family Papers, *Records of Ante-Bellum Southern Plantations*, Reel 41, Frame 223.
11. Devereux Family Papers, *Records of Ante-Bellum Southern Plantations*, Reel 37, Frame 617.
12. Devereux Family Papers, *Records of Ante-Bellum Southern Plantations*, Reel 37, Frame 620.
13. Devereux Family Papers, *Records of Ante-Bellum Southern Plantations*, Reel 37, Frame 621.
14. Devereux Family Papers, *Records of Ante-Bellum Southern Plantations*, Reel 37, Frame 621.
15. Devereux Family Papers, *Records of Ante-Bellum Southern Plantations*, Reel 41, Frame 231.
16. Devereux Family Papers, *Records of Ante-Bellum Southern Plantations*, Reel 37, Frame 233.
17. Devereux Family Papers, John William Devereux memorandum book, March 31, 1846.
18. Devereux Family Papers, *Records of Ante-Bellum Southern Plantations*, Reel 41, Frame 241.
19. Devereux Family Papers, *Records of Ante-Bellum Southern Plantations*, Reel 41, Frame 242.
20. Devereux Family Papers, John William Devereux memorandum book, May 30, 1846.
21. Devereux Family Papers, John William Devereux memorandum book, June 1, 1846.
22. Devereux Family Papers, John William Devereux memorandum book, June 4, 1846.
23. Devereux Family Papers, *Records of Ante-Bellum Southern Plantations*, Reel 41, Frame 803.
24. Devereux Family Papers, *Records of Ante-Bellum Southern Plantations*, Reel 37, Frame 574.
25. Devereux Family Papers, *Records of Ante-Bellum Southern Plantations*, Reel 39, Frame 948.
26. Devereux Family Papers, *Records of Ante-Bellum Southern Plantations*, Reel 39, Frame 948.
27. Devereux Family Papers, *Records of Ante-Bellum Southern Plantations*, Reel 39, Frame 948.
28. Devereux Family Papers, *Records of Ante-Bellum Southern Plantations*, Reel 39, Frame 948.

29. Devereux Family Papers, *Records of Ante-Bellum Southern Plantations*, Reel 39, Frame 967.
30. Devereux Family Papers, *Records of Ante-Bellum Southern Plantations*, Reel 39, Frame 967.
31. Devereux Family Papers, *Records of Ante-Bellum Southern Plantations*, Reel 39, Frame 977.
32. Devereux Family Papers, *Records of Ante-Bellum Southern Plantations*, Reel 39, Frame 948.
33. Devereux Family Papers, *Records of Ante-Bellum Southern Plantations*, Reel 39, Frame 971.
34. Devereux Family Papers, *Records of Ante-Bellum Southern Plantations*, Reel 39, Frame 962.
35. Devereux Family Papers, *Records of Ante-Bellum Southern Plantations*, Reel 39, Frame 977.
36. Devereux Family Papers, *Records of Ante-Bellum Southern Plantations*, Reel 39, Frame 1022.
37. Devereux Family Papers, *Records of Ante-Bellum Southern Plantations*, Reel 39, Frame 1022.
38. Devereux Family Papers, *Records of Ante-Bellum Southern Plantations*, Reel 39, Frame 1023.
39. Wyatt-Brown, *Southern Honor*, 404.

CHAPTER ELEVEN

1. Julien Sidney Devereux Family Papers, *Records of Ante-Bellum Southern Plantations from the Revolution through the Civil War*, Series G, Part 1, Reel 39, Frame 1014, Briscoe Center for American History, The University of Texas at Austin.
2. All data for this chart was drawn from John William Devereux's 1846 memorandum book on Reel 41, beginning with Frame 215.
3. All data for this chart was drawn from John William Devereux's 1846 memorandum book on Reel 41, beginning with Frame 215.
4. Devereux Family Papers, *Records of Ante-Bellum Southern Plantations*, Reel 41, Frame 281.
5. Devereux Family Papers, *Records of Ante-Bellum Southern Plantations*, Reel 41, Frame 282.
6. Fogel and Engerman, *Time on the Cross*, 208.
7. Fogel, *Without Consent or Contract*, 77.
8. Devereux Family Papers, *Records of Ante-Bellum Southern Plantations*, Reel 41, Frame 222.
9. Devereux Family Papers, *Records of Ante-Bellum Southern Plantations*, Reel 41, Frame 223.
10. Devereux Family Papers, *Records of Ante-Bellum Southern Plantations*, Reel 41, Frame 230.
11. Devereux Family Papers, *Records of Ante-Bellum Southern Plantations*, Reel 41, Frame 220.

NOTES

12. Devereux Family Papers, *Records of Ante-Bellum Southern Plantations*, Reel 41, Frame 219.
13. Devereux Family Papers, *Records of Ante-Bellum Southern Plantations*, Reel 41, Frame 219.
14. Devereux Family Papers, *Records of Ante-Bellum Southern Plantations*, Reel 41, Frame 226.
15. Devereux Family Papers, *Records of Ante-Bellum Southern Plantations*, Reel 41, Frame 219.
16. Devereux Family Papers, *Records of Ante-Bellum Southern Plantations*, Reel 37, Frame 698.
17. Devereux Family Papers, *Records of Ante-Bellum Southern Plantations*, Reel 41, Frame 727.
18. Devereux Family Papers, *Records of Ante-Bellum Southern Plantations*, Reel 41, Frame 727.
19. Devereux Family Papers, *Records of Ante-Bellum Southern Plantations*, Reel 41, Frame 727.
20. Devereux Family Papers, *Records of Ante-Bellum Southern Plantations*, Reel 41, Frame 727.
21. Devereux Family Papers, *Records of Ante-Bellum Southern Plantations*, Reel 41, Frame 727.
22. Devereux Family Papers, *Records of Ante-Bellum Southern Plantations*, Reel 39, Frame 523.
23. Devereux Family Papers, *Records of Ante-Bellum Southern Plantations*, Reel 38, Frame 773.
24. Devereux Family Papers, *Records of Ante-Bellum Southern Plantations*, Reel 39, Frame 561.
25. Julien Devereux receipt to Malone, date unknown, Box 2N214, File 8, Devereux Papers, Briscoe Center, Austin, Texas.
26. Devereux Family Papers, *Records of Ante-Bellum Southern Plantations*, Reel 39, Frame 229.
27. John Devereux's 1846 memorandum book, March 14, 1846, Box 2N214, File 5, Devereux Papers, Briscoe Center, Austin, Texas.
28. Devereux Family Papers, *Records of Ante-Bellum Southern Plantations*, Reel 41, Frame 228.
29. Devereux Family Papers, *Records of Ante-Bellum Southern Plantations*, Reel 41, Frame 231.
30. Devereux Family Papers, *Records of Ante-Bellum Southern Plantations*, Reel 41, Frame 744.
31. Devereux Family Papers, *Records of Ante-Bellum Southern Plantations*, Reel 42, Frame 023.
32. Devereux Family Papers, *Records of Ante-Bellum Southern Plantations*, Reel 42, Frame 023.
33. Devereux Family Papers, *Records of Ante-Bellum Southern Plantations*, Reel 42, Frame 023.

34. Devereux Family Papers, *Records of Ante-Bellum Southern Plantations*, Reel 42, Frame 023.
35. Devereux Family Papers, *Records of Ante-Bellum Southern Plantations*, Reel 42, Frame 023.
36. Devereux Family Papers, *Records of Ante-Bellum Southern Plantations*, Reel 41, Frame 932.
37. Devereux Family Papers, *Records of Ante-Bellum Southern Plantations*, Reel 39, Frame 943.
38. Devereux Family Papers, *Records of Ante-Bellum Southern Plantations*, Reel 41, Frame 932.
39. Devereux Family Papers, *Records of Ante-Bellum Southern Plantations*, Reel 41, Frame 932.
40. Devereux Family Papers, *Records of Ante-Bellum Southern Plantations*, Reel 41, Frame 932.
41. Devereux Family Papers, *Records of Ante-Bellum Southern Plantations*, Reel 39, Frame 068.
42. Devereux Family Papers, *Records of Ante-Bellum Southern Plantations*, Reel 39, Frame 525.
43. Devereux Family Papers, *Records of Ante-Bellum Southern Plantations*, Reel 39, Frame 525.
44. MeasuringWorth.com, accessed November 21, 2021, https://www.measuringworth.com/calculators/uscompare/relativevalue.php.
45. Devereux Family Papers, *Records of Ante-Bellum Southern Plantations*, Reel 42, Frame 025.
46. Devereux Family Papers, *Records of Ante-Bellum Southern Plantations*, Reel 39, Frame 535.

CHAPTER TWELVE

1. Julien Sidney Devereux Family Papers, *Records of Ante-Bellum Southern Plantations from the Revolution through the Civil War*, Series G, Part 1, Reel 41, Frame 683, Briscoe Center for American History, The University of Texas at Austin.
2. Devereux Family Papers, *Records of Ante-Bellum Southern Plantations*, Reel 42, Frame 049.
3. Devereux Family Papers, *Records of Ante-Bellum Southern Plantations*, Reel 39, Frame 915.
4. Devereux Family Papers, *Records of Ante-Bellum Southern Plantations*, Reel 38, Frame 145.
5. Devereux Family Papers, *Records of Ante-Bellum Southern Plantations*, Reel 38, Frame 145.
6. "Ex-Slave Stories (Texas)," Sanco-Young, *Federal Writers' Project: Slave Narrative Project,* Vol. 16, Texas, Part 4, 1936 (Manuscript/Mixed Material), accessed November 21, 2021, https://www.loc.gov/item/mesn164/.
7. Devereux Family Papers, *Records of Ante-Bellum Southern Plantations*, Reel 37, Frame 651.

8. Devereux Family Papers, *Records of Ante-Bellum Southern Plantations*, Reel 37, Frame 762.
9. Devereux Family Papers, *Records of Ante-Bellum Southern Plantations*, Reel 40, Frame 110.
10. Devereux Family Papers, *Records of Ante-Bellum Southern Plantations*, Reel 40, Frame 117.
11. Devereux Family Papers, *Records of Ante-Bellum Southern Plantations*, Reel 41, Frame 983.
12. Devereux Family Papers, *Records of Ante-Bellum Southern Plantations*, Reel 41, Frame 983.
13. Devereux Family Papers, *Records of Ante-Bellum Southern Plantations*, Reel 38, Frame 503.
14. Devereux Family Papers, *Records of Ante-Bellum Southern Plantations*, Reel 40, Frame 010.
15. Devereux Family Papers, *Records of Ante-Bellum Southern Plantations*, Reel 39, Frame 1014.

CHAPTER THIRTEEN
1. Julien Sidney Devereux Family Papers, *Records of Ante-Bellum Southern Plantations from the Revolution through the Civil War*, Series G, Part 1, Reel 39, Frame 1037, Briscoe Center for American History, The University of Texas at Austin.
2. Devereux Family Papers, *Records of Ante-Bellum Southern Plantations*, Reel 37, Frame 267.
3. "Ex-Slave Stories (Texas)," Harry Johnson, Image 220 of *Federal Writers' Project Ex-Slave Narratives Project*, Vol. 16, Texas, Part 2, Easter-King, Library of Congress, accessed November 14, 2021.
4. Devereux Family Papers, *Records of Ante-Bellum Southern Plantations*, Reel 41, Frame 216.
5. Devereux Family Papers, *Records of Ante-Bellum Southern Plantations*, Reel 41, Frame 216.
6. Devereux Family Papers, *Records of Ante-Bellum Southern Plantations*, Reel 41, Frame 751.
7. Devereux Family Papers, *Records of Ante-Bellum Southern Plantations*, Reel 41, Frame 804.
8. Devereux Family Papers, *Records of Ante-Bellum Southern Plantations*, Reel 41, Frame 793.
9. Devereux Family Papers, *Records of Ante-Bellum Southern Plantations*, Reel 41, Frame 728.
10. Devereux Family Papers, *Records of Ante-Bellum Southern Plantations*, Reel 41, Frame 731.
11. Devereux Family Papers, *Records of Ante-Bellum Southern Plantations*, Reel 41, Frame 804.
12. Devereux Family Papers, *Records of Ante-Bellum Southern Plantations*, Reel 41, Frame 805.

13. Devereux Family Papers, *Records of Ante-Bellum Southern Plantations*, Reel 41, Frame 02.
14. https://www.ancestry.com/search/collections/8055/?f-80100002=Julien&f-80100003=Devereux, accessed November 27, 2021.
15. "Ex-Slave Stories (Texas)," Millie Forward, Image 52 of *Federal Writers' Project Ex-Slave Narratives Project*, Vol. 16, Texas, Part 2, Easter-King, Library of Congress, accessed November 14, 2021.
16. Devereux Family Papers, *Records of Ante-Bellum Southern Plantations*, Reel 41, Frame 337.
17. John M. Barry, *The Great Influenza: The Epic Story of the Deadliest Plague in History* (New York: Viking Penguin, 2004). Part I of *The Great Influenza* has a good discussion of the development of professional medicine in America.
18. "History of Vaccines," accessed November 27, 2021, https://www.historyofvaccines.org/timeline#EVT_51.
19. Devereux Family Papers, *Records of Ante-Bellum Southern Plantations*, Reel 38, Frame 924.
20. Devereux Family Papers, *Records of Ante-Bellum Southern Plantations*, Reel 37, Frame 384.
21. Devereux Family Papers, *Records of Ante-Bellum Southern Plantations*, Reel 37, Frame 384.
22. Devereux Family Papers, *Records of Ante-Bellum Southern Plantations*, Reel 37, Frame 402.
23. Devereux Family Papers, *Records of Ante-Bellum Southern Plantations*, Reel 37, Frame 385.
24. Devereux Family Papers, *Records of Ante-Bellum Southern Plantations*, Reel 37, Frame 402.
25. Devereux Family Papers, *Records of Ante-Bellum Southern Plantations*, Reel 37, Frame 402.
26. Devereux Family Papers, *Records of Ante-Bellum Southern Plantations*, Reel 39, Frames 152-53.
27. Jessica Snider, in discussion with author, date unrecorded.
28. Devereux Family Papers, *Records of Ante-Bellum Southern Plantations*, Reel 39, Frame 154.
29. Devereux Family Papers, *Records of Ante-Bellum Southern Plantations*, Reel 39, Frames 193-95.
30. Devereux Family Papers, *Records of Ante-Bellum Southern Plantations*, Reel 39, Frame 252.
31. https://www.ancestry.com/search/categories/34/?name=Juilen_Devereux&death=1856_rusk-texas-usa_2569, accessed November 29, 2021.
32. Devereux Family Papers, *Records of Ante-Bellum Southern Plantations*, Reel 40, Frames 060-61.
33. Devereux Family Papers, *Records of Ante-Bellum Southern Plantations*, Reel 40, Frame 060.

34. Devereux Family Papers, *Records of Ante-Bellum Southern Plantations*, Reel 40, Frame 060.
35. Devereux Family Papers, *Records of Ante-Bellum Southern Plantations*, Reel 40, Frame 153.
36. Devereux Family Papers, *Records of Ante-Bellum Southern Plantations*, Reel 41, Frame 255.
37. Devereux Family Papers, *Records of Ante-Bellum Southern Plantations*, Reel 41, Frame 256.
38. Devereux Family Papers, *Records of Ante-Bellum Southern Plantations*, Reel 37, Frame 258.
39. Devereux Family Papers, *Records of Ante-Bellum Southern Plantations*, Reel 41, Frame 258.
40. Devereux Family Papers, *Records of Ante-Bellum Southern Plantations*, Reel 41, Frame 259.

CHAPTER FIFTEEN

1. Julien Sidney Devereux Family Papers, *Records of Ante-Bellum Southern Plantations from the Revolution through the Civil War*, Series G, Part 1, Reel 37, Frame 505, Briscoe Center for American History, The University of Texas at Austin.
2. Devereux Family Papers, *Records of Ante-Bellum Southern Plantations*, Reel 38, Frame 806.
3. Devereux Family Papers, *Records of Ante-Bellum Southern Plantations*, Reel 38, Frame 806.
4. Devereux Family Papers, *Records of Ante-Bellum Southern Plantations*, Reel 38, Frame 806.
5. Wyatt-Brown, *Southern Honor*, 408.
6. Devereux Family Papers, *Records of Ante-Bellum Southern Plantations*, Reel 41, Frame 335.
7. Devereux Family Papers, *Records of Ante-Bellum Southern Plantations*, Reel 39, Frame 954.
8. Devereux Family Papers, *Records of Ante-Bellum Southern Plantations*, Reel 37, Frame 573.
9. Devereux Family Papers, *Records of Ante-Bellum Southern Plantations*, Reel 37, Frame 573.
10. Devereux Family Papers, *Records of Ante-Bellum Southern Plantations*, Reel 37, Frame 573.
11. Devereux Family Papers, *Records of Ante-Bellum Southern Plantations*, Reel 39, Frame 942.
12. Devereux Family Papers, *Records of Ante-Bellum Southern Plantations*, Reel 39, Frame 942.
13. Devereux Family Papers, *Records of Ante-Bellum Southern Plantations*, Reel 39, Frame 948.
14. Devereux Family Papers, *Records of Ante-Bellum Southern Plantations*, Reel 39, Frames 942 and 953.

NOTES

15. Barr, *The African Texans*, 24.
16. Devereux Family Papers, *Records of Ante-Bellum Southern Plantations*, Reel 39, Frame 984.
17. Devereux Family Papers, *Records of Ante-Bellum Southern Plantations*, Reel 39, Frame 1002.
18. Devereux Family Papers, *Records of Ante-Bellum Southern Plantations*, Reel 39, Frame 1002.
19. Devereux Family Papers, *Records of Ante-Bellum Southern Plantations*, Reel 39, Frame 1002.
20. Devereux Family Papers, *Records of Ante-Bellum Southern Plantations*, Reel 39, Frame 953.
21. Devereux Family Papers, *Records of Ante-Bellum Southern Plantations*, Reel 39, Frame 961.
22. Devereux Family Papers, *Records of Ante-Bellum Southern Plantations*, Reel 39, Frame 961.
23. Devereux Family Papers, *Records of Ante-Bellum Southern Plantations*, Reel 39, Frame 984.
24. Devereux Family Papers, *Records of Ante-Bellum Southern Plantations*, Reel 39, Frame 1042.
25. Devereux Family Papers, *Records of Ante-Bellum Southern Plantations*, Reel 40, Frame 02.
26. Devereux Family Papers, *Records of Ante-Bellum Southern Plantations*, Reel 39, Frame 1022.
27. Devereux Family Papers, *Records of Ante-Bellum Southern Plantations*, Reel 39, Frame 1025.
28. Devereux Family Papers, *Records of Ante-Bellum Southern Plantations*, Reel 40, Frame 25.
29. Devereux Family Papers, *Records of Ante-Bellum Southern Plantations*, Reel 40, Frame 26.
30. Devereux Family Papers, *Records of Ante-Bellum Southern Plantations*, Reel 40, Frame 26.
31. Devereux Family Papers, *Records of Ante-Bellum Southern Plantations*, Reel 40, Frame 1046.
32. Franklin and Schweninger, *In Search of the Promised Land*, 55.
33. Devereux Family Papers, *Records of Ante-Bellum Southern Plantations*, Reel 40, Frame 26.
34. Devereux Family Papers, *Records of Ante-Bellum Southern Plantations*, Reel 40, Frame 27.
35. Devereux Family Papers, *Records of Ante-Bellum Southern Plantations*, Reel 42, Frame 032.
36. Devereux Family Papers, *Records of Ante-Bellum Southern Plantations*, Reel 39, Frame 1008.
37. Devereux Family Papers, *Records of Ante-Bellum Southern Plantations*, Reel 39, Frame 1028.
38. Devereux Family Papers, *Records of Ante-Bellum Southern Plantations*, Reel 39, Frame 1020.
39. Devereux Family Papers, *Records of Ante-Bellum Southern Plantations*, Reel 39, Frame 1020.
40. Devereux Family Papers, *Records of Ante-Bellum Southern Plantations*, Reel 39, Frame 970.

NOTES

41. Devereux Family Papers, *Records of Ante-Bellum Southern Plantations*, Reel 39, Frame 970.
42. Devereux Family Papers, *Records of Ante-Bellum Southern Plantations*, Reel 39, Frame 971.
43. Devereux Family Papers, *Records of Ante-Bellum Southern Plantations*, Reel 41, Frame 214.
44. Devereux Family Papers, *Records of Ante-Bellum Southern Plantations*, Reel 41, Frame 215.
45. Devereux Family Papers, *Records of Ante-Bellum Southern Plantations*, Reel 41, Frame 215.
46. Devereux Family Papers, *Records of Ante-Bellum Southern Plantations*, Reel 41, Frame 787.
47. Devereux Family Papers, *Records of Ante-Bellum Southern Plantations*, Reel 42, Frame 22.
48. Julien Devereux Notes, June 5, 1848, Box 2N214, File 8, Julien S. Devereux, Briscoe Center, Austin, Texas.

APPENDIX I

1. There is some confusion on Mahala. The Devereux Slave Community records clearly indicated her birth in 1838 and her inclusion in the slaves brought to Texas. Other documents mentioned her in Texas before 1846. However, her descendants have a family history of her birth in 1846 at Monte Verdi, and her headstone carries a birth date of 1846. There is not another Mahala.
2. Sally and Lucius were good examples of the break-up of families that occurred when Julien Devereux left Alabama for Texas. Sally and Lucius had a child born in 1833. Lucius was taken to Texas and his family was left behind. Even "good slave owners" sometimes split up families when it involved their pocketbooks. To put it another way, Julien Devereux stole the very person of Lucius. Julien broke up the marriage and forced Lucius to abandon his wife and son.

Bibliography

PRIMARY AND ARCHIVAL SOURCES

Chapman, John Jay. *William Lloyd Garrison.* 2d ed. Boston: The Atlantic Monthly Press, 1920.

Federal Writers' Project: Slave Narrative Project, Vol. 16, Texas, Part 2, 1936. Manuscript/Mixed Material. https://www.loc.gov/item/mesn162/.

Julien Sidney Devereux Family Papers, 1766–1908, Briscoe Center for American History, The University of Texas at Austin.

Julien Sidney Devereux Family Papers. *Records of Ante-Bellum Southern Plantations from the Revolution through the Civil War,* Series G, Part 1: Microfilm Reels 36-44. Briscoe Center for American History, The University of Texas at Austin.

Kennedy, Joseph. *Population of The United States in 1860; Compiled from the Original Returns of The Eighth Census.* Washington, DC: Government Printing Office, 1864.

Winkler, E. W., ed. *Journal of the Secession Convention of Texas, 1861.* In Documents of Texas History, edited by Earnest Wallace, David M. Vigness, and George B. Ward. Austin: Texas State Historical Association, 2002.

INTERVIEWS

Allison, Aldra Henry. Phone interview by Joleene M. Snider. April 2, 2018. Transcript by author.

Bowens, Art. Phone interview by Joleene M. Snider. April 9, 2018. Transcript by author.

Bowens, Carvell. Zoom interview by Joleene M. Snider. September 21, 2021. Transcript by Dr. Sandra Davidson.

Freeney, George Edward II. Zoom interview by Joleene M. Snider. March 2, 2021. Transcript by Dr. Sandra Davidson.

Freeny, Gerald. Zoom interview by Joleene M. Snider. May 16, 2021. Transcript by Dr. Sandra Davidson.

Hammons, Henry. Phone interview by Joleene M. Snider. October 25, 2018. Transcript by author.

Hammons, Martha. Interview by Joleene M. Snider. June 7, 2014. Nacogdoches, Texas. Transcript by author.

Henry, Anthony (Tony) Solomon. Zoom interview by Joleene M. Snider. February 26, 2021. Transcript by Dr. Sandra Davidson.

Mills, Jeri. Interview by Joleene M. Snider. October 13 & 14, 2021. Nacogdoches, Texas. Transcript by author.

Scott, Patricia Bowens. Phone interview by Joleene M. Snider. April 6, 2018. Transcript by author.

Spencer, Dr. Joi. Zoom interview by Joleene M. Snider. April 12, 2021. Transcript by Dr. Sandra Davidson.
Tatum, Cynthia. Interview by Joleene M. Snider. June 7, 2014. Nacogdoches, Texas. Transcript by author.
Williams, Brenda. Interview by Joleene M. Snider. June 8, 2014. Nacogdoches, Texas. Transcript by author.
Williams, Coretta. Interview by Joleene M. Snider. June 7, 2014. Nacogdoches, Texas. Transcript by author.

SECONDARY SOURCES

"Academic Disciplines Where African Americans Received Few or No Doctorates in 2019." *Journal of Blacks in Higher Education* (January 4, 2021). Accessed November 20, 2021. https://www.jbhe.com/2021/01/.
Baptist, Edward E. *The Half Has Never Been Told: Slavery and the Making of American Capitalism.* New York: Basic Books, 2014.
Barr, Alwyn. *Black Texans: A History of African Americans in Texas, 1528-1995.* 2nd ed. Norman: University of Oklahoma, 1973.
———. *The African Texans.* College Station: Texas A&M Press, 2004.
Barry, John M. *The Great Influenza: The Epic Story of the Deadliest Plague in History.* New York: Viking Penguin, 2004.
Beckert, Sven. *Empire of Cotton: A Global History.* New York: Alfred A. Knopf, 2014. Kindle.
Blassingame, John W. *The Slave Community: Plantation Life in the Antebellum South.* New York: Oxford University Press, 1979.
Camp, Stephanie M. H. *Closer to Freedom: Enslaved Women and Everyday Resistance In the Plantation South.* Chapel Hill: University of North Carolina Press, 2004. Kindle.
Campbell, Randolph B. *An Empire for Slavery: The Peculiar Institution in Texas, 1821-1865.* Baton Rouge: Louisiana State University, 1989.
———. *Gone to Texas: A History of the Lone Star State.* New York: Oxford University, 2003.
Clinton, Catherine. *The Plantation Mistress: Woman's World in the Old South.* New York: Pantheon, 1982.
Crouch, Barry A. *The Freedmen's Bureau and Black Texans.* Austin: University of Texas Press, 1999.
Dattel, Gene. *Cotton and Race in the Making of America: The Human Costs of Economic Power.* Lanham, Maryland: Ivan R. Dee, 2009. Kindle.
Davis, David Brion. *Inhuman Bondage: The Rise and Fall of Slavery in the New World.* New York: Oxford University Press, 2006.
———. *Slavery and Human Progress.* New York: Oxford University Press, 1984.
———. *The Problem of Slavery in the Age of Revolution 1700-1823.* Ithaca, New York: Cornell University Press, 1975.
———. *The Problem of Slavery in Western Culture.* Ithaca: Cornell University Press. 1966.
Deyle, Steven. *Carry Me Back: The Domestic Slave Trade in American Life.* New York: Oxford University Press, 2005. Kindle.

Eyerman, Ron. *Cultural Trauma: Slavery and the Formation of African American Identity.* Cambridge: Cambridge University Press, 2019. Kindle.

Faulkner, William. *Requiem for a Nun.* New York: Vintage International, 2011. Kindle.

Faust, Drew Gilpin. *The Ideology of Slavery: Proslavery Thought in the Antebellum South, 1830-1860.* Baton Rouge: Louisiana State University, 1981. Kindle.

Fogel, Robert William. *Without Consent or Contract: The Rise and Fall of American Slavery.* New York: W. W. Norton, 1989.

Fogel, Robert and Stanley Engerman. *Time on the Cross: The Economics of American Negro Slavery.* New York: W. W. Norton, 1974.

Ford, Lacy K. *Deliver Us From Evil: The Slavery Question in the Old South.* New York: Oxford University Press, 2009. Kindle.

Franklin, John Hope and Loren Schweninger. *In Search of the Promised Land: A Slave Family in the Old South.* New York: Oxford University Press, 2006.

Genovese, Eugene D. *Roll, Jordan, Roll.* New York: First Vintage Books, 1976.

Genovese, Eugene D. and Elizabeth Fox-Genovese. *Fatal Self-Deception: Slaveholding Paternalism in the Old South.* New York: Cambridge University Press, 2011.

Glymph, Thavolia. *Out of the House of Bondage: The Transformation of the Plantation Household.* Cambridge: Cambridge University Press, 2008. Kindle.

Grandin, Greg. *The Empire of Necessity: Slavery, Freedom, and Deception in the New World.* New York: Henry Holt and Company. Kindle.

Gregory, James Monroe. *Frederick Douglass the Orator.* Springfield, Mass: Willey Company, 1893. Google Play Books.

Gutman, Herbert G. *The Black Family in Slavery and Freedom, 1750–1925.* New York: Pantheon Books, 1976.

Harrigan, Stephen. *Big Wonderful Thing: A History of Texas.* Austin: University of Texas Press, 2019.

Johnson, Walter. *River of Dark Dreams: Slavery and Empire in the Cotton Kingdom.* Cambridge: Belknap Press of Harvard University Press. 2013. Kindle.

Jones, C. Allan. *Texas Roots: Agriculture and Rural Life Before the Civil War.* College Station: Texas A&M Press, 2005.

Jordan, Winthrop D., ed. *Slavery and the American South.* Jackson: University Press of Mississippi, 2003. Kindle.

Joyner, Charles. *Down by the Riverside.* Urbana: University of Illinois, 1984.

Kaye, Anthony E. *Joining Places: Slave Neighborhoods in the Old South.* Chapel Hill: University of North Carolina, 2007. Kindle.

King, Wilma. *Stolen Childhood: Slave Youth in Nineteenth-Century America.* Bloomington: Indiana University Press. 1995. Kindle.

Levine, Lawrence W. *Black Culture and Black Consciousness: Afro-American Folk Thought From Slavery to Freedom.* New York: Oxford University Press, 1977. Kindle.

Malone, Ann Patton. *Sweet Chariot: Slave Family and Household Structure in Nineteenth Century Louisiana.* Chapel Hill: University of North Carolina Press, 1992.

Olmsted, Frederick Law. *A Journey Through Texas: Or, a Saddle Trip on the Southwestern Frontier.* Austin: University of Texas Press, 1989.

Roberts, Alasdair. *America's First Great Depression: Economic Crisis and Political Disorder after the Panic of 1837*. Ithaca: Cornell University Press, Kindle.

Thomas, Hugh. *The Slave Trade*. New York: Simon & Schuster, 1997.

Torget, Andrew J. *Seeds of Empire: Cotton, Slavery, and the Transformation of the Texas Borderlands, 1800–1850*. Chapel Hill: University of North Carolina Press, 2015. Kindle.

Winfrey, Dorman. *Julien Sidney Devereux and his Monte Verdi Plantation*. Waco, Texas: Texian Press, 1962.

Wyatt-Brown, Bertram. *Southern Honor: Ethics & Behavior in the Old South*. New York: Oxford University Press, 1982.

Zinn, Howard. *A People's History of the United States*. Reissue edition. New York: Harper Perennial, 2015. Kindle.

Index

Aaron, 102, 201, 211, 219
abolitionist movement, 11, 13, 28
Adaline (older), 201, 203
Adaline (younger), 201
Advertiser, 113
Advocates Gazette, 113
Aleck, 202, 214
Alleck, 202
Allen (older), 202
Allen (younger), 202
Allison, Aldra Henry, 85, 101–3
Amanda, 202, 210, 218
Amy (Amey) (older), 32, 33, 69, 70, 97, 202
Amy (younger), 202, 213
Amos, 32, 202, 208, 213
Ancient City, 113
Anderson (older), 39, 47, 65, 69, 70, 75, 184, 203
Anderson (younger), 203, 215
Anthony (older), 103, 69, 70, 72, 75, 90
Anthony (younger), 203
Arnold, Dr. E. J., 87, 149
Arthur, 203, 211

Baptist, Edward, *The Half Has Never Been Told*, 12, 14, 20, 35, 37, 185
Barnett, Slade, 74
Barr, Alwyn, 95–96, 185
Ben (older), 191, 203
Ben (younger), 203
Berry, 203, 212, 218
Betty (oldest), 201, 203, 208, 211, 214
Betty (middle), 68, 70, 72, 75, 204
Betty (youngest), 204
Bill (William), 129, 136, 204
Birdwell, Mr., 191
Black Lives Matter, 3, 159, 169

Blassingame, John, *The Slave Community*, 43
Bond, William Baker, 30–31, 34–36
Bowens, Art, 103–4
Bowens, Carvell, 171–74
Brewer, Seaborn, 143
Briscoe Center for the Study of American History, 4, 88, 91–93, 201
Bureau of Indian Affairs, 19

Caddell, Anthony, 38, 58
Caddell Family Reunions, 4–5, 95, 194
Campbell, Randolph B., *Empire for Slavery*, 112, 197
Caroline, 204, 210
Celia, 204, 213
Cemetery Campground Springs, 58
Census
 of 1830, 10, 18;
 of 1850 slave schedule, 81, 89–9;
 of 1860, 23, 39, 81, 89, 111;
  Agriculture in the United States, 111;
  Manufactures in the United States, 112;
 slave schedule, 39, 81, 89
Chapman, John Jay, *William Lloyd Garrison*, 2d. edition, 9
Charity, 87, 89, 204
Charles
 in Slave Register, 202, 204;
 in lawsuit, 69–70, 72, 75;
 plantation carpenter, 140;
 to Texas, 32
Charlotte, 204, 208, 216
Cherokee land fraud, 18
Chestnut, Mary Boykin, 89–90
Choctaw, 124

INDEX

Civil War, 12–14
Colin (Collin)
 in Slave Register, 204, 206;
 in lawsuit, 65, 69–70, 72, 75, 81, 94;
 to Texas, 32
Cotton
 agriculture of, 2, 27–29, 116;
 amount raised, 117;
 economic value of, 19, 74, 111–13, 132, 135–36, 188;
 related to Devereux slaves, 17, 53, 91–92, 106, 128–30, 190;
 relationship to slavery, 10, 12, 183
Crystal Fount, 113
Cynthia (older)
 in Slave Register, 204, 218, 219;
 in lawsuit, 65, 69, 70, 72, 75, 80, 81;
 to Texas, 32, 39
Cynthia (younger), 205, 217
Cyrus (older)
 in Slave Register, 205, 217;
 in lawsuit, 65, 69, 70, 72, 75, 81;
 to Texas, 32
Cyrus (younger), 205, 216

Daniel (Dan) (older), 39, 69, 70, 72, 75, 129, 204
Daniel (Dan) (younger), 205
Dattel, Gene, *Cotton and Race in the Making of America*, 18–20
DeBow, J. D. B., *DeBow's Review*, 113
Democrat & Texas Register, 113
Dennis, 205, 208, 213
Depression of 1837, 18–20
Devereux, Adaline Bradley, 20–22, 25, 31, 33, 44
Devereux, Albert (older), 17
Devereux, Albert (younger), 42–43
Devereux, Alfred, 30–33, 36
Devereux (Garrison), Antoinette
 early life, 21–24, 28, 41;
 inheritance, 90, 202, 206–10
Devereux, John William
 early history, 2, 17;
 Lake Creek, 46–47;
 leaving Alabama, 21, 25, 29–31, 33, 40;
 support of Julien's second marriage, 45–46
Devereux, John William (in Rusk County)
 activities, 42, 61–64, 143, 146, 182;
 epidemic, 153–54;
 interaction with slaves, 62, 82, 125–27, 190–1;
 lawsuit, 69–73, 81;
 observation of overseers, 115, 125;
 recorder of daily life, 47, 62, 124–25, 142;
 wills, 64–66, 84
Devereux, Julien Sidney, Sr.
 Alabama years, 2, 17–18, 20–25;
 coming to Texas, 28–34, 36;
 Montgomery County years, 44–47
Devereux, Julien Sidney, Sr. (in Rusk County)
 as cotton planter, 2, 74, 111–13, 133;
 civic duties in Rusk County 2, 118, 184;
 finances, 18, 20–21, 130, 13;
 health, 42, 118, 152, 186–87;
 lawsuit, 61, 71–77, 82;
 Monte Verdi, 140;
 overseers, 48, 114–117;
 paternalistic slave master, 24–25, 42, 82, 180–82;
 relationship to slaves, 47–48, 86–87, 94, 127–29, 182–88
Devereux (Garrison), Sarah Ann Landrum
 as a slave owner, 11, 87, 90, 137;
 marriage years, 45–46, 63, 116–118, 138, 139;
 motherhood, 40, 42, 115;
 widowhood, 2, 43, 80, 116, 128
Devereux Slave Community
 as purpose, 16, 193, 199;
 descendants, 49, 95, 157, 165, 174;

families, 85, 88, 94;
  impact of lawsuit, 81–82;
  in Introduction, 1, 6;
  internal cohesion, 37, 39, 44, 97, 138, 181;
  move to Texas, 29, 35;
  plantation life, 142, 154;
  relationship to master, 20, 46, 118;
  work routines, 114, 116, 120, 124, 139–140
Devereux, Julien Sidney, Jr., 23–24
Deyle, Steven, *Carry Me Back, The Domestic Slave Trade in American Life*, 34
Diana
  in Slave Register, 205, 206–9, 211–12, 214–16;
  in lawsuit, 65, 69, 70, 72, 75
Dice, 205
Dikeman, Cyrus, 44
Dock, 47, 48
Dodson, Dr. Elijah
  business with Jesse, 2, 128;
  medical treatment, 149–52;
  on appraisal team, 74
Douglass, Frederick, 14, 16
Doughtery, Robert and William, 21, 22

Elisa, 206
Elisha, 214
Eliza (older)
  in Slave Register, 206, 208, 210, 213;
  part of community, 32, 126, 136, 150
Eliza (younger), 209
Elkins, Stanley, *Slavery: A Problem in American Institutional and Intellectual Life*, 15
Elmina (older), 31, 206, 215
Elmina (younger), 206, 211
Everett Selanus, 72

family slaves, 83
Faulkner, William, 9, 13, 158, 193
Few, C. A., 116, 127

Flora
  early history of, 32, 39;
  in Slave Register, 204, 206, 218–19;
  in lawsuit, 65, 69, 70, 72, 75;
  role in community, 44, 115, 149;
  with LDH, 81, 92, 94
Floyd, George, 159, 162–63
Fogel, Robert W., *Without Consent or Contract*, 37, 125
Fogel, Robert W. and Stanley Engerman, *Time on the Cross*, 124–25
Forward, Millie, 145
Frances, 206
Frank (older), 136, 207
Frank (younger), 207
Franklin, 207, 219
Franklin, John Hope and Loren Schweninger, *In Search of the Promised Land*, 187
Freedmen's Bureau, 38
Freeney, George Edward, 165–167
Freeny, Gerald, 158–60

Gage, Mr., 63
Galveston, 66, 40
Gincy
  as Holcombe slave, 25, 33, 67, 78–81;
  as kin to Devereux slaves, 25, 30–31, 84, 90, 188;
  her letter, 92–94;
  in Slave Register, 204, 206–7, 212–14
Genovese, Eugene and Elizabeth Fox Genovese, *Fatal Self-Deception*, 83
George (older), 92, 207
George (younger), 207
Graham's Magazine, 113
Godies (Godey's) Ladies Book, 113
Goffe (Gaff), Mr., 184
Green, 207
Greenwood District, Tulsa, Oklahoma, 192
Gutman, Herbert G., *The Black Family in Slavery and Freedom, 1750-1925*, 97

INDEX

Hal, 207
Ham (older), 32, 69, 70, 72, 75, 207
Ham (younger), 208
Hammons, Martha, 52–56
Hammons, Henry, 99–101
Haney, 202, 208
Haralson, Mr., 185
Harrison, 70, 208
Heard, A. C., 114–15, 128, 191
Henderson, Texas, 57, 73, 76, 102, 143
Henry (oldest)
    as companion to John Devereux, 62;
    early history of, 39;
    importance to book, 6, 120, 178, 179;
    in lawsuit, 69, 72, 75;
    in Slave Register, 202, 205–206, 208–209, 213, 215–16, 218–19;
    role in community, 49, 85–86, 95, 126, 136;
    relationship to masters, 37, 43, 128–29, 138, 190–91;
    to Texas, 32
Henry (middle), 208
Henry (youngest), 208
Henry, Anthony Solomon, 168–71
Hobson's Church, Alabama, 31
Holcomb, Henry B.
    business affairs, 22;
    lawsuit, 70–74;
    relationship to in-laws, 22, 25, 30–32, 64–67, 70;
    relationship to wife Louisiana, 74–75, 77–81
Holcombe, Louisiana Devereux
    after lawsuit, 76–81;
    Alabama years, 17, 25, 18, 22, 25, 26, 31–33;
    lawsuit, 51, 61–62, 64–67, 69–75;
    Texas years, 40, 84
Howerton, William
    Lake Creek overseer, 47–48, 114;
    Monte Verdi overseer, 24, 64, 76–77, 115–117, 119, 148, 151

Hugh, 208

Indian Removal Act, 18
Issac, 208

Jack, 30, 208, 128–29, 208, 213
Jack Shaw, 150–51, 181–82, 191, 209
Jamestown Colony (Virginia), 9
Jane, 20, 32, 206, 209, 211
Jenny, 87–88
Jeri Mills, x, 4, 53, 174–76, 194
Jerry, 30–31, 89, 206, 209–11, 215, 217–18
Jesse (older)
    business acumen of, 96, 128–30, 192, 195;
    in Slave Register, 202, 204, 205, 209;
    relationship to master, 49, 105, 118–19, 181–87;
    role on the plantation, 24, 43, 63–64, 135, 136, 171–72;
    to Texas, 32–33
Jesse (younger), 70, 72, 75, 205, 209
Jim, 30–31, 89, 136, 144, 186–87, 209, 215
Jim Crow, 139, 180, 192
Jincy, 209
Jinney, 210
Jinny, 209
Joanna (older), 30, 136, 210, 214
Joanna (younger), 210
Joe (older), 30–31, 89, 209, 210
Joe (younger), 210, 215
John, 75, 92, 210
Johnson, Harry, 142
Jones, Robert, 41, 91, 131, 189
Jourdan, Andrew, Sr., 181
Juba, 210, 213
Judy
    in Slave Register, 202, 207–8, 210–11, 215;
    plantation affairs, 136;
    purchase of, 88, 96
Julius, 210, 219

INDEX

July
in Slave Register, 201, 209, 211, 215;
punished, 115;
relationship to master, 62;
role in community, 89, 123, 129, 136;
runaway, 191;
to Texas, 30–31
Jumping the Broom, 38

Katy
in Slave Register, 201, 203, 206–7, 209, 211, 213–15, 217, 219;
to Texas, 32;
role in community, 95, 136
Kizzy (older)
bill of sale, 88, 96–97;
in Slave Register, 202–4, 210, 215, 217;
to Texas, 30
Kizzy (younger), 211
Koch, Cecilia and Joe, 46, 95, 141

Lake Creek, Montgomery County, Texas, 40, 44–48, 115, 143
Landrum, John, 45–46, 80, 87, 117, 120, 140, 148, 183–84
Landrum, Wells, 183
Law of 1830, 28
Levin, Jr., 211–12, 213, 216
Levin, Sr., 30, 86, 97, 129, 136, 213
Lewis, 129, 186, 212
Limas, 212
Little Scott, 72, 75, 81, 217–18
Little Tabby, 32, 204, 210–12, 219
Loftus, Sam, 125–26, 139
Lorenz, 212, 219
Louisa (older)
in lawsuit, 65, 69–70, 72, 74–75;
in Slave Register, 205, 212, 214, 218, 219;
role in community, 39;
to Texas, 32;
with LDH, 78, 80–81, 91–94, 188
Louisa (younger), 212

Lowell's fabric, 137
Lucius (older) (Frank), 30, 137, 207, 212, 218
Lucius (younger), 212
Lucy, 32, 65, 69–70, 72, 75, 81, 213, 216
Lucy Ann, 211, 213

Mahala (Helen)
ancestor, 38;
in lawsuit, 69–70, 72, 75;
in Slave Register, 202, 204, 213, 216, 245;
to Texas, 32
Malone, Mr., 127
Margaret, 203, 213, 216
Maria (Henry)
in Slave Register, 202, 205, 206, 208, 213, 215–16, 219;
role in community, 95, 126, 136;
to Texas, 32
Maria (Lev), 30, 86, 136, 207–13
Mariah, 213
Marshall Republican, 113
Marshall, Texas, 40, 77, 84, 92, 128
Martha
childhood use, 86–87;
in Slave Register, 202, 207, 208, 212–13, 215, 217–18;
role in community, 128, 136, 150–51;
to Texas, 30–31
Martin
family separation, 76, 90, 94;
importance of, 91, 129, 190;
in Slave Register, 207, 212, 214;
relationship to descendants, 95, 98, 171;
relationship to owners, 43, 63–64, 183, 188;
to Texas, 30–31;
work roles, 92, 188, 190
Mary (oldest)
in Slave Register, 203, 207, 214, 216, 218–19;
in lawsuit, 69–70, 72, 75;

255

role in community, 39, 90, 95, 136, 150;
  to Texas, 32
Mary (middle), 203, 214
Mary (youngest), 90, 205, 214–15
Mason, 214
Matilda
  in Slave Register, 203, 206, 208, 210,
    214, 218–17;
  in lawsuit, 65, 69–70, 72, 75;
  role in community 136;
  to Texas, 32, 39
Mats, 215
McKnight, John, 116–19, 181
McLarty & Son, 128
Mellissa, 210–11, 215
Mexican Law of 1830, 27
Mills, Jeri, 174–78
Milly, 205, 215
Mindah (older), 30–31, 89, 206–07, 209,
  210–12, 215, 218
Mindah (younger), 215
Mobile, Alabama, 70, 77–78, 80
Monte Verdi Plantation
  ancestors, 171, 175, 195;
  building of, 114, 140;
  Devereux home, 46, 70, 76, 115, 117,
    185, 187;
  general information about, 2, 132, 148;
  medical care at, 149, 152;
  present day, 49–50, 95–96, 139, 141,
    199;
  slaves' relationship to, 43, 84, 106, 111,
    115, 121, 188
Mount Enterprise, Texas, 62, 128–29, 135,
  138, 147–48
mulatto, 89–90

Nacogdoches (County), 126, 175
Negro Motorist Green Book, 176
Nelson, 208, 213, 215
New Orleans Delta, 113
New Orleans, Louisiana, 40, 128, 133, 188
Newton, 216, 218

Osnaburg fabric, 137
Ossian (older)
  in Slave Register, 215, 217;
  in lawsuit, 69–70, 72, 75;
  with LDH, 77–78, 80–81
Ossian (younger), 213, 216

paternalism
  in practice, 82, 84, 197;
  theory of, 11–12, 83, 132
Patrick, 216
Peninah, 32, 203–5, 208, 211, 213,
  216–17
Peter, 210, 216
Phebe, 69–70, 75, 208, 214, 216
Phillis, 216
Pitts, Eliza P., 87
Poe, Thomas, 76
Polk, James K., 28
Polly
  in Slave Register, 205, 213, 216–19;
  in lawsuit, 65, 69–70, 72, 75–76, 92;
  to Texas, 32, 39

racial relations, 3–4
Ramsey, S. S., 116–17
Ramer, Daniel & John , 86
Randal (older) (Randall/Randle), 69–70,
  72, 75, 136, 217
Randal (younger) (Randall/Randle), 209,
  217
Reagan, William, 72, 191
Reed, Mr., 42, 114
Renfro, J. B., 181
Republic of Texas, 12, 21, 24, 28, 36
Rhoda (Rhody)
  in Slave Register, 205, 209, 215, 217;
  trip to Texas, 22–24, 31
Richardson, Dr. P. T., 127, 152–53
Richmond (older), 92, 206, 214, 217
Richmond (younger), 216–17
Robert, 217, 211
Rolly, 211, 217

Rose, 211, 217
Rupel, Mr., 126

Sally, 203, 212, 218
Sam
   in Slave Register, 202, 218;
   in lawsuit, 69–70, 72, 75
Sarah, 202, 207–08, 214, 216, 218
Scott (older)
   early years of, 38;
   family of, 17, 39, 44, 77–78, 80–82, 85, 93–94;
   importance as influencers, 6, 37, 48, 81, 86, 94, 180;
   in Slave Register, 202–8, 214–19;
   in lawsuit, 61, 62, 69, 70, 72, 75, 76;
   in will, 65, 69;
   later years of, 43, 129, 137, 144;
   relationship with owners, 43;
   role in slave community, 4, 42, 88, 93–94;
   role in white family, 43, 83;
   year of 1846, 114;
   to Texas, 40, 111
Scott (younger), 72, 75, 81, 217–18
Scott, Andrew Gilbert, 22, 34
Scott, Patricia Bowens, 104–108
Shivey, Mr., 143
Shreveport Review, 113
Shreveport, Texas, 45, 63, 92, 106, 126, 128, 135, 188
Simms, 32, 218
Simonton, Mrs. E. M., 87
Singer, Issac, 137
slave trade
   commercial, 34–35;
   taken to Texas, 30–32
slavery
   growth of, 9, 10–11;
   historiography of, 14–16;
   importance of, 12
slave quarters, 20, 42–43, 181, 185, 189
slaves clothing, 40, 133–38

slave diets
   amounts, 132, 144–146;
   meats, 143–44;
   other than meats, 142
slave housing, 77, 125, 132, 139
slave/master relationship, 122, 128, 181–82, 179–92, 182–83
slave families
   break-up of, 29, 69–76;
   family slaves, 83;
   importance of, 43, 85–86;
   strength of, 1, 15, 49, 88–89, 92–97, 192
slaves in market economy, 106, 128–30, 138
slave births and deaths, 62, 92
slave work routines
   building, 113, 115, 121–22, 125–27, 144, 149;
   clearing land, 121–22, 125;
   field work, 121, 22, 10, 114;
   fencing, 121–22, 144;
   list of, 121–125;
   personal, 120, 127–129;
   picking and ginning, 91, 121–22, 123;
   travel, 92, 121–22, 188;
   weather, 122–23
slave health
   doctors' visits, 146–53;
   epidemics, 62, 92, 153;
   general health, 46–47, 142, 145–47, 188
Smith, James W., 134
Stephens, Lynnda Caddell, 38
Southern Press, 113
Southern women property rights, 65, 80–81
Spencer, Dr. Joi, 161–164
Spivy Enoch, 72
Stampp, Kenneth, *The Peculiar Institution*, 14
Stephen, 30–31, 89, 129, 209, 215, 218
Stern, H. F., 71–72
Stowe, Harriet Beecher, *Uncle Tom's Cabin*, 35

Stroud, Mark, 74, 116

Tabby (older)
    early years, 37–38;
    gendered roles, 40, 126, 137, 146, 195;
    family, 17, 39, 40, 44, 77–78, 80–82, 85, 93–94;
    importance as influencers, 6, 37, 48, 81, 86, 94, 180;
    in Slave Register, 202–8, 214–19;
    in lawsuit, 61, 62, 69, 70, 72, 75, 76;
    in will, 65, 69;
    later years, 129, 137, 144;
    relationship with owners, 43, 128, 144;
    relationship to descendants, 96;
    role in slave community, 4, 43, 88, 90, 93–94;
    role in white family, 42, 83;
    to Texas, 32, 111

Tabby (Little) (younger), 211, 212, 219
Tatum, Cynthia, 51–52
Taylor, Billy, 124
Taylor, Dr. William, 40, 76–77, 92, 94
Texas history, 26–29
Thirteenth Amendment, 111
Thomas, Hugh, *The Slave Trade*, 9
Thomas, James, 130
Tom, 32, 211, 219

United States Constitutional Convention
    slavery compromise, 9

Val Verdi Plantation, Alabama, 34–35
Vickers, James R., 87
Vinzent, Charles, 106, 128–30, 130, 135, 138

Walton, 32, 85, 208, 213, 219
Way, Barbara Scott, 21–24, 30, 45, 90
Winkler, *Journal of the Secession Convention of Texas*, 12
William, 211
Williams, Brenda, 56–58
Williams, Coretta, 49–51, 56
Willis, 219
Wornell, Mrs., 62
Wyatt-Brown, Bertram, *Southern Honor*, 119, 182

Zinn, Howard, *A People's History of the United States*, 18

About the Author

Courtesy of Fazia Rizvi.

Joleene Maddox Snider is a native Texan. She did her academic work at Southwest Texas State University (Texas State University) and the University of Texas. In 1969 Snider's master's thesis was the first revisionist work done on slavery in Texas. She holds numerous teaching awards from Texas State University.

CPSIA information can be obtained
at www.ICGtesting.com
Printed in the USA
BVHW090511261022
650169BV00009B/35